CONVEYANCING 2006

CONVEYANCING 2006

Kenneth G C Reid WS

Professor of Property Law in the University of Edinburgh

and

George L Gretton WS

Lord President Reid Professor of Law in the University of Edinburgh

with a contribution by Alan Barr of the University of Edinburgh

Avizandum Publishing Ltd
Edinburgh
2007

Published by
Avizandum Publishing Ltd
58 Candlemaker Row
Edinburgh EH1 2QE

First published 2007

ISBN 978-1-904968-17-7

British Library Cataloguing in Publication Data
A catalogue record for this book is available from the British Library.

Typeset by Waverley Typesetters
Printed and bound by Bell & Bain Ltd, Glasgow

CONTENTS

PREFACE

This is the eighth annual update of new developments in the law of conveyancing. As in previous years, it is divided into five parts. There is, first, a brief description of all cases which have been reported or appeared on the Scottish Courts website (www.scotcourts.gov.uk) or have otherwise come to our attention since *Conveyancing 2005*. The next two parts summarise, respectively, statutory developments during 2006 and other material of interest to conveyancers. The fourth part is a detailed commentary on selected issues arising from the first three parts. Finally, in part V, there are two tables. The first, a cumulative table of appeals, is designed to facilitate moving from one annual volume to the next. The second is a table of cases digested in earlier volumes but reported, either for the first time or in an additional series, in 2006. This is for the convenience of future reference.

We do not seek to cover agricultural holdings, crofting, public sector tenancies (except the right-to-buy legislation), compulsory purchase or planning law. Otherwise our coverage is intended to be complete.

We gratefully acknowledge help received from Shuiken Chan (Warners), Tom Drysdale, John Glover (Registers of Scotland), Professor W W McBryde, and Neil Tainsh (Lands Tribunal for Scotland). Our colleague Alan Barr wrote the text on stamp duty land tax and offered help and encouragement in many other ways.

Kenneth G C Reid
George L Gretton
22 March 2007

TABLE OF STATUTES

TABLE OF ORDERS, RULES AND REGULATIONS

TABLE OF CASES

PART I
CASES

CASES

The full text of all decisions of the Court of Session and of many decisions of the sheriff court is available on the Scottish Courts website: http://www.scotcourts.gov.uk.

Since 1 January 2005 all Court of Session opinions are numbered consecutively according to whether they are decisions of the Outer House or Inner House. Thus '[2006] CSOH 4' refers to the fourth Outer House decision of 2006, and '[2006] CSIH 15' refers to the fifteenth Inner House decision. This 'neutral' method of citation is used throughout this volume.

MISSIVES

(1) Middlebank Ltd v University of Dundee
[2006] CSOH 202

A dispute as to what had been sold. According to the seller, this was only the flats above the ground floor in a tenement. According to the buyer it was the whole tenement. Both views were arguable on the basis of the missives. The disposition, which would have cast light on the problem, had been sent to the Registers and, apparently, lost. **Held:** Only the upper flats had been sold. This was because (i) the provision which most favoured the other view had not been incorporated in the missives, (ii) the sale particulars related only to the flats, and (iii) considerations of commercial reasonableness supported the same view. On (i) see **Commentary** p 100. Lord Drummond Young's extensive judgment contains a helpful analysis of the proper approach to the interpretation of missives.

(2) Black v McGregor
2006 GWD 17-351 (Sh Ct) affd [2006] CSIH 45, 2006 GWD 31-668

A house was sold for £600,000 with entry on 28 November 2002. The missives contained the standard interest clause. The buyer having failed to pay the price, the seller rescinded on 16 December 2003 and sought interest of £60,928.79 in respect of the period from 28 November 2002 to the date on which the action was raised (27 January 2004). The house had not been resold. **Held:** No interest was due. In terms of the clause relied upon, interest was payable for the period between the date of rescission and the date of the resale. But there had been no resale, and might never be one. It was not enough for the seller to say that she was taking reasonable steps to obtain a resale. See **Commentary** p 87.

(3) Wipfel Ltd v Auchlochan Developments Ltd
[2006] CSOH 183, 2006 GWD 39-763

Similar facts, and result, to the previous case. The date of entry was 14 June 2004 and the price £536,000. The seller rescinded on 22 July 2004 and, eventually, entered into a resale contract which was contingent on the granting of planning permission. Before the condition could be purified, the seller raised this action, seeking interest on (some of) the price. **Held:** Following the previous case, the standard interest clause did not allow the payment of interest unless or until the property had been resold. Action dismissed. See **Commentary** p 88.

(4) Kenmore Homes (UK) Ltd v Cumming
[2006] CSOH 72, 2006 GWD 17-334

A builder sold one of its houses for £254,000, with entry on 31 August 2004. When the buyer failed to pay, the builder rescinded the contract and, eventually, resold at a loss. It sought damages under the following heads:

- contractual 'interest' at £67.45 per day for 294 days (31 August 2004 to 21 June 2005), a total of £19,830.30;
- shortfall in the resale price of £14,000;
- £2,560.10 as incentives paid to achieve the resale;
- £411.25 as solicitors' fees for the abortive sale.

The long period before achieving a resale will be noted. From a buyer's perspective, a possible difficulty in a case like this is that a builder may try to sell the other houses in the estate first. (There is, however, no suggestion from the judgment that this happened in this particular case.)

The buyer did not dispute the essential facts but challenged the amount claimed. In those circumstances the Lord Ordinary was willing to grant the summary decree sought by the builder only in respect of part of the amount claimed.

(5) McPhee v Black
31 July 2006, Ayr Sheriff Court, A1388/04

On examining the title deeds, after conclusion of missives, the buyers' agents wrote to the sellers' agents indicating dissatisfaction and that they intended to resile. This was in terms of the relevant clause in the missives by which:

> In the event of the Title Deeds disclosing any matter materially prejudicial to the purchasers' interests then they will be entitled to resile from the bargain without

expense but only by giving notice of the intention to do so in writing and that within ten working days from the date of receipt by you of the Title Deeds.

It appears, however, that rescission did not take place, although the price was not paid at entry (10 December 2004). The sellers sued for implement but at some stage decided it would be prudent to re-market the property. Before doing so, their agents wrote to the sellers' agents on 27 January 2005 that:

> In the meantime however standing the terms of your defences [to the action] we would advise that our client will be re-marketing the subjects. We trust that you have no objection.

The property was duly resold at a lower price. On 23 May 2005 a minute of amendment was lodged in which the sellers' craves were amended to seek damages for the buyers' breach of contract in failing to pay the price.

The main defences to this action were (i) that the sellers had failed to rescind the contract and so had no entitlement to damages, and (ii) that in any event the sellers were themselves in breach of contract in respect that the titles disclosed matters which were materially prejudicial to the buyers.

On (i), the sheriff principal (James A Taylor) considered the meaning of the requirement, in the interest clause, that the sellers could 'rescind the missives on giving prior written notice'. If effect was to be given to the word 'prior', this suggested a two-stage process, with written notice of an intention to rescind being followed, sometime later, by actual rescission. But in *Charisma Properties Ltd v Grayling (1994) Ltd* 1996 SC 556 a majority of the Extra Division had held, on similar wording, that the written notice could itself rescind the contract. In view of the fact that *Charisma* had not been cited to him, the sheriff principal put the case out for a further hearing so that he could be addressed on it. But his provisional view was that the wording did indeed require a two-stage process. If, however, *Charisma Properties* governed, the sheriff principal said that the letter of 27 January 2005 could not be read as effecting the rescission of the contract.

On (ii), the sellers drew attention to the requirement that the title deeds must 'disclose' the prejudicial matter, and offered to prove that the buyers knew of the matter alleged to be prejudicial even before missives were concluded. For, it was said, if they already knew of something, that thing could not be 'disclosed' by the title deeds. The sheriff principal accepted this interpretation of 'disclosed'. See **Commentary** p 98.

(6) Park Lane Developments (Glasgow Harbour) Ltd v Jesner
3 May 2006, Glasgow Sheriff Court, CA458/05

Missives were concluded for the sale of a new flat at 302 Meadowside Quay Walk, Glasgow. These were builders' missives, in standard form. In terms of the missives:

> The purchase price will also include title to an exclusive car parking space or in the case of the penthouse properties two exclusive car parking spaces.

In the event, the disposition offered to the buyer conveyed a right of common ownership in all the car parking spaces in the development together with a right of exclusive use of one of the spaces.

When the buyer purported to rescind, the seller sought implement, arguing (i) that the disposition properly implemented the missives and (ii) that, even if it did not, the buyer had known of the terms of the disposition for six months before settlement without objection and so was personally barred from doing so now. The sheriff (C A L Scott) rejected both arguments and dismissed the action. In relation to (i), he decided, plausibly enough, that 'title to an exclusive car parking space' meant sole ownership of that space.

It is not clear on what basis the seller purported to grant a right of exclusive use to a car parking space. Short of giving sole ownership, it is extremely difficult to structure exclusive rights of use. Thus even if the sheriff had been willing to regard the requirement of 'title' as fulfilled by common ownership, it is uncertain whether the seller could have delivered the exclusivity also required by the missives. The point, however, was not argued.

The personal bar aspects of this decision are discussed by Elspeth Reid at (2006) 10 *Edinburgh Law Review* 440–441.

(7) Aerpac UK Ltd v NOI Scotland Ltd
[2006] CSIH 20, 2006 GWD 18-365

As the buyer was already in possession before the date of entry, it simply retained possession after that date. But it failed to pay the price. For the purposes of a collateral contract, between different parties, it became important to know whether, after the date of entry, the buyer had a 'right to occupy' the property or whether its occupancy was unlawful. The missives contained the usual clauses entitling the buyer to entry but also providing for interest in the event of late payment of the price, with the option of rescission by the seller on giving written notice. No written notice was given. **Held:** In the absence of a notice of rescission, the buyer had a personal right to continue in occupation of the property. (On personal rights of occupation, see K G C Reid, *Law of Property in Scotland* (1996) para 128.) This affirms the decision of the Lord Ordinary on 31 March 2004 (*Conveyancing 2004* Case (1)).

(8) McNally v Worrell
2006 GWD 37-741, Sh Ct

Action for damages for what was said to be a fraudulent misrepresentation by the seller, made prior to missives, in relation to the adequacy of the private water supply serving the subjects of sale. The defender (seller) challenged the relevancy and specification of the pursuers' averments, arguing in particular that it was necessary to indicate the exact words on which the pursuers were relying. **Held:** that it was sufficient if the averments indicated the substance of the alleged misrepresentation, and so gave fair notice to the defender; and that that standard had been reached in the present case.

(9) Henderson v Marasa
1 December 2005, Glasgow Sheriff Court, A3429/03

Missives for the sale of a restaurant, held on leasehold tenure, contained the following supersession clause:

> [T]he missives of sale shall remain in full force and effect for a period of one year only following delivery of the Assignation of Lease in favour of your clients.

Although this clause omitted the usual qualification allowing enforcement if an action is raised within the stipulated period, it was held (i) that the missives could indeed be enforced provided that the action was raised within a year (which it had been), and (ii) that, although the pursuers' claim had now been amended from a purely delictual claim (based on misrepresentation) to include a claim based on breach of contract, the initial delictual claim was sufficient to defeat the one-year time limit, especially as the factual basis of both claims was the same. In the sheriff principal's view, it was not appropriate to apply here the stricter rules which affect statutory time limits under the Prescription and Limitation (Scotland) Act 1973.

FIXTURES

(10) Boskabelle Ltd v Laird
[2006] CSOH 173, 2006 SLT 1079

Missives were concluded for the sale of three fields on the outskirts of Edinburgh (near Little France) with entry and vacant possession on 26 March 2004. Before entry the seller had planted winter wheat and barley, and in August 2004 his employees took in the harvest without the permission of the buyer and new owner. When the buyer contacted the police, they refused to intervene. The buyer then sued for the value of the crop (£12,000).

The case raises directly the question of whether crops are heritable or moveable. The general rule is, of course, that crops – and plants, shrubs and trees – accede to the ground and so are heritable. That would mean that the wheat and barley belonged to the buyer. But the institutional writers are unanimous in their view that 'industrial growing crops' – crops which require annual seed and labour – do not accede and so are moveable. That would mean that the wheat and barley belonged to the seller (unless separately sold to the buyer).

A complication is that the decision of the Second Division in *Chalmers' Tr v Dick's Tr* 1909 SC 761 contains strong statements to the effect that industrial crops are heritable; but while this has been accepted by some commentators, it has been criticised by others (including one of us). In this new case Lord Turnbull had to choose between these competing views.

After a full argument, Lord Turnbull concluded that the remarks in *Chalmers' Tr* were *obiter* and that the institutional writers could and should be followed. That meant that the wheat and barley were moveable, that they remained the property of the seller, and that, on the principle that one can reap what one sows, the seller had been fully entitled to harvest the crop. The action was accordingly dismissed.

Of course, even moveable crops could have passed to the buyer if they had been included in the missives, whether expressly or by implication. In the present case they do not appear to have been mentioned expressly, but the buyer sought to argue that the requirement to give vacant possession included a requirement on the seller to remove its moveable property (as plainly it does), and that accordingly it could be inferred from the crops having been left behind that they were to be included in the sale. See eg K G C Reid, *Law of Property in Scotland* (1996) para 576. But this argument, which is not without merit, did not find favour with the court.

This decision is discussed by David Carey Miller in an article in the May 2007 issue of the *Edinburgh Law Review*.

COMMON PROPERTY

(11) Kenneil v Kenneil
[2006] CSOH 8, 2006 SLT 449; [2006] CSOH 95

This was an action of division or sale, which came before the court in two separate stages, in January and in June. The Ardpatrick Estate, Argyll, was co-owned by three brothers, Edan, Damon and Alistair Kenneil. Edan raised an action of division or sale. The court appointed a reporter to carry out the sale, and authorised any of the three brothers to bid. Damon submitted a bid for £3,700,000 and this was successful. On 20 September 2004 missives were concluded between the reporter and Damon. A deposit of 10% of the price was required by the missives and it was paid. The contractual date of entry was 1 December 2004. But Damon did not pay. The reporter rescinded the contract, having first obtained the authority of the court so to do, and found another buyer, Caledonian Trust plc, but at a lower price, £2,558,775. In the meantime Damon granted four standard securities over his one third *pro indiviso* share. Three of these were in favour of members of his family and the fourth in favour of his former solicitors.

A question now arose as to (i) the validity of the original contract between the reporter and Damon, (ii) whether the reporter could claim damages for breach, and (iii) whether the other *pro indiviso* owners could claim damages for breach.

In relation to (i), the Lord Ordinary (Glennie) said that, as a general rule, a contract between A, B and C and A would be invalid. But the reporter did not contract on behalf of the *pro indiviso* owners (para 30 of the January opinion):

> In my opinion a sale under Rule of Court 45 is not a sale by the parties at all. The Reporter does not act as their agent. Most of the ordinary incidents of agency are absent. The *pro indiviso* proprietors can give the Reporter no instructions; nor can they either add to or countermand his authority. The Reporter can procure dispositions in their name, against their will, signed in terms of Rule of Court 45.2(3) by the Deputy

Principal Clerk of Session. He accounts to the Court for the proceeds of sale, deducting therefrom (in accordance with the interlocutors of the Court) his expenses of sale. To my mind the proper analysis is that in conducting the sale of the subjects the Reporter acts in his own right as a Court authorised officer. He sells by authority of the Court. There is, therefore, no difficulty in him selling the subjects to one or more of the *pro indiviso* proprietors.

In relation to (ii), it was held that the reporter could not claim damages for breach, because the reporter had suffered no loss. This is a view we have difficulty in understanding. It means that a buyer in such a case could breach the contract with impunity. The same would presumably be true in sales by, for instance, trustees in sequestration, judicial factors, liquidators, company administrators, executors, and so on. This is not the law of Scotland. It is also difficult to reconcile this decision with the decision that the deposit (£370,000) should not be returned to Damon but should be added to the sale proceeds.

In relation to (iii), it was held that there could be no claim by the other *pro indiviso* owners for damages. In the first place, they were not parties to the contract. Nor, secondly, could they be said to have rights by virtue of the doctrine of *jus quaesitum tertio* (para 32 of the January opinion):

> Although in one sense it can be said that he [the reporter] contracts for the benefit of the owners of the property, in the sense that he is getting in the price for them, the reality and the form are both somewhat different. The price, less expenses of sale, are consigned into Court in terms of Rule 45.2(4)(a). They are distributed according to further order of the Court in terms of Rule 45.2(5)(a).... [I]t is wrong, in my opinion, to regard the consignation into Court as being the equivalent to payment to the owners of the property. The owners have no right to demand payment from the Accountant of Court. The nearest analogy may be that the Accountant of Court holds the proceeds of sale in trust. But whatever may be the precise legal analysis, it seems to me to be clear that the *pro indiviso* proprietors of the subjects could not sue the purchaser for the price. That would be to circumvent the need for further orders of the Court before the sale proceeds can be distributed. If that is so, I do not see how the owners can have a right to sue the purchaser directly for damages if he fails to pay the price and is, as a result, in breach of the missives.

In the third place (para 26 of the June opinion):

> Before the division and sale, the three parties to the action, as *pro indiviso* owners of the estate, had a legitimate expectation to receive the market value of the property. That was the limit of their 'entitlement' if it can be called an entitlement at all. If, for whatever reason, the second defender's bid were above the market value, that did not alter the legitimate expectation of the three parties.

This, however, seems questionable.

The sums for which the four standard securities were granted may – the point is unclear – have exceeded the share of the proceeds payable to Damon. If so that creates a difficulty, for a buyer will require an unencumbered title. But heritable creditors can refuse to sign discharges except against full payment.

[Another aspect of this case is digested at (44).]

(12) Apps v Sinclair
2006 GWD 16-316 (Sh Ct)

In 1989 the owner of a house in High Street, Dysart sold the house but reserved part of the ground to build a second house. The split-off disposition included, in the pertinents clause

> a right in common with me and my successors as proprietors of the subjects to the north-east of the subjects hereby disponed being retained by me (hereinafter referred to as 'said retained subjects') to the mutual accessway delineated and coloured blue on the said plan with access thereover on all necessary occasions.

Both houses changed hands more than once, but ultimately the old house came to belong to the defenders and the new house to the pursuers. Access to the pursuers' house was possible directly from the street, and there was hard standing which was large enough for four cars. For that reason it appears that the predecessors of the pursuers rarely used the mutual accessway. By contrast, the accessway was the only means of access to the defenders' house.

When the defenders attempted to restrict the pursuers' use of the accessway, the pursuers raised this action, seeking declarator of a right of common property, and interdict against the defenders from interfering with that right. The defenders counterclaimed, seeking a declarator that the pursuers' right of access was restricted in certain respects. In this appeal to the sheriff principal, which followed a debate, it was conceded by the defenders that the pursuers were entitled to a declarator as to common property.

As the sheriff principal (R A Dunlop QC) emphasised, the general rule for common property is that each co-owner can make any 'ordinary' use of the property; and an ordinary use of the accessway was, unsurprisingly, use for access. Thus far, the law favoured the pursuers. Why then should the pursuers' right be limited? The defenders argued that two sources of limitation could be identified.

In the first place, said the defenders, the meaning of 'ordinary' use depended to a considerable extent on past usage. As the sheriff principal pointed out, however, this was a misunderstanding of the role of past usage (para 22):

> Counsel for the appellants [and defenders] placed considerable reliance upon the statement in the Stair Encyclopaedia (Vol 18 para 24) that the dividing line between ordinary and extraordinary use will depend partly on the nature of the property and partly also on its recent history. In applying that statement to the circumstances of the present case however he appeared to overlook the reason that the author of that article gives for admitting consideration of recent history, namely that a use which begins its life as 'extraordinary' may, by passage of time, come to be accepted as 'ordinary'. That seems to be the *ratio* of *Wilson v Pattie* [(1829) 7 S 316] and of the few other authorities referred to in the article, which the author notes as the only reported decisions on this question. It is not suggested however that historic use may be relied upon to restrict a use which would otherwise be considered an ordinary use of the property in question.

Past usage, in other words, can be used to expand the range of ordinary uses, but it cannot be used to limit it.

The defenders' second argument turned on the closing words of the grant in the split-off disposition of 1989 ('with access thereover on all necessary occasions'). While, usually, *pro indiviso* owners can make ordinary use of the property, it is possible to agree on restrictions. This clause, the defenders argued, was an example of a restriction. The sheriff principal rejected this argument too on the basis (para 32) that 'the word "with" suggests something additional to the substantive right and not something restrictive of it'. To which we would add that it is not clear how an agreement, presumably personal in nature, between the parties to a disposition granted in 1989 could be binding on successors such as the pursuers and the defenders.

In any event, it is reasonably clear that, far from being an agreement, the words in question were intended to confer a servitude right of access. Naturally, this was incompetent, because the disponees were already (co-)owners of the supposed servient tenement (ie the accessway), and one cannot have a servitude over one's own property. It was also potentially misleading, giving rise to arguments of the kind mounted by the defenders. Nonetheless, it is surprising how commonly 'servitudes' are granted in cases where the grantee is also a *pro indiviso* owner.

SERVITUDES

(13) Bell v Fiddes
[2006] CSIH 15

This is a case of considerable complexity whose facts were set out in a very long opinion of the Lord Ordinary (Lord McEwan): see 2004 GWD 3-50, *Conveyancing 2004* Case (8). What seems to have happened was the following. The pursuers and the defender owned neighbouring crofts which were separated from the public road by a burn. Originally, access across the burn was by a ford, which was suitable for pedestrians and for off-road vehicles such as landrovers. In 1974, however, the pursuers built a bridge which led directly to their croft. A road to the east of the croft was added in 1983. It was possible to reach the defender's croft by vehicle by a combination of the bridge and the road.

At the time the bridge was built both crofts still belonged to the local estate. The pursuers bought their croft in 1979 and the defender's author bought in 1980. The 1979 disposition in favour of the pursuers reserved to the estate 'all existing rights and ways'. On the basis of this rather vague reservation the estate included in the 1980 disposition of the defender's croft an express servitude by reference to a line on a plan. The plan, however, was based on elderly OS maps which did not show the bridge. Whether for this or other reasons the route given in the plan for the servitude did not show a crossing of the burn at the point of the bridge.

It was accepted that the defender had a servitude over the pursuers' property. The question was the route. The defender argued for access across the bridge and along the eastern road. That would allow vehicular access. The pursuers argued for vehicular access up to and including the ford and for pedestrian access thereafter.

There had been various litigations; and the current action was made much more unwieldy by the fact that it took the form of a reduction of an earlier, undefended action in the sheriff court in which the defender (in that action the pursuer) had been granted a declarator of a servitude right of pedestrian and vehicular access along the line shown in a specially prepared plan which had now been lost.

Lord Marnoch, giving the opinion of an Extra Division of the Court of Session, takes up the story (paras 4–5):

> The Lord Ordinary has held, and there is now no dispute, that the pursuers could in no way be blamed for the failure to defend the Sheriff Court action and, accordingly, the only live question is or, at least, should be whether there was or was not a stateable defence which went unheard.
>
> Unfortunately, as the present action proceeded through the court, this simple question seems to have been lost sight of, with the result that the action has now been in court for more than ten years, evidence was taken on commission on two separate occasions, the evidence before the Lord Ordinary occupied ten days, the submissions of counsel occupied a further four days and the reclaiming motion before us was set down for four days of which, however, only two were in the event required. As the Lord Ordinary tells us, 'Many matters were explored in the days of the proof' and these seem to have included possible variations of the alleged right of way and the vexed subject of implied grants of servitude rights although it is fair to say that there is very little, if anything, in the pleadings relative to either of these concepts. Moreover, it transpired that the only real issue which the parties wished in the end to have decided was whether the right of access, as presently exercisable, had to be taken via a ford (in accordance with the Disposition plan) or via a bridge built over a stream running through the first pursuer's property, the bridge having been built by the first pursuer, *qua* tenant, in 1974. No doubt encouraged by counsel the Lord Ordinary did his best to answer that question but the sad truth is that, as was eventually made clear before us, the present process, having no declaratory conclusions of any sort, was, quite simply, not apt for deciding that matter.

The Extra Division had no difficulty in accepting that there had been a stateable defence to the sheriff court action, and refused the reclaiming motion.

(14) Skiggs v Adam
[2006] CSOH 73, 2006 GWD 17-352

Where a servitude of access was granted 'for all necessary purposes', these additional words were **held** to restrict its scope. See **Commentary** p 121.

(15) Candleberry Ltd v West End Homeowners Association
[2006] CSIH 28, 2007 SCLR 128, 2006 Hous LR 45

A deed of conditions recorded in 1989 provided that:

> Each proprietor shall have a heritable and irredeemable right of access for vehicular and pedestrian access over the 'public areas' which are shaded in yellow and pale green on the aforesaid plan.

Over the following years a number of feus were granted out of the area affected by the deed of conditions, title to the pursuer's feu being registered in 2001. In the pursuer's feu disposition the deed of conditions was referred to for burdens, in the usual way, but was not mentioned in the pertinents clause. Missing, therefore, was any statement to the effect that the subjects were conveyed 'together with the servitude specified in the deed of conditions aftermentioned'. As a result, no servitude was included by the Keeper in the property section of the title sheet. The defender, as the grantee of another feu, was owner of the putative servient tenement (ie the 'public areas'). The deed of conditions was referred to for burdens in the feu disposition granted in its favour.

In this action the pursuer sought declarator of the servitude, and interdict against obstruction by the defender. At first instance the sheriff held that the pursuer lacked a *prima facie* case sufficient for interim interdict. This was because the omission of the feu disposition from the pertinents clause was said to be fatal to the constitution of the servitude. We criticised that result in *Conveyancing 2005* pp 84–88, on the basis that a servitude could be included in the title of either the dominant or the servient tenement, that in the event it had been included in the title of the servient tenement (ie the defender's feu disposition), and accordingly that the servitude had been duly constituted. An Extra Division of the Court of Session has now adopted much the same reasoning, and result. Giving the opinion of the court, Lord Nimmo Smith said (at para 22):

> No doubt at the date when the Deed of Conditions was recorded and all the original land was in the ownership of the Secretary of State for Scotland [the granter of the Deed] it could not be said that there were a dominant and a servient tenement. But not only is the relevant provision of the Deed of Conditions set out in the burdens section of the pursuers' Land Certificate, it is also set out in the burdens section of the defenders' Land Certificate. There is no obvious reason why the pursuers' land should not have become the dominant tenement on the registration of the Feu Disposition in their favour.

Accordingly, the pursuer had a strong *prima facie* case. Further, and contrary to the view expressed by the sheriff and sheriff principal, it was held that the balance of convenience favoured the granting of interim interdict.

(16) Aberdeen City Council v Wanchoo
[2006] CSOH 196, 2007 SLT 289

For 20 years the defender and the defender's predecessor took access over land belonging to the pursuer. At the same time it held a lease over the land, restricted to a right of car-parking. The pursuer sought a declarator that no servitude existed in favour of the defender. **Held:** (i) that as the lease was confined to car-parking, the use of the land for access could not be attributed to the lease, and (ii) that as the pursuer was personally barred from denying access, the possession was 'as of right' and therefore qualified for the purposes of prescription. The defender was assoilzied. For (ii), see **Commentary** p 122.

Two other aspects of the judgment should be mentioned. First, there was a gap of about a year between the time when the defender began to take access and the time when the defender's predecessor ceased to take access. During this period any access taken would have been slight. Nonetheless, Lord Glennie (para 22), following D J Cusine and R R M Paisley, *Servitudes and Rights of Way* (1998) p 342, decided that there was no interruption to the possession.

Secondly, there was some discussion of an *obiter dictum* by Lady Smith, in *Nationwide Building Society v Walter D Allan Ltd* 2004 GWD 25-539 at para 35, that servitudes, even those which are created by prescription, 'emanate from grants. They are given, not taken'. Lord Glennie (at para 31) took a different view:

> [H]aving had the benefit of full citation of authority on this point, I should say that, had I required to decide the point, I would have inclined towards the view that there was no additional requirement on a person claiming a servitude right to establish, directly or by inference, that there had been a grant. It seems to me that, if Lord Young's opinion in *Grierson* [*v The School Board of Sandsting and Aithsting* (1882) 9 R 437] is to the effect that there is such a requirement, it did not find favour with the majority of the Second Division in that case. Nor is it consistent with the speeches in the House of Lords in *Mann v Brodie* [(1882) 12 R (HL) 52]: see, in particular, per Lord Blackburn at p 54 and Lord Watson at p 57. Although that case was concerned with the establishment by prescription of a public right of way, there can, in my opinion, be no relevant distinction in this respect between such a case and the establishment of a servitude right. However, since it is not necessary to decide the point I say no more about it.

We would agree with that view: see *Conveyancing 2004* pp 89–90.

(17) Neumann v Hutchinson
2006 GWD 28-628, Sh Ct

For more than 20 years the pursuer took access to the rear of his house over property belonging to the defenders. He claimed a servitude. **Held:** (i) that as the pursuer was unable to prove an absence of tolerance on the part of the defenders and their predecessors, no servitude had been established by prescription, and (ii) that although the pursuer had carried out a certain amount of building work on his own property in reliance on the access, the amount expended (c £2,500) was far too small to create a right founded on acquiescence.

On (i), see **Commentary** p 124.

(18) Peart v Legge
2006 GWD 18-377 affd 2007 SCLR 86, Sh Ct

A servitude of way which could only be exercised by first breaching a wall on the dominant tenement was **held** to be *res merae facultatis* and hence not extinguished by non-exercise for 20 years. See **Commentary** p 128.

(19) Spella v Scottish Enterprise Ltd
16 May 2006, Glasgow Sheriff Court, A1015/02

The pursuer owned a private road which was subject to a servitude, in favour of a property immediately to the west, to take a pipe from the property to the publicly adopted sewer underneath the road. Subsequently, the defender, who owned land further to the west, reached agreement with the owner of the dominant tenement to connect into his drainage system. What happened next was unclear, and had not yet been the subject of a proof. On one version, all the work carried out by the defender took place within the dominant tenement. On another version work upgrading the system took place in the servient tenement (ie the pursuer's road). All this happened some years before. The pursuer sought damages in respect that he had lost the opportunity to realise the commercial value of his property.

This argument was substantially rejected by the sheriff principal (James A Taylor). (i) The pursuer's case was based on encroachment. But on the first version of the facts there was no encroachment. (ii) On the second version, the defender was merely doing what Scottish Water had both a power and a duty to do under ss 1–4 of the Sewerage (Scotland) Act 1968. That being the case, the pursuer was not in a position to extract a ransom from the defender.

It is not clear why, under (i), the use of a pre-existing pipe to send additional sewage was not thought to count as encroachment. After all, the legal basis for resisting the increased use of a servitude is precisely that, if the use is beyond the terms of the servitude, the dominant owner is encroaching (or trespassing) on the servient tenement. The answer, if there is one, may lie in the speciality that, under s 16(1)(c) of the 1968 Act, the pipe was vested in Scottish Water, so that, arguably, such encroachment as there was did not affect the property of the pursuer.

REAL BURDENS

(20) Hanover (Scotland) Housing Association Ltd v Reid
[2006] CSOH 56, 2006 SLT 518

This decision marks the final shots in a dispute which began in 1989 and which has led to arbitration, and also to previous litigation both in the sheriff court and in the Court of Session: for the latter see *Hanover (Scotland) Housing Association Ltd v Sandford* 2002 SCLR 144, discussed in *Conveyancing 2001* p 11. The dispute concerns the governance of a sheltered/retiring housing development at Millbrae Gardens, Glasgow. The superior, Hanover Housing, was at loggerheads with some of the owners. Originally, Hanover had factored the development, but, following complaints about costs, and an arbitration award, it appointed other factors. The new factors were not acceptable to a majority of owners, who refused to pay their service charge and, as soon as the Title Conditions (Scotland) Act 2003 s 28 came into force, replaced them with other factors. In this action Hanover, as superior, together with the factors it had appointed, was suing for arrears of payments.

The action was dismissed. (i) Under the deed of conditions, as amended, new factors could be appointed only if the property council was consulted. This had not been done (although the owners had been written to individually). Hence the factors had not been properly appointed and had no title to sue. The deficiency was not cured by s 65 of the Title Conditions Act because the action had been raised before the Act came into force. (Lord Reed was not, however, fully addressed on this last point and he regarded his views as tentative.) (ii) Equally, Hanover had no title to sue. In terms of the deed of conditions, enforcement rights lay with the factors; but in any event the money was not properly due because, under the deed, a demand for payment must be issued by the factors, by which was meant factors who had been properly appointed. (iii) Since relations between the parties were regulated by the deed of conditions, there could be no question of setting that deed's conditions at naught by claiming the money due under the law of unjustified enrichment.

(21) Faeley v Clark
2006 GWD 28-626, Lands Tribunal

A real burden in a disposition prohibited further building without the consent of an immediate neighbour. In 1990 this consent was given in the form of a minute of agreement between the two sets of owners. Under the agreement, a further house was to be allowed 'provided always that external additions shall not be made to the said dwellinghouse and no other erections shall be constructed upon 7A Rockland Park without our prior written consent'. Were these additional provisions independent real burdens, or were they merely personal to the parties in question? It was **held** that they were merely personal. See **Commentary** p 114.

[Another aspect of this case is digested at (29).]

(22) At.Home Nationwide Ltd v Morris
11 December 2006, Lands Tribunal

A condition in a deed of conditions in respect of a retirement housing development provided that an owner who wished to sell or change the use of a flat must first satisfy the superior that the flat would continue to be used as accommodation for the elderly. **Held:** now that feudal superiors had ceased to exist, the condition was no longer valid or enforceable. See **Commentary** p 111.

[Another aspect of this case is digested at (31).]

(23) Halladale (Shaftesbury) Ltd
20 June 2005, Lands Tribunal

The Title Conditions Act s 90(1)(a)(ii) confers on the Lands Tribunal a new jurisdiction, in relation to a real burden (only), 'to determine any question as to its validity, applicability or enforceability or as to how it is to be construed'. This is the first case in which the jurisdiction has been used.

The application concerned Shaftesbury House in Glasgow, situated at the junction of Hope Street and Waterloo Street. The title included a disposition granted by the Royal Bank of Scotland which provided that:

Our said disponees and their foresaids shall not carry on in the subjects hereby disponed or any part or parts thereof or sell or let the same for the purpose of carrying on therein the business of bankers.

The applicants sought a determination that the burden was not enforceable or, alternatively, the discharge of the burden. Since the application was unopposed, the applicants were entitled to a discharge without further inquiry, and the application could have been disposed of on this ground. However, on the basis of the written application and (or so it appears) without legal argument, the Tribunal decided that the burden was indeed unenforceable because there was no benefited property and, even if there had been, there was no interest to enforce.

(24) Sheltered Housing Management Ltd v Jack
5 January 2007, Lands Tribunal

This is the first case to consider whether real burdens are void as 'repugnant with ownership' under s 3(6) of the Title Conditions (Scotland) Act 2003 – although the test derives from the former common law as to which there is a certain amount of authority, collected in K G C Reid, *Law of Property in Scotland* (1996) para 391. The burdens in question were contained in a new deed of conditions prepared for an existing sheltered housing development. They read:

> The House Manager's Apartment and Office shall not be used otherwise than for occupation and use by the House Manager.
> The Guest Rooms shall not be used otherwise than for occasional occupation by guests of or visitors to the Proprietors or occupiers of Flats.

The deed of conditions was imposed by a two-thirds majority of owners in the development, acting under s 33 of the 2003 Act, and was opposed by Sheltered Housing Management Ltd, the former superior and manager which also owned the apartment, office and guest room, and wished to be able to use it for another purpose. Among other arguments, it sought to have it found that the burdens were repugnant with ownership. Unsurprisingly, the Lands Tribunal disagreed (p 29):

> Real burdens are generally perpetual in nature and therefore liable to restrict to some degree, in perpetuity, the owner's right to exclusive occupation and use. Restrictions in the use of property which are conceived in the legitimate interests of other property owners are recognised and permitted.... The extent of interference with the owner's exclusive enjoyment of his property will obviously vary with the terms of the restriction but will also vary with the nature of the property. Ancillary property is by its nature likely to be permanently shackled by a restriction, in the interests of the owners of the principal property, to ancillary use. It seems to us that the owners of the principal property, here the sheltered flats, have a proper and legitimate interest in establishing such a restriction, and we are not persuaded that there is anything in any way unusual or objectionable in these proposed burdens, which appear typical of modern provision in such property communities. The applicants as owners of the residual property will not be prevented from selling, or leasing, or granting security over, the residual property.

[Another aspect of this case is digested at (35).]

VARIATION ETC OF TITLE CONDITIONS BY LANDS TRIBUNAL

(25) Regan v Mullen
2006 GWD 25-564 (merits), 1 September 2006 (expenses), Lands Tribunal

The applicants owned a large penthouse flat – five bedrooms and four bathrooms, some 4,500 square feet in all – at Speirs Wharf, Glasgow. This was a conversion, completed in 1989, of warehouses on the Forth and Clyde Canal, resulting in the creation of some 176 units, a mixture of flats and offices. Clause eighteenth of the Deed of Conditions provided that 'none of the said dwellinghouses forming part of the said buildings shall at any time hereafter be subdivided'. The applicants, wishing to subdivide, sought variation of this condition. The Residents' Committee unanimously agreed to oppose the application, and the owners of more than 60 flats registered objections.

The application was granted. Although the purpose of the condition (Title Conditions (Scotland) Act 2003 s 100, factor (f)) was to prevent the creation of more and smaller flats, the applicants' flat was 'one-off', being much larger than the others. (It was originally created for a director of the developer.) There was little benefit to the other owners in maintaining the condition as it applied to that particular flat (factor (b)). And the condition plainly impeded a reasonable use of the flat by the applicants (factor (c)), even although evidence that the flat in its current form was difficult to sell was unimpressive.

Under factor (j) ('any other factor'), the Tribunal acknowledged the importance of preserving the deed of conditions (pp 13–14):

> We appreciate and acknowledge the importance of the deed of conditions where there are so many proprietors at this particular development. The residents and the factor need to know that the deed of conditions can be relied upon and will be upheld. The narrower aspect of this is on the specific issue of sub-division. Here, we are completely clear that allowing sub-division of this property should not be seen as any form of precedent. It may sometimes be a legitimate concern that the character and amenity of a housing scheme is threatened when an owner becomes the first to apply to sub-divide, extend, etc because of the prospect that others may follow, but in this case the unique nature, and in particular size, of this property makes it impossible to suggest that there are any other comparable properties.

On expenses, the Tribunal noted (p 3) that:

> The correct approach, applying Section 103(1) of the Act of 2003, to claims for expenses by applicants who have been successful in opposed applications for discharge or variation of title conditions is not straightforward. The unsuccessful opponents are 'benefited proprietors' seeking to uphold their legal rights. It is not at all surprising that they will be unhappy at the prospect of not only losing the rights but also having to pay the sometimes very substantial professional expenses of the party who had purchased property on the basis that it was burdened by those rights.

Nonetheless, s 103 required the Tribunal to depart from its former practice of not awarding expenses in cases of reasonable opposition. And, roughly speaking, the new rule was that expenses follow success. But here, as in general litigation, there were exceptions where either the court disapproved of some aspect of the successful party's conduct or there was divided success. Examples of the *first* exception would include an application which was vague or not justified by detailed averments or evidence until shortly before the hearing, or, sometimes, where no effort had been made towards reaching agreement. In application of the *second* exception, it would be wrong to tot up a list of successes or failures in relation to the list of factors set out in s 100 of the 2003 Act. But where an argument took up a great deal of time without impressing the Tribunal, this would be a ground for modifying expenses. In the present case, that would be true of the argument that an undivided flat could not be readily sold. Accordingly, while the applicants should be awarded their expenses – though only from the point at which the application was opposed – the amount should be reduced by 50%, bearing in mind that the weak argument also caused expense to the respondents in opposing it.

(26) Daly v Bryce
2006 GWD 25-565, Lands Tribunal

The applicant owned a house in a 1960s housing estate at Blairston Avenue, Bothwell. In terms of the governing feu charter, of 1961, the feuar was bound to erect a dwellinghouse not exceeding two storeys in height. Furthermore:

> No other buildings or erections of any kind whatever except the wall and other enclosures shall ever be erected on the said plot of ground without the consent in writing of us or our successors....

The applicant had planning permission to replace the existing bungalow with two houses. The feudal system having been abolished, the superiors were no longer there to give their consent. Hence the application for a variation or discharge. An immediate neighbour objected. Although the Tribunal did 'not find it easy to decide this case' (p 22), ultimately it was willing to grant the application. The Tribunal's reasoning was as follows.

The purpose of the condition (Title Conditions (Scotland) Act 2003 s 100, factor (f)) was, in a broad sense, to preserve the amenity of the neighbourhood as a whole, in particular by maintaining residential use and preventing over-development. Against this background the crucial question was whether the benefit of the condition to the respondents (factor (b)) outweighed its burden to the applicants (factor (c)). On balance it did not.

On factor (c), it was plain that the house was outmoded and that something needed to be done. Of course this might take the form of renovation and extension, as had happened elsewhere on the estate. And indeed (p 20):

> The applicants accepted that their personal reasons for their preference are not relevant and did not indicate any particular reasons related to the property for building two houses rather than extensively refurbishing (or perhaps completely rebuilding) the one. This seems to us to be something of a gap in the applicants' case.

However, it seemed from the evidence that refurbishment would be very expensive so that (pp 20–21):

> Abiding by the restriction to one house would, standing the clear requirement to do something fairly major, apparently be onerous. This is not a case in which the subjects could simply be enjoyed in their existing state and the proposal to demolish and replace with two new houses was motivated only by financial profit.

Factor (b) was less strong. While the condition struck at over-development, the applicants' main concern was actually with preserving light, particularly to their sittingroom. But while one of the new houses would be much closer and would restrict light, there was nothing in the condition which would have prevented the existing house from being built so close.

(27) J & L Leisure Ltd v Shaw
28 March, 25 August (merits) and 30 October 2006 (expenses),
Lands Tribunal

In 1958 a split-off disposition of property in Dunbar imposed a height restriction of 15 feet 6 inches on new buildings. At the time the reserved property – the benefited property in the burden – was a hotel, and the purpose of the restriction was evidently to preserve the hotel's sea views. Ultimately, the buildings on the burdened property became derelict, and the owner received outline planning permission to build two-storey housing. But the burden stood in the way, because the proposed buildings would be 3 metres higher than the permitted limit. So the owner applied to the Tribunal for variation of the burden to the extent of allowing the development.

By this time the hotel had been converted into flats, and the application was opposed by the owner of the flat which formed the upper level of a rear extension. The owner's view at present, though towards the sea, was unprepossessing because of the derelict state of the applicant's buildings. But the proposed new buildings would further block the view and the light.

The Tribunal granted the application, apparently without much difficulty. It was true that the original purpose of the burden – to preserve the sea view – remained in place (Title Conditions (Scotland) Act 2003 s 100, factor (f)). But the burden seriously impeded the enjoyment of the burdened property (factor (c)): the existing buildings were now derelict; as this was a conservation area there were limited options as to their replacement; it could readily be accepted 'that single storey housing firstly might not be approved by the planners and secondly would be uneconomic' (p 9). Furthermore (p 14):

> the proposed housing development seems not only eminently reasonable but also the only type of development which can be seriously considered. Accordingly, the burden on the applicants of the title condition restraining development to this height is very considerable.

As against that, the Tribunal considered that the benefit of the condition to the respondent (factor (b)) was of lesser weight. The proposed development would bring advantages as well as disadvantages. Admittedly, the effect on the respondent's sittingroom gave cause for concern (pp 10–11):

> In the sittingroom, however, we are clear that there would be a substantial adverse impact. There was not much of a view from that room, but the respondent is understandably concerned as much if not more by the light than the view. We do consider that in that room the light, already weak, would be considerably affected. The direct outlook would be completely dominated by the end of the development. The view of the sky would be all but obliterated.

But this was one room only. And the very fact that the Act makes provision for compensation in respect of 'substantial loss and disadvantage' as a result of a successful application (s 90(7)(a)) shows that it was contemplated that applications could be granted which had a material impact on the benefited owner.

Other factors also favoured granting the application, particularly the age of the burden (factor (e)) and the fact that planning permission had been granted (factor (h)). On the other hand, the Tribunal rejected as irrelevant in relation to this burden the suggestion (under factor (j)) that the development would improve the amenity of other properties.

The Tribunal awarded compensation which was ultimately fixed at £5,600. In doing so it rejected the valuation evidence for the respondent that the value of his property would be reduced by £30,000. It is worth noting that the applicant had tried to buy the respondent off shortly before the hearing with an informal offer of £8,000.

Only the respondent sought expenses. The Tribunal awarded £750, primarily in respect of a second hearing that was made necessary by an alteration to the application, but also having regard to the respondent's success in respect of compensation.

(28) McPherson v Mackie
2006 GWD 27-606 rev [2007] CSIH 7, 2007 GWD 10-189

The applicants owned a house in an 11-house estate near Helensburgh, overlooking the Gareloch, which had been built in 1990. The applicants wished to demolish their house so that it could be used for the construction of a road which would lead from the estate to a proposed new estate of some 15 houses. This was contrary to the deed of conditions, which required the maintenance of the existing house.

The application was refused, mainly on the ground that the benefit which the conditions conferred on the benefited properties, ie the neighbours (Title Conditions (Scotland) Act 2003 s 100, factor (b)) exceeded the extent to which they impeded the enjoyment of the burdened property (factor (c)). Indeed the enjoyment was not really impeded, for the proposed development was not on the burdened property but on adjoining land. In the Tribunal's view (p 18):

> [T]he conditions do not in any way at all impede the ordinary, normal use of this house or diminish its value as a house or garden. To the contrary, they underpin that value. This is not a case in which, for example, a house or garden has become too large or in some other way unattractive or uneconomic in modern conditions.

At most, the conditions prevented the windfall benefit which would result if the plot were sold to the neighbouring developer free of the conditions.

By contrast, factor (b) was more strongly established. It was true that the proposed road would be largely unobtrusive and would not carry much traffic. It was also true that the developer of the estate had at one time held a plot back with a view to using it for the very road which was now being proposed, although this aspect could not be given much weight. On the other hand, the immediately adjacent house would be subject to considerable disruption during the construction period, which might last for as long as four years. Admittedly (p 16):

> [t]his is not generally a material consideration, because such disturbance is usually quite short-lived, for example when a neighbour wishes to build an extension, house in the garden or the like. Here, however, what is involved is not only the actual construction work at the subjects but also the construction traffic using the estate road.

In the Tribunal's view, the other statutory factors were less important. The purpose of the conditions (factor (f)) was 'to preserve the amenity and character of the estate' (p 14). The availability of planning permission for the new development – something which seemed unlikely in 1990 – was a change in circumstances (factor (a)). Planning permission had been granted (factor (g)), but this only showed that the proposed development was reasonable from the viewpoint of the general public.

The applicants appealed to the Court of Session, and an Extra Division of the Court allowed the appeal and remitted the application to the Lands Tribunal for reconsideration. The decision was based on three main grounds.

First, the Tribunal was mistaken in its view that an important purpose of the conditions (factor (f)) was to protect the owners of the estate from traffic, and in particular from construction traffic. After all, a plot had originally been held back for use as a road. And in any event, there was nothing in the conditions to stop an owner in the estate from demolishing his house and building another – something which would inevitably involve construction traffic. Similarly, if a house was destroyed by fire, the deed of conditions required that it be re-built.

Secondly, construction traffic was in any event a temporary difficulty whereas the purpose of real burdens was to deal with the long-term use of property. In the words of Lord Eassie (at para 16, giving the opinion of the court):

> Title conditions such as those in issue in the present case are directed towards continuing long-term user – the ultimate user – rather than transitional matters such as construction disturbance. If the long-term user is acceptable it will usually be difficult to deny its allowance on the basis of short-term construction disturbance.

In England the Court of Appeal had recently taken a similar view, in *Shephard v Turner* [2006] EWCA Civ 8.

Finally, the Tribunal had been wrong to disregard what it termed the 'windfall' benefit to the applicants from being able to realise the development value of the plot. Lord Eassie again (para 23):

[W]here variation or discharge of a title condition is sought it will often be the case that the burdened property is the fortuitous beneficiary of its situation in changing circumstances or is the beneficiary of the discovery of some other feature which enhances its value if that feature were to be exploited. Discovery of gold under farmland may be a wholly fortuitous benefit to the farmer, who bought the farm for farming purposes and who could happily and profitably continue to farm there, but the fortuitous nature of the benefit would not, in our view, be a good reason for denying discharge of the title conditions impeding the mining of gold. We therefore think that in its characterisation of the development value as 'windfall', with the possible moral judgment implied in the selection of that adjective, the Tribunal may have fallen into error if that were material to its reasoning. We would add that we do not think it possible to consider reasonableness of the development of the appellants' property for the construction of the access road in isolation from the potential public benefit of the development of the Bergius land for housing in accordance with the detailed planning consent.

This is an important decision, the first by the Inner House under the new legislation. In general, the approach taken by the Lands Tribunal to the legislation is not challenged (although, admittedly, it was not challenged by counsel for the appellants: see para 8). But in admitting windfall benefit as a relevant consideration for factor (c), while at the same time upholding (if only by implication) the Tribunal's view (deriving from *Church of Scotland General Trustees v McLaren* 2006 SLT (Lands Tr) 27) that factor (b) is limited by factor (f) – that, in other words, a benefit is relevant only where (unlike freedom from construction traffic in the present case) it is within the original purpose of the condition – the Inner House has tipped the balance in favour of those seeking to have conditions discharged. After this decision (even) more applications will meet with success, and in a battle between developers and neighbours, victory will usually go to the developers.

(29) Faeley v Clark
2006 GWD 28-626, Lands Tribunal

A break-off disposition of property in Largs ('Broomcraig'), granted in 1967, provided that:

Any further erections or buildings on the solum or ground of the subjects hereinbefore disponed other than what are already in being shall require the written consent and approval first had and obtained of me and my successors in the ownership of Broomcroft [the property retained by the disponer].

Over the years Broomcraig was divided and some further buildings were allowed. The applicants, who owned part of Broomcraig, obtained planning permission for the erection of a second house in their back garden and now sought variation of the title condition just quoted. The application was opposed by the owners of Broomcroft.

In considering this application, the Tribunal set out its general approach in the following passage (p 14):

As with many cases under this jurisdiction involving proposals to build additional houses in garden areas contrary to existing title conditions, this case comes down in large measure to the Tribunal's assessment, on the evidence and their impression at the site inspection, of the effect of the building proposals on the benefited proprietors, in the light of the purpose of the conditions and the other factors relevant to the issue of reasonableness.

In the present case, as so often, the purpose of the condition was to preserve the amenity of neighbours – in particular a spectacular view over the Clyde to Cumbrae. And, as so often, the task of the Tribunal was to balance the benefit of the condition to the objectors (Title Conditions (Scotland) Act 2003 s 100, factor (b)) against the burden which it imposed on the applicants (factor (c)). Often the Tribunal's conclusion has been that the burden exceeds the benefit and that the condition should be discharged. But in this case, rejecting evidence led by the applicants, the Tribunal concluded – largely on the basis of a site visit – that the proposed house, although built at a lower level, would have a serious impact on Broomcroft. Not only would it obstruct the sea view, but 'the substantial mass of building so close would considerably affect the particular setting of Broomcroft' (p 19). By contrast, factor (c) was less compelling. It was true, of course, that the title condition prevented the development for which the applicants had planning permission; but it did not prevent all developments, because the owners of Broomcroft had, in the past, been willing to allow reasonable additional buildings. By contrast, the house proposed in the present case 'is too high to make the objection from the Broomcroft proprietors, who have demonstrated their reasonableness in considering development proposals on previous occasions, unreasonable' (p 23).

[Another aspect of this case is digested at (21).]

(30) West Coast Property Developments Ltd v Clarke
28 June (merits) and 6 October 2006 (expenses), Lands Tribunal

Number 11 Turnberry Road, Glasgow is the end terrace of a block of four Victorian terraced houses. The terrace is subject to a feu contract of 1875 which, after an obligation to build a house on each plot, provides that:

> no stables or dung pits shall be erected or set down on and no offensive use or occupation made or allowed of the back green and no erections shall be placed thereon except the necessary ashpit accommodation for each lodging and a stable with a loft thereto on each of the plots of ground before disponed for the use of the proprietor thereof the height of any of which at the highest point shall not exceed twenty five feet from the level of the Meuse lane behind....

The applicant, who had planning permission for a two-storey house in the rear garden, sought the discharge of this condition. The application was opposed by a number of neighbours. The Tribunal granted a variation to the extent of allowing the proposed house but refused a complete discharge, on the basis that the condition might still have some life in it. A claim for compensation was refused because, while there was evidence of possible loss of value as a result of the proposed development, this was not tied in to the relaxation of the condition in the 1875 deed.

The Tribunal's decision turned mainly on the change in circumstances (Title Conditions (Scotland) Act 2003 s 100, factor (a)): all of the terraced houses were now flatted, and – contrary to the 1875 deed – mews houses had been built in the gardens. Indeed this last point was important in relation to factor (b) because, while it was certainly true that the loss of amenity which the applicant's development would cause would be greatest in respect of the mews houses, 'we doubt the reasonableness of insisting on that [amenity] benefit when the mews houses themselves go against the 1875 scheme' (p 24). On factor (c), the Tribunal accepted that '[i]nability to proceed with a substantial development which has planning permission ... is a significant impediment when the subjects have otherwise little or no prospect of any other valuable use' (pp 24–25); but the Tribunal also accepted that 'this may simply be a speculative development with a view to realising profit' and that 'there is a difference between situations in which some factor such as the passage of time has created problems for the original permitted use of the property and situations which simply involve a new development use' (p 25).

Almost as an aside, the Tribunal commented that factor (b) 'raises the issue of degree of interest, which, although similar, is not identical to the test of interest [to enforce] under Section 8(3)(a)' (p 16).

The application having largely succeeded on its merits, those objecting to the application were ordered to pay 70% of the applicant's costs from the time that they made their objections. The Tribunal's opinion of 6 October 2006 contains a valuable discussion of the issue of expenses.

(31) At.Home Nationwide Ltd v Morris
11 December 2006, Lands Tribunal

A condition in a deed of conditions in respect of a retirement housing development provided that an owner who wished to sell or change the use of a flat must first satisfy the superior that the flat would continue to comply with a second condition in the deed. The second condition provided that the flat must be used as accommodation for the elderly. The applicant, who owned nine of the 19 flats, applied for a discharge of the first condition but not of the second. In the event, the Tribunal decided that, following the abolition of the feudal system, the condition was no longer enforceable. But it indicated that it would not have been willing to discharge the condition if it had been still alive. It was true that the condition was burdensome for the applicants, particularly if the requirement to obtain the superior's consent had now to be read as a requirement to obtain the consent of all flat-owners. But it conferred a benefit on the two owners who had entered objections which was different from the benefit conferred by the second condition. This is because it was preventative in nature. Further, the Tribunal would have been unwilling to discharge the condition just for the applicants' flats, and in the absence of a proposal to put some equivalent but more workable condition in its place.

The Tribunal refused to make an award of expenses because (i) this was a particularly novel and difficult question under new legislation, (ii) the applicants gave no indication that any effort had been made to resolve the problem before making the application, and (iii) the applicants' arguments were in any event not all successful.

[Another aspect of this case is digested at (22).]

(32) Ventureline Ltd
2 August 2006, Lands Tribunal

Whereas an application to vary or discharge a *real burden* must, if it is unopposed, be granted without further inquiry (Title Conditions (Scotland) Act 2003 s 97), the same rule does not apply to applications in respect of *servitudes*. This was one such. Two dispositions of 1972 purported to create 'a right to use' certain ground. Whether so vague a right can be constituted as a servitude is open to doubt, but the new legislation (unlike the old) allows the Tribunal to consider the application anyway (2003 Act s 90(1)(a): 'purported title condition'). In the absence of opposition, the Tribunal had little difficulty in granting the application, principally on the ground that the condition prevented re-development, and so impeded the enjoyment of the applicant's property (factor (c)).

(33) Perkins v Moffat
16 January 2006, Lands Tribunal

This was a combined application (i) for discharge and (ii) for a declaration as to the validity or enforceability of a burden. When the application was intimated by advertisement, the respondents objected. Thereafter the application was withdrawn. **Held** that it must follow from the withdrawal of the application that the applicants were liable for the respondents' expenses.

(34) Hornbuckle Mitchell Trustees Ltd v Sundial Properties (Gilmerton) Ltd
13 February 2006, Lands Tribunal

Where a real burden is more than 100 years old, the owner of the burdened property can obtain its discharge by the service and registration of a notice of termination. This is the so-called 'sunset rule' set out in ss 20–24 of the Title Conditions (Scotland) Act 2003. But a notice of termination can be opposed by the owner of any of the benefited properties by making an application to the Lands Tribunal for a renewal of the burden (2003 Act s 90(1)(b)). The application then proceeds much like a normal application for variation and discharge, except that the applicant (on whom the onus of proof rests) is the benefited owner and not the burdened.

This is the first case in which a notice of termination was opposed. But the opposition did not get very far because, while an application for renewal was duly made, it was withdrawn some three weeks before the hearing date. The question then became one of liability for expenses. The respondent (which had served the original notice of termination) sought expenses taxed on the Sheriff Court Defended Ordinary Action scale but increased to 150% to reflect the amount of research involved on what were still novel points of law. The applicant sought to avoid an award of expenses by arguing that, following service of the notice of termination, it had had little choice but to apply for renewal in order to preserve its position and to allow negotiations to take place.

The Tribunal awarded expenses to the respondent at the ordinary rate. On the one hand, expenses were plainly due, because it could not really be said that the applicant did not have sufficient time after the notice of termination; but on the other hand, the costs of research were properly attributable to the notice of termination and not to opposing the Tribunal application.

(35) Sheltered Housing Management Ltd v Jack
5 January 2007, Lands Tribunal

This is the first case to test the validity of a new deed of conditions adopted by a sheltered housing development. It is also the first case to challenge a variation of community burdens carried out under s 33 of the Title Conditions (Scotland) Act 2003.

The application concerned a sheltered housing development known as Dunmail Manor, Dunmail Avenue, Cults, Aberdeen. Until the appointed day for feudal abolition (28 November 2004), the development was factored by the superior, Sheltered Housing Management Ltd ('SHML'). After the appointed day the owners replaced SHML with Peverel using their powers under s 28(1) of the 2003 Act. They also drew up a new deed of conditions to replace the original one, which had been couched in feudal terms and had involved the management of the development by the superior.

One of the key changes in the new deed was a provision that certain parts of the development which belonged to SHML – which owned the warden's flat, warden's office, guest bedrooms, a garage, a potting shed and certain store rooms – were to be used only for purposes ancillary to the development. Thus the warden's flat, for example, was to be used only for occupation by the warden. In exchange, the other owners were to pay SHML £6000 a year, with a provision for upwards adjustments in line with the RPI.

Naturally, SHML was opposed to the change. But under s 33 of the 2003 Act – read, in the case of sheltered housing, with s 54(5)(b) – existing community burdens can be varied by the owners of two thirds of the units in the community. In the present case, two thirds of the owners had signed the deed. Changes made under s 33 can be challenged by means of an application to the Lands Tribunal under s 90(1)(c), and SHML duly applied to have the existing deed of conditions preserved unchanged. The application was refused.

In terms of s 98, the Tribunal can grant an application for preservation under s 90(1)(c) only if it is satisfied, having regard to the factors set out in s 100, that the proposed variation – in this case, the new deed of conditions – is either (i) 'not in the best interests of all the owners (taken as a group) of the units in the community' or (ii) 'unfairly prejudicial to one or more of those owners'. Naturally, the discussion in the present case focused mainly on (ii).

The Tribunal drew attention to what it saw as the broad thrust of certain provisions of the 2003 Act (pp 35–36):

> The 2003 Act goes some way beyond simply re-formulating and re-stating title conditions to enable them to work in a world without feudal superiors. It appears to us that there is a clear statutory intention to facilitate changes in the operation of property communities. The provisions of sections 52 to 54, particularly section 53, give new enforcement rights to proprietors within the community and able to demonstrate a real interest. Beyond that, however, there are provisions about management and there is this new right of majorities to impose additional burdens provided this is in the interest of the community as a whole and not unfair to the minority, particularly individual owners. This seems to involve recognition of a possible need to supplement or alter the titular arrangements entered into between developers and individual purchasers: a monopoly over management arrangements may have been created or title conditions may be seen as tilted in favour of the developer who either remains owner or is put in a position to deal in residual property. In the sheltered housing context, the evidence before us suggests that much current practice in the industry reflects a need to respond to such concerns.

The Tribunal noted that, until now, it had always been clear that SHML's property was to be used for the purposes of the development. And indeed if a choice now had to be made between imposing a use restriction on SHML and forcing the owners to buy replacement accommodation elsewhere, fairness would point in favour of the former.

The Tribunal accepted that, in assessing whether the proposed changes were unfairly prejudicial within s 98, it was required to have regard to the statutory factors set out in s 100. These factors were designed with variation or discharge in mind and there was a certain artificiality in using them in the present context. But that was what s 98 required. The Tribunal found a number of the factors to be of particular assistance. In respect of factor (a) there had been significant changes since the original deed of conditions was registered in 1986, including (i) the abolition of superiorities, (ii) the replacement of SHML by Peverel, and (iii) the move within the sheltered housing sector generally from owning managers (such as SHML) to managers who were responsible to the owners.

Factor (c) also pointed in favour of allowing the new deed of conditions (p 38):

> [O]n the applicants' approach that the residual property can now be viewed as available to be exploited separately, the individual sheltered flats are almost uninhabitable, and certainly not usable as sheltered housing, because there is no access to, for example, the main electrical equipment or the central alarm systems. The unreality of such a situation might seem of itself to justify the imposition of burdens restricting the use of the residential property to its present use, even although this is clearly a considerable fetter on the applicants' ownership.

Other statutory factors also pointed in the same direction.

On the evidence, the Tribunal was satisfied that the proposed annual payment was reasonable. And taking the circumstances as a whole, it concluded that the new deed of conditions was not unfairly prejudicial to SHML. It followed that the application for preservation of the old deed of conditions must be refused.

[Another aspect of this case is digested at (24).]

(36) George Wimpey East Scotland Ltd v Fleming
2006 SLT (Lands Tr) 59

At an earlier hearing, the Lands Tribunal granted an application to vary a servitude of way, to the effect of diverting an access road: see 2006 SLT (Lands Tr) 2, *Conveyancing 2005* Case (12). The diversion would make it possible for the applicant to build 115 houses on its land. Fifteen neighbours claimed £4,000 each in compensation for the temporary disruption caused by the work to the road. **Held:** that, while the fact that loss was temporary did not of itself prevent a claim for compensation, in the present case that loss could not be said to be 'substantial', as required by s 90(7)(a) of the Title Conditions (Scotland) Act 2003. Compensation was therefore refused.

PUBLIC RIGHTS OF WAY AND ACCESS RIGHTS

(37) Hamilton v Dumfries and Galloway Council
[2006] CSOH 110

A short stretch of a public road was stopped up in 1989 but continued to be used by members of the public. Ultimately it was re-adopted by the local authority (as roads authority). The owner of the road challenged the authority's right to do so. Under the relevant legislation (Roads (Scotland) Act 1984 s 16) only a 'private road' can be adopted; and 'road' is in turn defined (s 151(1)) as 'any way (other than a waterway) over which there is a public right of passage'. It was argued for the owner that a 'public right of passage' could only be acquired by 20 years' use (by analogy to public rights of way). Hence the stretch of former road was not a 'road' under the legislation and could not be adopted.

This argument was rejected by the Lord Ordinary (Lord Kingarth). He thought that the requirements for adoption under the 1984 Act were in substance the same as those under the Roads (Scotland) Act 1970, where the wording used was ways 'to which the public has access'. On the authority of *Cheyne v Macneill* 1973 SLT 27, that wording meant access arising out of permission or tolerance. But even if that was wrong, it was equally wrong to interpret the 1984 Act as requiring the establishment of a full public right of way: see *Cowie v Strathclyde Regional Council* (unreported, 8 July 1986, First Division). Apart from anything else, as some public roads provided access to private property, it was impossible for them to meet two of the requirements of public rights of way, namely use from end to end on a continuous journey, and public termini. It was, Lord Kingarth supposed, possible that the rules for public rights of way applied to the extent of requiring that the use be of right and not by tolerance, but that requirement was met where (as here) the use was substantial. But he did not accept that the use had to be for 20 years.

It is worth adding that in *Melfort Pier Holidays Ltd v The Melfort Club* [2006] CSOH 130, 2006 GWD 28-627 (digested as the next case), Lord Hodge (at para 17) expressed a similar view:

> A local authority may, under the Roads (Scotland) Act 1984, adopt a road over which there is no public right of way but the use of which by the public has merely been on tolerance by the landowner (see *MacKinnon v Argyll and Bute Council* [2001 SLT 1275]).

But even if tolerance is enough to allow adoption, the question remains, what happens *after* adoption. Does the right of the public continue to depend on tolerance, in which case it can be withdrawn by the owner at any time? Or does the act of adoption confer a right on the public, more substantial than the flimsy right which allowed adoption in the first place – and, if so, what is the nature of that right? See further *Conveyancing 2000* pp 50–51. Conveyancers, naturally enough, operate on the assumption that the latter must be correct; and indeed if public money is being used to maintain a road, it would be strange if the public were denied its use. But the issue has not been the subject of express decision.

(38) Melfort Pier Holidays Ltd v The Melfort Club
[2006] CSOH 130, 2006 GWD 28-627 affd [2006] CSIH 61, 2007 GWD 7-115

Both the pursuer and the defenders owned and operated holiday complexes at Loch Melfort, near Kilmelford, by Oban. The defenders' complex had a restaurant. The pursuer obtained planning permission for a restaurant of its own, although the application was opposed by the defenders on grounds including difficulty of access. Access was indeed a problem. The properties of both parties were reached by a single-track public road which finished at a dead end. The pursuer's property lay beyond that of the defenders. Immediately before the defenders' property was a bridge. Beyond the bridge the road turned sharply. In order for large vehicles to get round the corner it was necessary for them to reverse over the bridge and into the private driveway belonging to the defenders. When the defenders began to place bollards across the driveway, the pursuer sought interim interdict against the obstruction.

The pursuer's case was (i) that the public right of way which already existed over the main road could be extended on to private land where this was necessary for reasonable passability, and (ii) that in any event a public right of way had been established over the driveway by positive prescription. The Lord Ordinary (Lord Hodge) rejected (i) but accepted (ii) and granted interim interdict. On appeal, the First Division upheld the Lord Ordinary.

A difficulty with (ii) was the rule that a public right of way must lead from one public place to another, whereas in the present case the detour led straight back to the place from which it had started (which was itself admittedly a public place). On the whole, Lord Hodge thought that this difficulty might be disposed of (para 16):

> Where there is a public road and the users of that road encroach upon a small area of private land when traversing the road for the prescriptive period, I consider that it is arguable that their so doing could create a public right of way over the area of private land. The right of way would be an adjunct to the public road. In the present case it is not likely that the wheels of large vehicles which enter the driveway to effect the manoeuvre will leave the driveway at exactly the same spot as they entered it. Thus, while it is a technical point, a vehicle will usually move from one public place on the public road to another. I am not persuaded therefore that it is a legal impossibility for there to be a public right of way over the driveway as an adjunct to the public's right of passage over the public road.

On appeal, however, Lord President Hamilton, giving the opinion of the court, criticised this approach (para 8) as tending

> to look in isolation at the route across the driveway as a right of way. The better approach is to view the larger picture of the public right of way being the public road as a whole, together with the variant sought to be established as a public right of way by reason of prescriptive user.

A difficulty with this 'better approach', however, is that it assumes that the public had a public right of way in respect of the public road itself, as opposed to some other, and possibly lesser, right. In fact this issue was canvassed in argument by the defenders and was the subject of some helpful discussion by Lord Hodge. But the law here, although important, remains under-researched and unclear.

(39) Caledonian Heritable Ltd v East Lothian Council
2006 GWD 22-487, Sh Ct

This was an appeal against a notice issued by East Lothian Council under s 14 of the Land Reform (Scotland) Act 2003.

The pursuer owns Archerfield Estate, an area of some 500 acres near Gullane. The area is currently being developed to provide two golf courses and housing. During this development work the pursuer had sought to keep the public out by removing a bridge over a burn, putting a barbed wire fence along one side of the estate where there is a strip of woodland, and erecting signs warning of prosecution if people entered the 'construction site'. The justification was public safety, although it was clear that some parts of the estate, including one of the golf courses, were not or were no longer subject to development.

The Council's response was to serve a notice requiring removal of the signs, reinstatement of the bridge, removal of the barbed wire, and the unlocking of gates. Its power to do so derived from s 14 of the 2003 Act which prohibits certain acts if they have the purpose of preventing or deterring the exercise of access rights. By s 14(2):

Where the local authority consider that anything has been done in contravention of subsection (1) above they may, by written notice served on the owner of the land, require that such remedial action as is specified in the notice be taken by the owner of the land within such reasonable time as is so specified.

This stage of the proceedings was concerned with a preliminary plea that the notice was lacking in specification and should be quashed. In particular, the pursuer argued that (i) the plan attached to the notice showed the whole of the Archerfield Estate and did not indicate which parts were subject to access rights, and (ii) the location shown for the bridge was incorrect. The Council's response was that, due to the development work, the area over which access rights could be taken varied almost from day to day, that the notice was perfectly intelligible, that in reality the pursuer was in no doubt as to what it had to do, and that matters would be clarified by a proof. The sheriff (Mhairi M Stephen) allowed a proof, partly because it would be premature to quash the notice without hearing evidence, and partly because the word 'anything' in s 14(2) suggested that a notice could be broken down to its constituent parts so that failure in one part would not be fatal to the rest of the notice. For a discussion, see (2006) 70 *Greens Civil Practice Bulletin* 4. In the event, the case settled on the eve of the proof, with the pursuer substantially complying with the notice. See http://www.ramblers.org.uk/scotland/accessN/casestudies/archerfield-may06.html.

In the course of a very long opinion, the sheriff had something to say about s 9(g) of the Act, which excludes from access rights 'being … on land which is a golf course'. As she pointed out (at p 27), this prevented only the right set out in s 1(2)(a) (the right to be on land) and not that set out in s 1(2)(b) (the right to cross land). So the Archerfield golf courses could still be crossed by members of the public, although

> there is no right to stop, to get out an easel and make a painting of the course or indeed to stop and fly a kite or have a picnic. There is no right to be on the golf greens for any purpose.

At the same time the sheriff rejected the Council's suggestion that, because of their nature, certain parts of a golf course might not fall within s 9(g), with the result that they would be fully available to the public (p 29):

> To seek to categorise and separate different areas within a golf course would be artificial and contrary to the very specific provisions of the Act excluding all but rights of traverse from a golf course. This is reiterated in the Access Code. To interpret otherwise would indeed be an affront to common sense and lead to a plethora of disputes/confrontations and likely litigation. Unless specific features exist such as a course being intersected by a public highway for instance, a golf course has to be regarded as a whole and not merely a collection of individual holes (tee, fairway and green). A wooded area is as much part of a golf course as a bunker, both being hazards of the game and features of the course.

The sheriff also considered the question of whether, in the course of a single excursion, access rights can be both lost and retrieved (p 27):

The access taker may well have access rights as he is behaving responsibly by remaining on roads and paths until he decides to closely inspect the interior design of a house by pressing his/her face to the window when he or she loses them by entering the garden and peering into the window. There seems to be little difficulty in accepting that the location is excluded land and the behaviour is indicative of not exercising rights responsibly. Then, rather like a halo, do the rights float back over the walker when he proceeds onwards down the road? Are the rights capable of being lost and reacquired?

This appears to be the first decision on part 1 of the Land Reform Act but others are in the pipeline:

- *Tuley v Highland Council*, Dingwall Sheriff Court. The owner of Feddanhill Wood, who is committed to public access rights, erected barriers across a track to keep out horses which, he feared, would cause unacceptable damage. A notice was served by Highland Council under s 14 of the Land Reform Act requiring removal of the barriers. This is the appeal against the notice. A proof was heard in late November 2006 and judgment is now awaited. See http://www.scotways.com/news/detail.php?newsid=94. This is apparently the first case on part 1 of the Act to go to proof.

- *Snowey v Stirling Council*, Stirling Sheriff Court. This concerns the 70-acre Boquhan Estate, west of Stirling. This is also an appeal against a s 14 notice, which sought to prevent the owner from locking all the gates and so denying access to the public. In addition, the owner has sought a ruling under s 28 of the Act to the effect that there are no public access rights. A proof is due to be heard in May 2007. See http://www.scotways.com/news/detail.php?newsid=91.

- *Gloag v Perth & Kinross Council*, Perth Sheriff Court. This is an action for a ruling that roughly one half of the grounds of Kinfauns Castle lying within a security fence is land excluded from access rights under s 6(1)(b)(iv) of the Act because it comprises 'sufficient adjacent land to enable persons living there to have reasonable measures of privacy in that house or place and to ensure that their enjoyment of that house or place is not unreasonably disturbed'. Perth & Kinross Council is defending the action and has proposed an alternative boundary line for exclusion of a smaller area of land from access rights. See http://www.scotways.com/news/detail.php?newsid=87.

WARRANDICE

(40) Holms v Ashford Estates Ltd
2006 SLT (Sh Ct) 70 affd 2006 SLT (Sh Ct) 161

A split-off disposition conveyed to the pursuers (i) a flat, (ii) a car parking space, and (iii) a servitude right of access to the car parking space over the car parking area (which included other car parking spaces). It turned out that the pursuers could only reach their own space by means of the neighbouring space; but, naturally, the neighbouring space was sometimes in use. So they sought damages against the seller for breach of warrandice. **Held:** that the pursuers had been evicted, and so damages were due. See **Commentary** p 141.

STATUTORY NOTICES

(41) Gardner v Edinburgh City Council
2006 SLT (Sh Ct) 166

This is the latest in a long-running series of cases in which Mr Gardner has sought to prevent the carrying out of common repairs to the tenement 143–147 Bruntsfield Place, Edinburgh, in which Mr Gardner owns a flat. The parties indeed are old adversaries. Mr Gardner had previously challenged statutory repairs notices issued in 1986 (*Edinburgh District Council v Gardner* 1990 SLT 600), 1990 (*Gardner v Edinburgh District Council* 1991 SC 402), and the late 1990s. Only the second challenge was successful, on the ground that the notice did not give sufficient specification. Following the third notice, the other proprietors embarked on a common repairs scheme which, so Mr Gardner argued, went beyond the terms of the notice. An attempt to interdict the architect from carrying out the agreed work failed before the sheriff and then on appeal to the Inner House: see *Gardner v Macneal* 2000 GWD 38-1430, 2001 Hous LR 8, discussed in *Conveyancing 2000* pp 6–7. One aspect of that scheme was the installation of the entryphone system with which the current litigation is concerned.

Unluckily, the entryphone system broke down almost from the start and for the past six or so years the door to the common stair has been without a lock. Mr Gardner would not agree to a repair, and eventually the owners of other flats approached Edinburgh Council to serve a statutory notice. This was done in August 2005 under powers conferred by s 24(1) of the City of Edinburgh District Council Confirmation Act 1991. Mr Gardner appealed against the notice and, as usual, was not legally represented. Having failed before the sheriff he appealed to the sheriff principal. His argument turned on the alleged unlawfulness of the installation of the entryphone system. This, Mr Gardner said, was beyond what was required by the original repairs notice. It would have been stopped by interdict in the litigation against the architect (mentioned above) had not the interdict come too late – the basis, he said, of the decision against him in the Inner House. But it remained unlawful, and he could not be made to pay for its repair.

There may be merit in the suggestion that the entryphone system was unlawfully installed. Under the Tenements (Scotland) Act 2004 sch 1 rule 3.1(f), a majority of owners can insist on an entryphone system. But that is new law. At the time when the system was installed in Bruntsfield Place, a decision to do so would probably have required the agreement of all the owners, including Mr Gardner – at least assuming that it involved interfering with common property. Initial illegality, however, would not have been enough to help Mr Gardner, for the question of how something was installed is different from the question of who can be made to pay for its maintenance. And, as the sheriff principal (Edward F Bowen QC) pointed out, the Council's statutory powers were sufficient to cover the case. To which we would add that Mr Gardner was one of the owners of the entryphone system by virtue of s 3(4)(b) of the Tenements (Scotland) Act 2004.

The appeal therefore failed. On only one matter did the sheriff principal hesitate (although the point was not raised by Mr Gardner). In terms of s 24(1) of the City of Edinburgh District Council Order Confirmation Act 1991, the Council could serve a notice in respect of repairs only where the disrepair was 'from decay, or in consequence of a storm or otherwise'. If 'otherwise' was *ejusdem generis* with the preceding words, then it could not be extended to cover the present case where the repair was necessitated by a deficiency at the time of installation. However, the sheriff principal concluded that the preceding words could not be said to have some common or dominant feature, so that the *ejusdem generis* rule did not apply.

REGISTRATION OF TITLE

(42) Foster v Keeper of the Registers of Scotland
[2006] CSOH 65, 2006 SLT 513

Applications for registration in respect of two adjoining properties ('A' and 'B') were made at about the same time. Although the Opinion does not say, it seems likely that these were first registrations. The applicants were in dispute with each other as to the ownership of a small piece of ground between the two properties, and the Keeper was aware of the dispute. Faced with this dispute, the Keeper registered the owner of property B as owner, without exclusion of indemnity. Presumably he had decided that there was no legal basis for its inclusion within property A; and indeed the owner of property B was in possession and had recently obtained an interim interdict against the owner of property A.

The owner of property A sought judicial review of the Keeper's decision in which she sought declarator (i) that 'the entries made by the Keeper are *ultra vires*, unlawful, void and of no effect', and (ii) that the making of these entries 'breach the Petitioner's rights in terms of Article 6 and Article 1 of the First Protocol of the ECHR and that by making the entries in the manner complained of the [Keeper] acted contrary to section 6(1) of the Human Rights Act 1998'. She also sought reduction of the entry, to the effect of removing the disputed ground from the title sheet of property B.

The petition was dismissed. The temporary judge (J Gordon Reid QC) accepted that judicial review was competent in principle. But if reduction of an entry in the Register were to be allowed, this would defeat the protection for proprietors in possession painstakingly created by s 9(3) of the Land Registration (Scotland) Act 1979. Assuming the Register to be inaccurate, the proper remedy of the petitioner was to apply for rectification, failing which for indemnity.

(43) David W S Mackay v Keeper of the Registers of Scotland
1 February 2006, Lands Tribunal

The Mackay family had possessed a field for over 70 years. The current possessor was David Mackay. But neither he nor anyone else in his family had ever had any actual title. A company called G S Brown Construction Ltd successfully applied for first registration. Mackay then submitted to the Keeper an admittedly *a non domino* disposition in his own favour, and applied for registration. When the Keeper rejected his application, he appealed to the Lands Tribunal. His case was that the GRS title on which the company had based its application did not in fact extend to the field in question. **Held:** that the GRS title, though admittedly subject to considerable obscurities, did in fact extend to the field, and appeal was accordingly refused.

Thus far, fact-specific. But the case also touched on a small but significant legal point. It is the Keeper's practice, when rejecting an *a non domino* application, to base his rejection on s 4(2)(c) of the Land Registration (Scotland) Act 1979, ie the ground that the application is 'frivolous or vexatious', and that is what he had done in this case. The Tribunal held, however, that Mr Mackay's application could not be categorised as frivolous or vexatious, but without specifying any other provision of the 1979 Act as the basis for the Keeper's lawful rejection. One of the problems about the 1979 Act is that it does not expressly say that the Keeper can reject an application by someone who has no right to be registered – hence the Keeper's reliance on the 'frivolous or vexatious' provision.

TRANSFER OF OWNERSHIP

(44) Kenneil v Kenneil
[2006] CSOH 8, 2006 SLT 449; [2006] CSOH 95

This was an action of division or sale, which came before the court in two separate stages, in January and in June. As one of the co-owners had successfully offered for the property, the question then arose as to whether a disposition by A, B and C in favour of A would be valid. Previously, in *Board of Management of Aberdeen College v Youngson* [2005] CSOH 31, 2005 SC 335 (*Conveyancing 2005* Case (45)), it had been held that an A to A disposition was not a valid foundation writ for the purposes of prescription. In *Kenneil*, however, the Lord Ordinary (Glennie) was satisfied that the disposition would be valid. He accepted the analysis in the *Aberdeen College* case (para 31 of the January opinion):

> in the case of an ordinary transaction. But in the context of a sale by the Court, or under the authority of the Court, it is the Reporter who enters into missives and in terms of the missives undertakes to procure a disposition. In those circumstances the signature of the owner of the subjects on the disposition is effectively ministerial. It can be dispensed with altogether if the DPCS [Deputy Principal Clerk of Session] signs the disposition. Although he signs on behalf of the owner, he does so at the instance of the Reporter. There is in such a case delivery and transfer by the Reporter to the purchaser, even where the purchaser is one of the *pro indiviso* proprietors whose

property the Reporter is selling under the authority of the Court. Accordingly I see no difficulty in there being a sale by the Reporter in his own name to one of the owners of the property, even though that requires a disposition signed in name of the owner in favour of himself.

As the sale to one of the co-owners did not in the event proceed, these remarks were *obiter.*

In fact it is hard to know why it was thought necessary to have a disposition by A, B and C to A, B and C – unless there was a special destination which required to be evacuated (as to which see *Conveyancing 2005* pp 74–78). For A was already the owner of a one third *pro indiviso* share, and all that was needed was a disposition by B and C of their respective shares (only).

[Another aspect of this case is digested at (11).]

(45) Nabb v Kirkby
24 February 2006, Stranraer Sheriff Court, A169/01, rev 2007 SCLR 65

Lucille Nabb, Stewart Douglas and Helen Nabb, the owners of Knocknassie House Hotel, Kirkcolm, Wigtownshire, concluded missives to sell it to Paul and Jayne Kirkby. The price was to be paid in two instalments, the first being for £150,000 and the second for £60,000. The second was to be paid a few weeks later, and the buyers were to grant a standard security to the sellers over the property, securing the unpaid balance. A ranking agreement was also to be entered into in relation to another security (in favour of Royal Bank of Scotland plc) being granted by the buyers.

The first instalment was duly paid by cheque, and the sellers' solicitors banked it, and at the same time posted the dispositions (the property was in two parts, and two dispositions were used), with this covering letter:

> Thank you for your letter of 15 August 2001 and we acknowledge safe receive [sic] of your cheque in respect of the initial instalment of the purchase price. We are presenting this to the bank today on the basis that it was only this morning (16 August 2001) that our clients signed the relative deeds.
>
> In that connection we are pleased to enclose herewith the following:- 1.Title deeds following [sic] to be delivered. 2. Two executed dispositions....
>
> Please acknowledge safe receipt of the enclosures which should be held by you as undelivered pending your confirmation that you hold the executed standard security in favour of our client and pending return to us of the completed Minute of Agreement.

What then happened was that the buyers registered the disposition in the Land Register without delivering to the sellers the standard security and ranking agreement. Nor did they pay the balance of the price. (This narrative of the facts is based on the pursuers' pleadings.) The sellers raised an action for payment of the balance, but later amended their action so as to seek rectification of the Land Register by deleting the names of the buyers and restoring their own names, on the basis that since the disposition had never been delivered the buyers had no right to register it. They also sought violent profits at the rate of £80,000 per annum.

The buyers counterclaimed for £150,000 damages, on the footing that they had been induced to buy the property by misrepresentations by the sellers.

The missives are not quoted in the judgment but it seems that there was disagreement as to how they should be interpreted. (In fact the sheriff doubted whether any contract had actually been concluded, though both parties took the view that there had been.) Seemingly the buyers considered that delivery of the standard security was not a condition of settlement, so that, having paid the first tranche of the price, they were entitled to register the dispositions in their favour. The sellers took the view that delivery of the standard security was a condition of settlement, but that even if it had not been, the simple fact was that the disposition had not been delivered in a legal sense and therefore could not lawfully be registered. The buyers argued, *inter alia*, that the sellers were not entitled to impose unilaterally the 'to be held as undelivered' clause and that in any event they had personally barred themselves from denying that the transaction had settled, mainly by encashing the cheque for the first instalment.

The sheriff dismissed the claim for violent profits, but for the rest allowed proof before answer. The pursuers appealed, arguing that decree for rectification should have been granted without proof and that the counterclaim should have been dismissed as irrelevant. The sheriff principal allowed the appeal in respect of the admissibility of the claim for violent profits, but otherwise dismissed the appeal. The result is that all matters in contention between the parties will proceed to a proof. As the sheriff principal said (para 53):

> There requires to be evidence before the court can consider (a) the effect of the cheque of £150,000 being sent as undelivered, as averred by the respondents, in terms of a letter of 15 August 2001, (b) the effect of the dispositions being said to be held as undelivered in terms of the letter of 17 August 2001, (c) the effect of subsequent correspondence and actings by the parties and their solicitors, (d) the question of whether the respondents' pleas of personal bar and waiver can be sustained, and (e) whether at present there is an inaccuracy in the Land Register and, if so, the nature of that inaccuracy and (f) whether there has been fraud or carelessness or neither on the part of the respondents and their solicitors.

COMPETITION OF TITLE

(46) Bain v Bain
[2006] CSOH 142, [2006] CSOH 189, 2007 GWD 6-84

A long dispute between two parties, involving much arcane law. See **Commentary** p 148.

(47) 3052775 Nova Scotia Ltd v Henderson
[2006] CSOH 147, 2006 GWD 32-675

The core of this dispute is a disposition, dated 12 February 2001, by Letham Grange Development Co Ltd to 3052775 Nova Scotia Ltd. The latter applied for registration on the same day, but the application is still pending and the Keeper has neither accepted nor rejected it.

For a parallel litigation, see 2006 SC (HL) 85, noted as Case (86) below. In that action (action no 1), Mr Henderson is the pursuer, and he seeks, as liquidator of Letham Grange Development Co Ltd, reduction of the disposition as a gratuitous alienation. In the action in which Mr Henderson is the defender (action no 2), 3052775 Nova Scotia Ltd seeks declarator that it is entitled to possession of the Letham Grange property, and damages against the defender for alleged unlawful possession.

In the current phase of action no 2, 3052775 Nova Scotia Ltd sought an interim order for possession. Counsel for the pursuer 'submitted that the pursuers held the personal fee in the subjects and that they had a "quasi-real right" in them'. The Lord Ordinary (Lord Hodge), in rejecting the pursuer's motion, commented that (para 11):

> It is clear from Lord Rodger's speech in *Burnett's Trustee* [2004 SC (HL) 19] at paragraph 105 and from that of Lord Hope at paragraphs 16 to 19 that the disponee who has not registered his title enjoys no real right in the subjects. Scots law does not recognise a right that lies between a real right and a personal right: see the decision of the Whole Court in *Young v Leith* (1847) 9 D 932. Lord Hope discussed this in some detail in his seminal opinion in the Inner House in *Sharp v Thomson* 1995 SC 455. It is noteworthy that when that case reached the House of Lords, no challenge was made to the analysis of property law by the judges of the First Division (see Lord Clyde's speech at 1997 SC (HL) 66, 80B). Thus, in my opinion, Lord Hope's exposition of the law of property in *Sharp v Thomson* is the leading modern statement on the subject and is supported by the decision of the House of Lords in *Burnett's Trustee*. There is no such thing as a 'quasi-real right'.

(48) Sexton and Allan v Keeper of the Registers
17 August 2006, Lands Tribunal

This is the latest (and last?) round of a battle that has been going on for more than 30 years about the ownership of 27 and 29 Main Street, Coatbridge. (For a recent previous round, see *Sexton v Coia* 2004 GWD 17-376, 2004 GWD 38-781, discussed in *Conveyancing 2004* pp 117–121.) The Keeper eventually registered Carmela Coia and Mark Coia as owners. John Sexton and Maureen Allan then sought rectification. When the Keeper declined to rectify, they appealed to the Lands Tribunal. The Lands Tribunal has now refused the appeal, observing that even if there could be doubt about the right of the Coias, Sexton and Allan had not put forward any coherent case that they themselves had right. An odd feature of this case is that the Coias did not seek to defend. We do not know why. Possibly they were confident that the Keeper would protect their interests. Or possibly they were of the view that if the decision went against them, they could claim indemnity.

RIGHT-TO-BUY LEGISLATION

(49) Williamson v Fife Special Housing Association
2006 Hous LR 80, Lands Tribunal

An application to buy was refused because the applicant had previously assigned the tenancy to his wife, this assignation having been consented to by the landlord.

(50) Dorman v Edinburgh City Council
2006 SLT (Lands Tr) 37, 2006 Hous LR 74

The Housing (Scotland) Act 1987 sch 2 para 8(1) provided that a tenancy is not a secure tenancy (and so there is no right to buy) 'if the house forms part of, or is within the curtilage of, a building which' is primarily not for housing. A school had burnt down, but the janitor's house was undamaged. **Held:** that the exception nevertheless applied. (Sch 2 para 8(1) has been repealed, but this case was on the old law. The current, and similar, provision is sch 1 para 9 of the Housing (Scotland) Act 2001.)

(51) Fee v East Renfrewshire Council
2006 GWD 27-610, Lands Tribunal

Schedule 1 para 9 of the Housing (Scotland) Act 2001 provides that a tenancy is not a secure tenancy (and so there is no right to buy) 'if the house forms part of, or is within the curtilage of, a building which' is primarily not for housing. A janitor had a house on a school site. It was separated from the rest of the site by a 'low ranch-style fence'. **Held** that it was within the curtilage, and application to buy dismissed.

(52) Fletcher v South Lanarkshire Council
2006 SLT (Lands Tr) 51

There were three houses in a row, with gardens to the rear. The tenant of the middle house (No 61) used a path across the garden of No 63 to get her wheelie bins etc in and out to the road. She bought her house in 2003, and was granted a servitude over this path. The tenants of No 63 then applied to buy. The Council duly offered to sell, subject to the servitude. They objected, and sought in the present action to compel the Council to offer the property to them without the servitude. The Tribunal held that the tenancy of No 63 had indeed been subject to access in favour of No 61, but only for certain purposes. It ordered the Council to offer No 63 for sale to the tenants subject to a limited servitude.

Given that an unlimited servitude was already in existence, the effect of the decision is that the Council will find itself in breach of contract, unless it can persuade the owners of No 61 to agree to a limitation of the servitude. The Tribunal was aware of this, but the decision is in conformity with previous Tribunal decisions in such cases. As the Tribunal notes, there might be the possibility of a rectification of the conveyance to the owners of No 61: in this connection the Tribunal refers to *Higgins v North Lanarkshire Council* 2001 SLT (Lands Tr) 2. (For discussion of this important but problematic case, see *Conveyancing 2000* pp 105–107.)

(53) Johnston v Dundee City Council
2006 Hous LR 68, Lands Tribunal

The right to buy does not exist if the applicant was not in occupation for the relevant period. An application was refused on this ground.

(54) Hutchison v Graham's Exrx
[2006] CSOH 15, 2006 SCLR 587

Not about the right-to-buy legislation as such but about a contract made between the purchasing tenant and other family members. See **Commentary** p 114.

LEASES

(55) Advice Centre for Mortgages Ltd v McNicoll
[2006] CSOH 58, 2006 SLT 591, 2006 SCLR 602, 2006 Hous LR 22

A complex case about the formation of the contract of lease, about the Requirements of Writing (Scotland) Act 1995, about personal bar, about purchase options in leases and whether they bind a successor landlord, and about the offside goals rule. See **Commentary** p 102.

(56) Ashford and Thistle Securities LLP v Kerr
(1) December 2005; (2) 2006 SLT (Sh Ct) 37, 2006 Hous LR 6;
(3) 2006 SCLR 873

This case has resulted in three opinions. The second concerned the landlord's motion that the defender be required to find caution for violent profits: this motion was refused. The substance of the dispute between the parties is to be found in the first and third opinions, the latter being an appeal to the sheriff principal. The landlord was seeking declarator of irritancy for non-payment of rent.

In 2004 the defender took a five-year lease of property at 138 High Street, Dalkeith from Parkcross Ltd. The lease contained a standard 21-day irritancy clause. Notwithstanding the terms of the lease, the defender allegedly agreed with the landlord that no rent would be paid, but that the tenant would restore the property instead. This agreement was not in writing. Shortly thereafter Parkcross Ltd went into receivership and the property was sold to Ashford and Thistle Securities LLP. Immediately on acquiring the property, the new landlord served an irritancy ultimatum, under s 4 of the Law Reform (Miscellaneous Provisions) (Scotland) Act 1985, and followed it up with a notice of irritancy. When the tenant did not remove, the landlord raised this action for declarator of irritancy.

At first instance the sheriff pronounced decree in favour of the pursuer on the ground that the defender had not relevantly pled a case for saying that the alleged unwritten agreement about rent not being payable could bind a singular successor.

On appeal to the sheriff principal, the focus of the dispute shifted somewhat. The defender argued that the landlord's s 4 notice failed to comply with the requirements of the 1985 Act, because it failed to state whether the rent allegedly due was payable to the previous landlord or to the new landlord. The sheriff principal emphasised a different objection. He took the view that irritancy for non-payment of rent is competent only if the unpaid rent is due to the irritating landlord. In this case the allegedly unpaid rent had been due to the original landlord: in order to be payable to the new landlord, the arrears would have needed to be assigned. But either they had not been or at least the pursuer had no averments that they had. In the words of the sheriff principal (para 13):

> If, however, I am wrong in that view [about s 4] and all that such a notice requires is to inform the tenant that there are arrears and that they require to be settled, it nevertheless appears to me that as a matter of pleading the pursuers have failed to disclose why it is that rent allegedly due prior to [the transfer of the property] should have been paid to them.

Moreover, the sheriff principal seems to have considered that the alleged agreement, if it could be proved, would bind the new landlord:

> It would be open to the defender to prove, in a question with the original landlord, that there was no sum 'which she had failed to pay'. I accept the defender's Counsel's proposition that a successor landlord cannot be in a better position to enforce an obligation of a lease than his predecessor.

Whether this is correct is unclear. The whole issue of what terms, and under what circumstances, will bind a successor is deeply problematic. For another case this year on this issue, see *Advice Centre for Mortgages Ltd v McNicoll* 2006 SLT 591, noted immediately above.

(57) Burgerking Ltd v Rachel Charitable Trust
[2006] CSOH 13, 2006 SLT 224

This case was about whether a landlord's refusal of consent to a sublease was reasonable or not. The lease was of premises in Paisley's High Street. Trading conditions had deteriorated over the years, and Burgerking was losing money. It wished to close, and either (a) surrender the lease or (b) assign it or (c) sub-let. Any of these options would involve buying itself out of its position, because the rent it was paying (£112,000 per annum) was higher than what the current market rent would be (about £75,000 per annum), and the ish was not until 2009. (Although there was a rent review clause, it was no doubt of the usual upward-only type.)

Burgerking decided to sub-let. But the lease contained this provision:

(2) The Tenants shall not ... grant sub-tenancies except with the prior written consent of the Landlords such consent not to be unreasonably withheld or delayed in the case of a substantial and respectable ... sub-tenant ... who is of sound financial standing and is in the reasonable opinion of the Landlords demonstrably capable of performing ... the tenants' obligations under the proposed sub-lease....

It also provided:

(3) Every permitted sub-lease granted in pursuance of this Clause shall be granted subject to the whole conditions contained in this Lease (other than as to the amount of rent payable hereunder) and such other reasonable conditions as the Landlords shall have previously approved in writing, in consideration of a full market rent (calculated without taking any fine, premium, grassum or other lump sum payment which the Tenants may have obtained into account).

Burgerking found a sub-tenant in a company called Quids In. The sub-rent was agreed as being £112,000 but with a counter-payment of £100,000, so the net rent was £12,000. The landlord refused consent to the sub-lease, and Burgerking raised the present action to have it declared that the refusal was unreasonable.

The landlord gave two reasons for the refusal. The first concerned the proposed sub-tenant's financial standing. The court **held** that this objection was unreasonable.

The other reason was that the sub-rent was below the current market rent. It was **held** that this was a reasonable objection. The rent was so low that it could be regarded as commercially damaging. The court therefore did not find it necessary to decide whether the device of a nominal rent of £112,000 with a counter-payment of £100,000 did or did not comply with sub-clause (3), for, even if it did, it was not a provision that a reasonable landlord could be required to accept.

The Lord Ordinary also noted (para 33) that

in England and Wales the onus rests on the landlord of proving that his decision was reasonable. In Scotland the onus is on the tenant to prove that the decision was unreasonable. The present case is, I think, fairly close to the margin, and is one where the onus is of some significance.

(58) Drimsynie Estate Ltd v Ramsay
[2006] CSOH 46

This action for removing from a holiday chalet at Lochgoilhead was raised as a test case: there appear to be a substantial number of similar cases. In this phase of the dispute the issue was one as to the appropriate court. The defender moved to have the case, which had been competently raised in the Court of Session, remitted to the sheriff at Dunoon. The motion was granted.

(59) Bell v Inkersall Investments Ltd
[2006] CSIH 16, 2006 SC 507, 2006 SLT 626

Bell occupied property owned, directly or indirectly, by Woodcock. Some parts of the land were in Woodcock's name and others were in the name of two companies he controlled, Inkersall Investments Ltd and Prosper Properties Ltd. The parties fell out, and Woodcock and his companies raised sheriff court actions to remove Bell. Bell defended those actions and at the same time raised a Court of Session action against Woodcock and his companies seeking interim interdict against interference with his possession, averring that Woodcock was seeking to oust him without due process of law. After interim interdict was refused ([2005] CSOH 50, *Conveyancing 2005* Case (28)) the pursuer reclaimed. The Inner House has now affirmed the Lord Ordinary's decision. Bell had produced no evidence that he was threatened with ejection *brevi manu*. Moreover his pleadings were irrelevant. His possession had been based on a series of written seasonal grazing leases, which did not attract security of tenure under the Agricultural Holdings (Scotland) Act 1991.

This decision has generated interesting discussion: see Craig Anderson (2006 SLT (News) 221 and 262), Robert Sutherland (2006 SLT (News) 249) and Alasdair Fox ((2006) 51 *Journal of the Law Society of Scotland* Dec/42). What appears to happen sometimes in practice, and what seems to have happened in this case, is that although the lets are expressed as being seasonal ones, the tenant is *de facto* allowed to keep his beasts on the land throughout the year. The facts in *Bell* predated the Agricultural Holdings (Scotland) Act 2003. That Act continues the rule that grazing lets do not attract security of tenure. But s 4(2) says:

> Where the tenant remains in occupation of the land after the expiry of the term of a tenancy to which section 3 applies [seasonal grazing lets] with the consent of the landlord, the tenancy continues to have effect as if it were for a term of –
>
> (a) 5 years; or
> (b) such period of less than 5 years as the landlord and tenant may agree to,
>
> and the tenancy is, by virtue of this subsection, a short limited duration tenancy.

This new provision means that where there is a seasonal grazing let and the tenant in fact continues occupation round the year, the result *may* be to upgrade the grazing let into a short limited duration tenancy. Whether it does so will depend on the precise facts. In practice much may depend on how the word 'consent' should be construed. If s 4(2) does operate, that is bad news for the landlord, but not as bad news as it might be: the upgrade is to the middle-of-the-range short limited duration tenancy and not to the top-of-the-range 1991 Act agricultural tenancy. For instance, a short limited duration tenancy does not carry with it the right to buy.

Section 4(2) and *Bell* thus to some extent pull in opposite directions but to some extent pull in the same direction. They pull in opposite directions in as much as if the facts of *Bell* were to occur now, in 2007, the tenant would have the possibility of arguing that he had acquired something more than a seasonal grazing let. But they pull in the same direction in as much as they both confirm that a seasonal grazing tenant who stays in possession after the end of the season cannot claim a top-of-the-range 1991 Act agricultural tenancy.

Of particular importance is what is said in *Bell* about *Morrison-Low v Paterson* 1985 SC (HL) 49. According to Lord Justice Clerk Gill (paras 23–24):

Counsel for the pursuer relied on *Morrison-Low v Paterson* ... in submitting that the pursuer's alleged tenancy was constituted by his continuous occupation of the land over a period of years and by his payment of rent therefor.... That submission is based on a misunderstanding of the law. In *Morrison-Low* ... there was no document constituting the lease claimed by the defenders; but there was evidence of continuous occupation by the defenders over several years with payment of annual rents. The House of Lords held, in the words of Lord Keith of Kinkel, that 'where a proprietor admits someone into the possession of an agricultural holding, or maintains him in such possession without any pre-existing right thereto, and regularly accepts rent from him, there is an inescapable inference that a tenancy has been brought into existence, and it is of no moment that no particular occasion can be pointed to upon which the parties agreed to the one granting and the other taking a tenancy'. This is not such a case. In this case there is a series of grazings lets, each signed by the pursuer, which prima facie qualify under the former s 2(2) of the 1991 Act. The pursuer does not suggest that any of these lets was a sham transaction. He does not aver that he made any payments of rent other than those due under the lets. His allegedly continuous occupation of the land to which the lets relate is consistent with his having been in breach of clause 4 in each case. Likewise, his unspecific averments that he has occupied, repaired and renewed buildings and carried out works of improvement on the estate are consistent with his having illegally exceeded his rights under the lets. Since the pursuer does not attack the validity of the lets, it is not open to counsel for the pursuer to submit, in the face of them, that the pursuer occupies the land to which they relate under an entirely different form of contract.

(60) O'Donnell v McDonald
2006 GWD 28-615, Sh Ct

A lease was entered into, the tenant having the use of certain buildings and also having the right to graze horses. The tenant used the property as a riding school. Over the years the activities of the riding school declined and the predominant use came to be grazing. The question was whether the lease was (i) an agricultural tenancy or (ii) a lease of a riding school, with ancillary grazing rights. This was evidently not an easy case to decide. The sheriff decided that it was an agricultural tenancy, but on appeal the sheriff principal came to the opposite conclusion.

(61) Ben Cleuch Estates Ltd v Scottish Enterprise
[2006] CSOH 35, 2006 GWD 8-154

This case was about whether a break option had been validly exercised. Scottish Enterprise ('SE') held a 25-year lease of premises at 45 North Lindsay Street, Dundee at an annual rent (at the time of the litigation) of £210,700. The lease contained this provision:

[T]he Tenants shall be entitled at any time prior to [2 February 2005] to give to the Landlords at least one year's written notice of termination of this lease, such notice to take effect on [2 February 2006] whereupon this Lease shall absolutely determine....

This break option was, as such options commonly are, a cliff-edge provision. If the tenant wished to bring the lease to an end (or, rather, in the gobbledygook of the lease, to 'an absolute determination') then the notice had to be served, and validly served, by 2 February (old Candlemas) 2005. Otherwise the tenant would be tied in until 2016.

In 1991 the owner was Faraday Properties Ltd. That company later transferred the property to Fiscal Estates Investments Ltd. That company later transferred it to Pacific Shelf 977 Ltd (later called Bonnytoun Estates Ltd). That company then transferred it to Pacific Shelf 1145 Ltd (later called Ben Cleuch Estates Ltd). SE was informed of these successive transfers, though it was not informed about the change of name from Pacific Shelf 1145 Ltd to Ben Cleuch Estates Ltd.

SE decided to exercise the break option. On 29 November 2004 its in-house solicitor wrote to SE's law firm:

> I thank you for your letter of 2 November 2004 and would be pleased if you would serve, prior to 2 February 2005, a Break Notice in respect of SE's lease of the above subjects. This Notice should be served on:
>
> 1. Bonnytoun Estates Limited, PO Box 14, Linlithgow, West Lothian, WH49 7JZ. For the attention of Scott Cairns.
> 2. Colliers CRE, Surveyors, 45 West Nile Street, Glasgow, G1 2PJ. For the attention of Anne Forrester.

(Colliers was the landlord's agent.)

The notice was served on 6 January 2005. But of course the landlord was not Bonnytoun Estates Ltd but Ben Cleuch Estates Ltd. The two companies were, however, closely linked. Ben Cleuch Estates Ltd was a wholly-owned subsidiary of Bonnytoun Estates Ltd. They had the same registered office, namely Pacific House, 70 Wellington Street, Glasgow. (SE's law firm checked at Companies House for the registered office of Bonnytoun Estates Ltd and served the notice at that address.) Mr Cairns was a director of both companies. Ben Cleuch Estates Ltd thus knew that the break option notice had been served. But it did not wish the lease to end. So it decided to keep silent about the tenant's mistake until the deadline of 2 February 2005 had passed, by which time it would be too late.

The matter came before the court in the form of an action of declarator by Ben Cleuch Estates Ltd that the lease remained in force. Decree was granted in the pursuer's favour. The notice was invalid because it was not served on the landlord. The main line of defence was that the invoices for the rent had been issued by Colliers on behalf of Bonnytoun Estates Ltd. Since Colliers were also the agents of Ben Cleuch Estates Ltd, the latter company had, it was said, misled the tenant into thinking that Bonnytoun Estates Ltd was still the landlord. This argument failed on the ground that SE knew that the property had been transferred by Bonnytoun Estates Ltd. Thus although the invoices had indeed constituted a misrepresentation, nevertheless SE had only itself to blame.

The Lord Ordinary (Reed) comments (para 151):

A reasonable person in the position of the defenders, in the circumstances of the present case, would not have been expected to rely on the invoices and other communications in deciding on whom the notice should be served.

And he also says (para 138):

The break notice was not validly served. This result may be thought to confer an adventitious bonus on the pursuers, enabling them to take unmeritorious advantage of the defenders' error when they realised perfectly well that the defenders intended to exercise their entitlement under the break clause. This criticism however misses the point that the parties have agreed, as it were, on the key which is to be capable of turning the lock: if the tenant has not used the right key, then the lock will not turn. The absence of confusion or prejudice on the part of the landlord is irrelevant. If the parties had intended that the break clause should require no more than that the tenant should evince a clear intention to terminate the lease, which should come to the attention of the landlord, then they could have said so in their contract. They did not; and it is not for the court to re-write their contract for them.

The law firm checked the Companies Register. But it seems that it did not check the Land Register. Stewart Brymer, writing at (2006) 82 *Greens Property Law Bulletin* 3, asks:

Is that sufficient? According to Lord Reed it was. What would the ordinary solicitor exercising reasonable skill and care have done?

(62) Superdrug Stores plc v Network Rail Infrastructure Ltd
[2006] CSIH 4, 2006 SC 365, 2006 SLT 146

The Tenancy of Shops (Scotland) Act 1949 s 1 provides that:

If the landlord of any premises consisting of a shop and occupied by a tenant gives or has given to the tenant notice of termination of tenancy ... and the tenant is unable to obtain a renewal of his tenancy on terms that are satisfactory to him, he may, at any time before the notice takes effect and not later than the expiry of twenty-one days after the service of the notice ... apply to the sheriff for a renewal of his tenancy.

This case turned on the question of whether the application had met the 21-day deadline. The sheriff principal held that it had not: 2005 SLT (Sh Ct) 105, *Conveyancing 2005* Case (35). By a 2–1 majority the Inner House has now reversed that decision.

(63) Central Car Auctions Ltd v House of Sher (UK) Ltd
[2006] CSOH 137

The pursuer held a lease of a building at Scotland Street in Glasgow. The owner, without the tenant's permission, allowed T-Mobile to install telecommunications equipment on the roof. The pursuer's solicitors served this notice on the landlord:

We act on behalf of Central Car Auctions Ltd of 44 Easterhouse Road, Swinton, Glasgow. We refer to the Lease between you House of Sher (UK) Limited dated 23rd

December 1996 and 22nd January 1997 which relates to the whole subjects at 15 and 33 Scotland Street, Glasgow, including the roof, with a minor exclusion from an Advertising Hoarding. We are advised that you have allowed possession of part of the subjects leased to our clients to be removed from our clients and given to T-Mobile. We understand that T-Mobile have erected a substantial structure on the roof of the building with substantial supporting conduits for cables which also occupy part of the subjects let to our clients under the Lease. We have made enquiry and believe that a Lease has been granted in favour of T-Mobile for a period of twenty years. As such our clients maintain you are in material breach of contract in allowing possession of part of the subjects let to be taken by T-Mobile. This action is entirely inconsistent with the continuing existence of a contract of lease between you and our clients of the subjects let in terms of the Lease. In these circumstances our clients treat your breach as material and as a repudiation of the Lease and hereby intimate that in light of your repudiatory conduct our clients treat themselves as no longer bound by the obligations under the Lease. The keys of the property are being delivered to your clients' Property Agents NAI Gooch Webster separately.

Thereafter Central Car Auctions Ltd raised an action of declarator that they had validly rescinded the lease. (The background circumstances are unclear but it may be that the tenants wished to get out of the lease for other reasons.) After a proof, it was held that the landlord was indeed in breach of contract, but that the breach was not sufficiently material to allow the tenant to rescind.

(64) Westbury Estates Ltd v Royal Bank of Scotland plc
[2006] CSOH 177, 2006 SLT 1143

Premises at 26 St Andrew Square, Edinburgh were let in 1979 on a 25-year lease. At the ish in 2004 the landlord claimed that the premises were not in the condition required by the terms of the lease. The landlord carried out various works to the lift, fire alarm system, electrical wiring, boiler and heaters and then sued the tenant for the cost, plus damages for loss of rental income during the time that the works were being carried out. The two heads of damages were £572,254 and £73,022. Thus far, the case sounds like an ordinary dilapidations dispute. But it was not. The pursuer admitted that everything was in good condition at the ish. But, argued the pursuer, the various items were all nearing the end of their economic life and therefore required to be replaced.

The action was dismissed, for two reasons. One was that the property standards that the pursuer was founding on were not in use in 1979, and as the Lord Ordinary (Reed) said (para 38), 'a lease, like any other contract, is to be interpreted in the sense which the words bore at the time it was entered into; its meaning cannot change as a result of changes in circumstances arising ex post facto'.

The second reason was that even if the modern standards had been the applicable ones in 1979, the tenant was not in breach, because of the terms of the lease. The relevant clause was:

The Tenants accept the Let Subjects in their present condition notwithstanding all (if any) defects therein whether latent or otherwise and are held to have satisfied themselves that in all respects the Let Subjects are fit for their purposes and throughout the whole currency of this Lease the Tenants shall at all times uphold, maintain, repair and renew the Let Subjects both externally and internally so as to keep the Let Subjects in good and substantial repair and condition, it being declared that the Tenants' obligations shall extend to all work necessary upon the Let Subjects whether structural or otherwise and whether of the nature of maintenance, repair, renewal or rebuilding and whether normally the obligation of a Landlord or of a Tenant, the Landlords having no duties, liabilities or obligations in respect of such work or the cost thereof and further that the Tenants' obligations shall extend to the maintenance, repair, renewal and if necessary replacement of all services within and external to but serving the Let Subjects (either alone or in common with other subjects) including lifts, heating installations, ventilation or air conditioning systems, drainage system and gas, electricity and water supplies and any other services.

The Lord Ordinary noted (para 33) that 'In relation to the replacement of services elements, the test is one of necessity: replacement, rather than "maintenance, repair [or] renewal", is required only "if necessary"'. He concluded, therefore (para 36), that 'it therefore appears to me that the fact that an item is at the end of its economic life, in the particular sense in which that expression is defined in the pursuers' averments, does not entail that the tenant is necessarily obliged under the repairing covenant to replace it'.

(65) Mack v Glasgow City Council
[2006] CSIH 18, 2006 SC 543, 2006 Hous LR 2

A residential tenant sued her landlord. Her flat, she said, was damp, and that constituted breach of contract. She sued both for damage to her moveable property, and for inconvenience. The question for decision was whether inconvenience should be regarded as 'personal injury', in which case the pursuer's claim would have been outwith the triennium. *Fleming v Strathclyde Regional Council* 1992 SLT 161 was authority that such a claim is indeed for 'personal injury', but the Inner House overruled *Fleming*, holding that the pursuer's claim was not time-barred.

(66) Ferns v Scottish Homes
20 December 2006, Airdrie Sheriff Court, A1388/04

The pursuer was a tenant of the defender. Her flat was in an area where the defender was boarding up and then demolishing properties. Hers was one of the last to be occupied. Vandals were active. One day when she was out vandals broke into her flat and caused serious damage to her moveable property. She sued her landlord for failing to provide sufficient security. The sheriff, following *Maloco v Littlewoods Organisation Ltd* 1987 SC (HL) 37, dismissed the action as irrelevant. The pursuer appealed. The decision of the sheriff was affirmed by the sheriff principal.

(67) Stephen v Innes Ker
[2006] CSOH 66, 2006 SLT 1105

The landlord in two agricultural tenancies (Meikle Geddes, Nairn and Broomhill Farm, Piperhill, Nairn) served notices to quit. The tenant raised an action for declarator that he was the lawful tenant in both tenancies and for reduction of the notices to quit. The landlord's case, based on *Smith v Grayton Estates Ltd* 1961 SLT 38 and *Coats v Logan* 1985 SLT 221, was that the tenant's succession to half of the tenancy from his late grandmother had prevented the lease from continuing by tacit relocation. The Lord Ordinary (Clarke) rejected the landlord's argument. It is understood that the decision is being reclaimed.

(68) Salvesen v Graham
25 July 2006, Scottish Land Court

A case similar to *Stephen v Innes Ker* 2006 SLT 1105, digested above, and with a similar result. It is understood that an appeal has been lodged.

(69) Harbinson v McTaggart
2006 SLT (Lands Tr) 42

Section 20 of the Land Registration (Scotland) Act 1979 provides that 'a tenant-at-will shall be entitled ... to acquire his landlord's interest'. The rules about the price are complex, but in the normal case the tenant-at-will receives a mouth-watering 96% discount.

What is a tenant-at-will? It is (s 20(8)):

a person –

    (a) who, not being tenant under a lease or a tenant or occupier by virtue of any enactment, is by custom and usage the occupier (actual or constructive) of land on which there is a building or buildings erected or acquired for value by him or any predecessor of his;

    (b) who is under an obligation to pay a ground rent to the owner of the land in respect of the said land but not in respect of the building or buildings on it, or would have been under such an obligation if the ground rent had not been redeemed; and

    (c) whose right of occupancy of the land is without ish.

Certain people occupied, and paid rent for, holiday huts at Rascanel Bay, near Castle Douglas. They claimed to be tenants-at-will and accordingly entitled to acquire ownership of the properties. In such matters the Land Tribunal has jurisdiction.

'It has been said', comments the Tribunal, 'that trying to understand what a tenancy-at-will is, is like "trying to hold water in your hand"', citing an unreported 1992 case, *Conochie v Watt*. Indeed. The subject may be ultimately beyond comprehension but the present case is a most valuable contribution, even if much of the discussion is probably to be classified as *obiter dicta*. The Tribunal dismissed the applications as irrelevant and lacking in specification, and did so for a particular reason. It was accepted that over the years the rent for these huts had changed from time to time. Although the Tribunal did not think that variable rent necessarily meant that a tenancy was not a tenancy-at-will, it considered that it did throw on an applicant a burden of explanation, and since the applicants' pleadings did not offer any explanation, dismissal had to be the consequence. The applications thus never reached the stage of proof. Whether there will be new applications with amended pleadings remains to be seen.

(70) Dean v Freeman (No 3)
[2006] CSOH 91, 2006 GWD 22-492

For earlier stages of this case, see *Conveyancing 2005* Case (23). After a tenant went into liquidation, the landlord claimed against the tenant's cautioner. After proof it was **held** that no sums were due by the cautioner.

(71) William Collins & Sons Ltd v CGU Insurance plc
[2006] CSOH 87, 2006 SLT 728 rev [2006] CSIH 37, 2006 SLT 752

The pursuer held premises on a 35-year lease created in 1990. In 1991–92 it sub-let the premises on a 15-year lease. The annual sub-rent was £616,000. The pursuer wished to carry out major works to the building, and requested access to the subjects so as to be able to carry them out. The sublessee refused access. The commercial reason for doing so was that there would be major disruption to its business: it estimated the likely loss at over £1,000,000. The legal reason was that the terms of the sub-lease did not, in all the circumstances of the case, allow the pursuer to insist on access. The pursuer raised the present action to compel the defender to allow access. The pursuer also sought an order for interim access on the basis of s 47(2) of the Court of Session Act 1988.

The Lord Ordinary granted the interim order but the Inner House reversed. The case has thus gone back to the Outer House for further procedure. The case – at least thus far – is therefore only of limited significance. But it does contain some interesting points.

One concerns s 47(2). That provision allows a court to make an interim order about possession. But the Inner House held that what the pursuer was seeking was not *possession*, and so s 47(2) could not be invoked. There is much fuzzy thinking (and loose usage) about the concept of possession, and also about the conception of re-possession, and the Inner House's insistence on clarity is therefore welcome. One might add that if the pursuer had indeed obtained possession, that would presumably have brought the sub-lease to an end, for it is difficult to see how a landlord can resume possession and still assert that a lease exists. Moreover, one may observe that the pursuer in any case had civil possession, but presumably s 47(2) is not about civil possession but about natural possession.

Glasgow became operational for the Land Register in 1985. In an operational area a long lease has to be registered in order to be a real right and hence bind singular successors of the landlord: Land Registration (Scotland) Act 1979 s 3(3). Yet this lease was not registered in the Land Register but only in the Books of

Council and Session. This seems to be a not uncommon phenomenon. It is unclear whether that is because those involved do not appreciate the implications of s 3(3), or because they wish to save expense, or because they consider that the common law, whereby a lease is only a personal right, is acceptable.

(72) Valente v Fife Council
2006 GWD 38-752, Sh Ct

Adriana Valente wished to let out a flat in St Andrews to students. For this she needed an HMO licence under the Civic Government (Scotland) Act 1982 (Licensing of Houses in Multiple Occupation) Order 2000, SSI 2000/177. Residents objected on the grounds that to have student neighbours would be intolerable, especially because of round-the-clock noise. Fife Council refused the application, and against that decision she successfully appealed, and the Council was ordered to grant a HMO licence. The sheriff (G J Evans) said:

> By ignoring the marginal nature of the change proposed by the granting of this HMO licence, by rejecting out of hand the conditions proposed that would go a long way to meet the objections made and by acting inconsistently with their previous grant in respect of properties elsewhere in the street, where similar objections were made, the respondents have exercised their discretion in an unreasonable manner and the appeal should accordingly be allowed on that ground.

(73) Little Cumbrae Estates Ltd v Island of Little Cumbrae Ltd
April 2006, Glasgow Sheriff Court, CA305/05

There was a lease of (and here we quote the sheriff principal, James Taylor) 'the island of Little Cumbrae, the motor vessel named Bean Mhadh and the dumb barge'. In January 2005 there was storm damage. (It is not clear what parts of the leased subjects were damaged.) The landlord claimed on the insurance policy, and a payment was received from the insurance company. But it did not cover the full cost of repairs. The tenant argued that the shortfall for the repairs was the responsibility of the landlord, while the landlord argued that it was the responsibility of the tenant. When the tenant began to withhold the rent, and insurance premiums, the landlord sued for payment.

It was held by the sheriff principal, affirming the sheriff, that on a proper interpretation of the lease the repairs in question were the landlord's responsibility, and that in the light of the landlord's failure to effect the repairs the tenant was justified in withholding payment. It is understood that an appeal to the Inner House has been lodged.

(74) Abacus Estates Ltd v Bell Street Estates Ltd and
Clinton Cards (Essex) Ltd
[2006] CSOH 192, 2007 GWD 2-31

A unit in a building at 18 High Street, Paisley was leased. The subjects of let were defined in such a way as to include not only the unit itself but also the common parts of the building. Clause 3(iv) of the lease bound the tenant 'to repair ... the subjects let'. Clause 3(v) bound the tenant 'to bear and pay all costs and expenses payable by either the landlord or the tenant in respect of the subjects let' but the remaining words of the sub-clause showed that it was dealing with the common parts.

Repairs were needed to the common parts. The question before the court was which of the sub-clauses was applicable. There was a sub-lease in similar terms and the same issue thus arose as between lessee and sub-lessee. A proof before answer was allowed.

(75) Standard Commercial Property Securities Ltd
v Glasgow City Council
[2006] UKHL 50, 2006 SLT 1152, 2007 SCLR 93

Although we do not cover planning law litigation in this series, this high-profile case merits some mention. Glasgow City Council has for some years been seeking the redevelopment of a block bounded by Buchanan Street, Bath Street, West Nile Street, Nelson Mandela Place and West George Street. The plan was to acquire the whole site (which was in multiple ownership) and then have it developed by a particular developer. A rival developer challenged the whole arrangement as *ultra vires*. This claim was rejected at first instance. The rival developer reclaimed. The Inner House reversed. The Council in turn appealed. The House of Lords has now reversed the Inner House's decision.

STANDARD SECURITIES

(76) Unity Trust Bank plc v Frost
[2006] CSIH 14

This was an action to enforce certain standard securities. The defender, a party litigant, advanced a variety of unusual defences, all of which were rejected by the Lord Ordinary: see 2003 GWD 21-888, *Conveyancing 2003* Case (43), and also [2005] CSOH 33. The defender reclaimed to the Inner House, without success. (The defender has since been declared a vexatious litigant: *HM Advocate v Frost* [2006] CSIH 56.)

(77) Wilson v Dunbar Bank plc
[2006] CSOH 105, 2006 SLT 775, 2007 SCLR 25

Section 25 of the Conveyancing and Feudal Reform (Scotland) Act 1970 says that if a standard security holder enforces the security by sale, then 'it shall be the duty of the creditor to ... take all reasonable steps to ensure that the price at which all or any of the subjects are sold is the best that can be reasonably obtained'. Debtors not infrequently complain that creditors sell at too low a price, but such claims are seldom successful. This was an exception.

The pursuer had carried out a development called 'The Harriers' at Fernieside Avenue, Edinburgh, with the assistance of secured finance from the defender. The pursuer's affairs having become embarrassed, the defender enforced the security and sold the flats. The pursuer argued that the flats had not been adequately marketed and had accordingly failed to achieve a fair value.

After a proof, Temporary Judge C J Macaulay QC agreed, and awarded £66,400 as damages, this being the estimated amount by which the actual sale figure fell short of the amount that could have been 'reasonably obtained' by the defender. The judge also noted that there had been vandalism and commented (para 188) that 'the damage caused by vandalism … occurred during the period when the settlement of the transaction was being unnecessarily delayed and at a time when D M Hall [the marketing agents] were in control of the property. In my opinion the defenders require to bear responsibility for that loss'.

The proof established that the marketing agents had not marketed the properties satisfactorily. That raised the question of whether a heritable creditor should be liable for the negligence of an agent employed to market the security subjects. It was **held** that the defender had itself been negligent, in as much as it had been aware of D M Hall's inadequate marketing. Nevertheless, the opinion was expressed that a heritable creditor can be liable, even without fault on its own part, in this respect following *Bisset v Standard Property Investment plc* 1999 GWD 26-1253 (discussed in *Conveyancing 1999* p 52.)

For commentary on this decision, see Ken Swinton, 'A selling creditor's duty of care – *Wilson v Dunbar Bank*' (2006) 74 *Scottish Law Gazette* 76.

SOLICITORS, ESTATE AGENTS AND SURVEYORS

(78) McDonald-Grant v Sutherland & Co
[2006] CSOH 171

Mr Barclay owned a house at Boat of Garten. In 1993 he disponed it gratuitously to his son, reserving to himself a liferent. Shortly thereafter he married for a second time. In 1998 he died. The second Mrs Barclay, acting through Quantum Compensation Specialists, sued her late husband's solicitors for £350,000. This was said to be the loss she suffered because her husband on his death had had only a liferent and not full ownership. The solicitors argued that the claim was irrelevant, and also pled prescription. The Lord Ordinary (Lord Dawson), giving a brief opinion, allowed a proof before answer. It is not easy to understand why the plea to the relevancy was not sustained.

(79) Legal Services Centre Ltd v Miller Samuel LLP
[2006] CSOH 191

This case was about alleged negligence in the drafting of a rent review clause. Property in Glasgow was owned by Glasgow City Council. It was leased to the Scottish Development Agency, which sub-leased it to the pursuer, which carried out the development of the site and sub-sub-leased part of it to the Secretary of State on a term of 60 years. The pursuer claimed that the rent-review clause had been drafted negligently with the result that the return on its investment would be diminished. The total loss over the term of the sub-sub-lease, stated as a lump sum in current money, was estimated at £3,500,000, and this was the sum sued for. The sub-sub-lease was granted in 1990 and the defender raised a preliminary plea of prescription. Proof before answer allowed.

(80) Bennett & Robertson LLP v Strachan
1 May 2006, Cupar Sheriff Court, A442/04

This was an action by a firm of solicitors for payment of their fees. Mr Strachan bought a newly-built house at Tayport in Fife. Before settlement it emerged that part of the property (in fact nearly half) belonged not to the seller (the building company) but to the neighbouring farmer. Nevertheless settlement took place, on the basis of a price reduction, coupled with a retention of a further tranche of the price until the title problem had been resolved. It appears that the sellers were still contractually bound to ensure that the buyer would receive a land certificate for the whole area, without exclusion of indemnity. But matters dragged on, partly because the Keeper declined to complete registration until the Ordnance Survey map for the area had been updated. Mr Strachan's relationship with his then law firm broke down and he then retained the pursuer to deal with the problem. But relations with the pursuer deteriorated and eventually the latter withdrew from acting. It rendered a fee note, which was not paid. Hence the action. The defender pled breach of contract. After proof, decree was granted to the pursuer.

(81) Connolly v Brown
[2006] CSOH 187

Mr and Mrs Connolly owned some land in West Lothian. They thought it might have development value. In 1995 they agreed with Mr Brown that he would try to find a buyer. Eventually they sold it to Mr Brown himself. When he resold it soon afterwards at a substantial profit they sued him, either on the basis that he was their agent and thus barred from making a profit at their expense, or on the basis that, although he had ceased to be their agent by the time he bought it, he remained under certain duties to them.

In 2004 it was held that by the time that Mr Brown bought the property from the Connollys he was no longer their agent: *Connolly v Brown* 2004 GWD 18-386, *Conveyancing 2004* Case (48). But a proof was considered necessary on the alternative branch of the pursuers' case. This has now happened, and decree of absolvitor has been pronounced. Whether an ex-agent continues to be under duties to his ex-principal depends on the whole facts and circumstances of the case. It was **held** that by the time that Mr Brown bought the property from the Connollys, he was no longer under any duties to them.

COHABITATION AND MATRIMONIAL PROPERTY

(82) Satchwell v McIntosh
2006 SLT (Sh Ct) 117

A claim based on the law of unjustified enrichment. See **Commentary** p 119.

(83) Smith v Barclay
27 August 2006, Dundee Sheriff Court, A 1459/04

A claim based on the law of unjustified enrichment. See **Commentary** p 119.

(84) McKenzie v Nutter
2007 SLT (Sh Ct) 17, 2007 SCLR 115

A claim based on the law of unjustified enrichment. See **Commentary** p 120.

COMMUNITY RIGHT TO BUY

(85) Holmehill Ltd v The Scottish Ministers
2006 SLT (Sh Ct) 79

This is the first reported case about the 'community right to buy' created by part 2 of the Land Reform (Scotland) Act 2003. It has been a politically charged one and has attracted media attention.

Holmehill is a green area in Dunblane extending to about five hectares. It belonged to a hotel group, which owned it as part of the Dunblane Hydro. The group decided to sell it. Although there was no planning permission for development, the property was marketed on the basis that such permission might be obtainable. Local feelings ran high. Holmehill Ltd, a non-profit company, was established, and it sought to register an interest in the Register of Community Interests in Land. The problem was that the community right to buy, unlike the crofting community right to buy in part 3 of the 2003 Act, is only a pre-emption, ie a right to buy if the property happens to come on the market. If a property is *already* on the market, it is in principle too late. The 2003 Act does, however, have a regime for late applications in s 39, and Holmehill Ltd applied under that provision.

All right-to-buy procedure under the 2003 Act is subject to approval by Scottish Ministers. Scottish Ministers did not approve. The company responded by raising this action to compel Ministers to consent. The action failed. The sheriff (J C C McSherry) took the view that Ministers had a broad discretion under the Act and that the refusal of consent in this case was within that discretion.

The decision in itself seems correct. But it raises at least three concerns. The first is whether Ministers are using their discretion in too restrictive a manner. This is a political question. The second is that in practice, as here, it will often be only when a property is put on the market that the local community wakes up.

Section 39 is thus an important section in practice. How Ministers treat it, and whether the Act itself should be amended to make late applications easier: these again are political questions. The third concern relates to the following passage from the sheriff's opinion (at p 101 H–I):

> The purpose of the community right to buy is that of sustainable development of communities. If the purpose of an application to register a community interest in land is the desire to prevent or frustrate development by a potential purchaser, I would agree that it is not unreasonable for the Scottish Ministers to take this into account and regard the application as being incompatible with the policy aims of the legislation.

That passage – which reflects an argument addressed to the court by counsel for Scottish Ministers – has caused some concern. If it is right – as to which we express no view – then the community right to buy is narrower in scope than many had believed. Here too the issues become political.

For a valuable study of the decision, see an article by Malcolm M Combe published at (2007) 11 *Edinburgh Law Review* 109. In this article Mr Combe also discusses another 2006 case on the community right to buy, *Earl of Glasgow v Fairlie Land Acquisition Co Ltd*, but about this litigation no detailed information appears to be in the public domain.

DILIGENCE AND INSOLVENCY

(86) Henderson v 3052775 Nova Scotia Ltd
[2006] UKHL 21, 2006 SC (HL) 85, 2006 SLT 489, 2006 SCLR 626

This reverses the decision of an Extra Division of the Court of Session: 2005 1 SC 325, digested as *Conveyancing 2005* Case (47). The reversal only concerns a procedural question, namely whether summary decree should have been granted. The case continues. For a parallel litigation between the same parties (but with the company as the pursuer), see [2006] CSOH 147, noted above as Case (47).

BARONY TITLES

(87) Hamilton Ptr
15 May 2006, Lyon Court

Mrs Margaret Hamilton petitioned the Lord Lyon (i) for official recognition in the name of Margaret Hamilton of Rockhall, Baroness of Lag, and (ii) for a grant of Arms together with additaments appropriate to the dignity of Baron in the Baronage of Scotland. The Lord Lyon recognised Mrs Hamilton as Baroness of Lag, and agreed to grant Arms, but without the baronial additaments.

In respect of (i) the main difficulty arose from the Abolition of Feudal Tenure etc (Scotland) Act 2000 s 63. Prior to the abolition of the feudal system, the title of baron was attached to land and was transferred with that land. The right to a barony title could thus be determined by inspecting the property registers.

Since feudal abolition, the title of baron has been severed from the land, and is transferred by assignation: see s 63(2). In order to make proof of title easier, Brian Hamilton, who is active in the barony market, has been instrumental in setting up a Register of Scottish Baronies: for further details, see *Conveyancing 2004* p 50. In the present case, the petitioner's title was hardly in doubt. The Barony of Lag was previously held by Brian Hamilton, and his title was recognised by the Lord Lyon in an interlocutor issued shortly before feudal abolition. Thereafter Mr Hamilton assigned the title to the petitioner (his wife), and registered the assignation in the Register of Scottish Baronies. It seems worth noting that the assignation included the following declaration as to title:

> And I do solemnly and sincerely swear that, as at 28 November 2004, I held the relevant interest in land on my Barony Title as narrated above and was entitled to the Dignity of the Barony, that the Entitlement to the Dignity of the Barony has not been sold or transferred since that date and that I am not aware of any competing claims to the Entitlement to the Dignity of the Barony.

While, however, the Lord Lyon had no difficulty with Mrs Hamilton's title, he gave a strong indication that other titles were likely to be less straightforward and might require to be established by court declarator. In particular, Lyon suggested that little credence could be given to the Barony Register:

> I do not consider that a private Register, managed by a person appointed by a private company with no public scrutiny, and operated under terms which allow complete discretion as to what evidence is to be provided, is an acceptable source of evidence in an application before the Court of the Lord Lyon.

In respect of (ii), the main issue was entitlement to the baronial additaments, notably the red chapeau and the mantle. The petitioner argued (a) that under the law as it was before the appointed day, barons were entitled to the additaments, and (b) that the position was preserved by the 2000 Act s 63(1) which provided that 'nothing in this Act affects the dignity of baron', 'dignity' itself being defined (in s 63(4)) to include 'any quality or precedence associated with, and any heraldic privilege incidental to, a dignity'.

The Lord Lyon rejected both arguments. The conferral of additaments was a matter of discretion and not of right, and the exercise of the discretion dated only from about 60 years ago. In Lyon's view, the baronial additaments reflected the heritable jurisdiction of barons, and ceased to be appropriate once that jurisdiction was abolished (as it was under the 2000 Act). Further, the practice of granting additaments arose at a time when barony titles were associated with a major estate of land, but now the title had been severed from the land.

In relation to s 63(1) – the second argument – Lyon took the view that:

> A heraldic privilege in the context of a barony would be a heraldic right which the holder of the barony enjoyed by right, by virtue of being the holder of the barony. It would not be a heraldic feature which might be granted by Lyon to such a holder if he were to apply for it and if Lyon decided to grant it.

Even before this decision, the issue of whether a petitioner could now – after feudal abolition – insist on baronial additaments had been a matter of some controversy: see Sir Crispin Agnew of Lochnaw, 'Baronial Heraldic Additaments' 2004 SLT (News) 179; Peter Drummond-Murray of Mastrick, 'Baronial Heraldic Additaments' 2005 SLT (News) 161. And Sir Crispin Agnew, the Rothesay Herald, who represented Mrs Hamilton, was obliged to disavow the opposition to the granting of additaments which he had expressed in his article.

It is arguable that in reaching his decision the Lord Lyon under-played the effect of s 63(1). For if the practice of granting of the additaments is tied to the baron's heritable jurisdiction, now abolished by the 2000 Act, such abolition should not, according to s 63(1), affect the heraldic privileges or, one might assume, the practice adopted by Lyon. That apparently was the view of the Scottish Law Commission, because in its commentary on the provision which became s 63 the Commission notes that 'dignity' in subsection (4) includes 'matters of heraldry and precedence incidental to a dignity, such as the addition of baronial additaments to a coat of arms': see Scottish Law Commission, Report on *Abolition of the Feudal System* (Scot Law Com No 168, 1999) p 205. Paragraph 200 of the official explanatory notes to the 2000 Act is to the same effect. The Lord Lyon, however, rejected this reading:

> The implication from the wording of the note is that the Act is to be read as meaning that nothing in the Act affects the addition of certain baronial features to a coat of arms. I do not believe that the intention of section 63 of the Act was either to fetter the operation of the system of heraldry in Scotland or to enshrine into Scottish heraldic law a requirement that baronial features were to be a legal right. If that had been the intention then much more specific wording would have to have been adopted in the 2000 Act than the wording used as part of the definition of 'dignity' in subsection (4).
>
> In my view the intention of the Scottish Law Commission proposals, and of the Act as subsequently passed, was not to interfere with current heraldic practice. The Act did not create any heraldic right that did not already exist. I do not accept the submissions that the terms of the Scottish Law Commission Report or the Act imply that a legal right to additaments exists. I accept that there has been over recent years a practice by Lord Lyons of granting additaments and that the Act did not seek to interfere in this practice. But that is very different from the assertion that by virtue of the 2000 Act Lyon is precluded from departing from this practice.

MISCELLANEOUS

(88) Cahill's Judicial Factor v Cahill
[2006] CSIH 26, 2006 GWD 19-409

Following his father's death, the defender took possession of the family home, and claimed the right to continue possession on grounds which are not entirely easy to understand, one of them being an alleged agreement with the judicial factor on his father's estate. The judicial factor has been litigating since 1994, attempting to gain possession. The Inner House has now affirmed the sheriff's decision, in favour of the judicial factor, noted as *Conveyancing 2005* Case (49).

(89) Findlay's Exr, Ptr
[2006] CSOH 188

This case is primarily about administrative law, but it will also be of interest to conveyancers. In 1967 Robert Findlay sold 14 acres to West Lothian County Council. This was not a CPO as such, but the Council had said that if he did not sell the land then it would compulsorily purchase it. The Council's proposed development of the land never took place. In such cases there is a principle of administrative practice that the property should be offered back to the previous owner at market value. This convention is constituted by the Crichel Down Rules (so called because they resulted from the Crichel Down scandal in 1954.) These rules are laid down in a formal Scottish Executive policy document (SE Circular 38/1992), which, though not binding as a matter of private law, nevertheless can be the basis for a 'legitimate expectations' claim against the public authority in question.

West Lothian Council at first was simply going to sell the land on the open market, but it withdrew when threatened with judicial review by Robert Findlay's executor. An informal agreement was then reached whereby the executor would buy the land for £1,820,000. But missives were not concluded, and matters dragged on. With land prices rising, the Council then said that the price would have to be increased to £2,388,000. The executor rejected this. The Council said that it would put the land on the open market. The executor raised the present petition for judicial review.

The petition failed. The Lord Ordinary (Hodge) held that the challenge to the Council's interpretation of SE Circular 38/1992 could not be sustained, and that the petitioner's legitimate expectations had not been unlawfully frustrated.

(90) Beriston Ltd v Dumbarton Motor Boat and Sailing Club
[2006] CSOH 190, 2007 SLT 227

The question of whether local authorities have wrongfully alienated land is one which crops up regularly, and possibly more often now than in the past. One such case was *Wilson v Keeper of the Registers of Scotland* 2000 SLT 267 (*Conveyancing 1999* Case (33)). Sometimes issues of common good law are involved, and fortunately a book has now been published on that obscure subject: Andrew Ferguson, *Common Good Law* (2006).

The present dispute attracted some publicity, as such cases often do. The pursuer had a completed title in the Land Register and sued in the Court of Session to remove the defenders, these being a sailing club and various of its office bearers. Temporary Judge C J MacAulay QC held that 'no relevant defence has been pled to challenge the pursuers' right to possess the enclosure' (para 45), but nevertheless found for the defenders on a technical point: the action should have been raised in the sheriff court. (The jurisdictional rules about actions of removing and of ejection are by no means straightforward.)

PART II

STATUTORY DEVELOPMENTS

STATUTORY DEVELOPMENTS

Housing (Scotland) Act 2006 (asp 1)

Though receiving the Royal Assent in 2006, this Act completed its Parliamentary stages at the end of 2005, and it was covered in *Conveyancing 2005* pp 26–29 and 122–130. There have been some developments since.

Single surveys and purchaser's information packs

For conveyancers, one of the most important changes introduced by the Act is the planned introduction of single surveys and purchaser's information packs. See *Conveyancing 2005* pp 124–130. These are the equivalent of the home information packs which are to be introduced in England and Wales on 1 June 2007. To considerable surprise, however, it was announced on 18 July 2006 that home information packs would extend, for the moment at least, only to an energy efficiency rating, searches and title deeds. The relevant regulations, the Home Information Pack Regulations 2006, SI 2006/1503, are to be amended to withdraw the requirement to include a 'home condition report' (ie single survey). Officially this is just a more gradual phasing-in of HIPs: see www.homeinfor mationpacks.gov.uk/home.aspx. But *The Times* for 19 July 2006 presented it as abandonment of home condition reports due to (i) negative reports by private consultants engaged by the Government, (ii) CML's statement to Ministers that many lenders would not be able to rely on home condition reports as they would not include information about subsidence, flood risk or land contamination, and (iii) not enough home inspectors having been trained – only a few hundred when 7000 were needed.

The relentlessly breezy press release from the Department of Communities and Local Government presents bad news as good and is a masterpiece of obfuscation:

> The Government today announced plans for the introduction of Energy Performance Certificates as part of the phased roll-out of Home Information Packs to help consumers cut costs and waste when buying a home and help the environment too. In the light of the plans for testing and concerns about the readiness of industry, the Government announced new proposals to phase the introduction of HIPs, prioritising the delivery of energy efficiency information with further testing later this year on the other aspects of HIPs.
>
> This means that HIPs will be introduced in June next year with searches and energy performance information, enabling buyers and sellers to get A–G ratings on their

homes similar to fridge ratings as well as a list of practical measures to cut their fuel bills and carbon emissions at the same time.

The Energy Savings Trust estimates that by following the proposals in the Energy Performance Certificate, the average homeowner will save £300 a year on fuel bills. Government also believes that the information could be used to support the growth of green mortgages and other incentives.

However on the basis of detailed consultations with industry and the latest market and testing information, the Government has decided to phase the roll-out of other aspects of Home Information Packs, introducing the rest of Home Condition Reports on a market-led basis in the first instance, in order to ensure a smooth implementation with clear benefits for consumers ...

The dry run aims to ensure that HIPs deliver the maximum benefits to consumers by looking at costs, the savings from avoiding waste and duplication, consumer attitudes to the Packs, failed transactions and transaction times, and people's willingness to sell with HIPs in place. It will begin with further consumer research in the summer as well as analysis of over 14,000 HIPs produced so far, in order to inform area-based trials later in the year which will be independently monitored.

Ministers are determined to avoid the risks to consumers and to the implementation of Energy Performance Certificates from a 'big bang' introduction in June next year. In particular, further testing is needed on the costs and impacts of Home Condition Reports and the Government does not want to see early roll-out of Energy Performance Certificates jeopardised by late amendments or delays to the rest of the scheme.

The latest information casts doubts on the readiness of the industry to be able to pass on the benefits to consumers from next June. There are concerns about the number of home inspectors who will be in place in time. In addition evidence from the Council of Mortgage Lenders shows that many lenders will not be in a position to make maximum use of Automated Valuation Models which will support the use of the Home Condition Report. The Government is keen to avoid risks to consumers from industry delays and potential late changes to the implementation timetable next year.

Therefore, the Government will begin by promoting the take-up of HCRs on a market-led basis – including examining the case for pump priming and other incentives. Mandatory introduction of Home Condition Reports remains on the table, however the Government wants to encourage market-led take-up first, in order to allow a more flexible roll-out that responds to consumer demand and the results of further testing. The Government will urgently review with key stakeholders what support is needed to ensure that there are sufficient home inspectors in place, and that consumers are fully protected.

Thus far, the Scottish Executive has continued to insist that it will press ahead with purchaser's information packs, including the single survey. The Law Society of Scotland, previously neutral on the issue, has now called for the single survey to be dropped: see (2006) 51 *Journal of the Law Society* Dec/26. In place of PIPs the Society advocates the much simpler property sale questionnaire which also derives from the Scottish Executive's Purchaser's Information Advisory Group and is being piloted in various parts of the country: see p 48 of the November *Journal*, and an article by Stewart Brymer in (2007) 85 *Greens Property Law Bulletin* 5. Single surveys were attacked by Duncan Collinson in the October issue of the *Journal* (p 9) and defended in the December *Journal* (p 8) by Sarah O'Neill, the Legal Officer of the Scottish Consumer Council.

Commencement

Four commencement orders have so far been passed, as follows:

- **Housing (Scotland) Act 2006 (Commencement No 1) Order 2006, SSI 2006/14** commences ss 176 and 177 on 29 January 2006.
- **Housing (Scotland) Act 2006 (Commencement No 2) Order 2006, SSI 2006/252** commences ss 178 and 180 on 17 May 2006.
- **Housing (Scotland) Act 2006 (Commencement No 3) Order 2006, SSI 2006/395** commences ss 70, 175, 185, 193 and 194 on 5 July 2006 and ss 52–54, 64(6) and 65(3), (4) on 4 December 2006.
- **Housing (Scotland) Act 2006 (Commencement No 4) Order 2006, SSI 2006/569** commences ss 55-57, 63(1), 181(1)(c), (5), 182, 184, and 186–189 on 4 December 2006.

Family Law (Scotland) Act 2006 (asp 2)

Though receiving the Royal Assent in 2006, this Act completed its Parliamentary stages at the end of 2005, and its conveyancing aspects were covered in *Conveyancing 2005* pp 72–74 and 78–84. Subject to some transitional arrangements, the Act came fully into force on 4 May 2006: see the **Family Law (Scotland) Act 2006 (Commencement, Transitional Provisions and Savings) Order 2006, SSI 2006/212**.

Planning etc (Scotland) Act 2006 (asp 17)

This Act brings about major changes to planning law. One change of interest to conveyancers is that the standard duration for planning permission is reduced from five years to three: s 20. Another is that there are changes to s 75 agreements: s 23. (On this aspect, see an article by Robin Priestley and Martin Whiteford in the *Journal of the Law Society of Scotland* in March 2006 (p 49).) One aim of the Act is to facilitate major developments. Conservationists are worried. An issue of some political prominence was whether third party rights of appeal would be introduced into the planning system, but at the end of the day the Act did not include them.

Bankruptcy and Diligence (Scotland) Act 2007 (asp 3)

See **Commentary** p 131.

Consumer Credit Act 2006 (c 14)

This extensively amends the Consumer Credit Act 1974. One change is that hitherto the legislation did not affect loans over a prescribed sum (latterly £25,000). There will now be no ceiling. This change is relevant, among other things, for standard securities.

Finance Act 2006 (c 25)

For changes to stamp duty land tax, see **Commentary** p 153.

Companies Act 2006 (c 46)

This replaces the Companies Act 1985. It is partly a consolidation measure, but it also introduces new law. It is expected to be brought into force gradually in the course of 2007 and 2008. With one important qualification, the new law does not seem to affect conveyancers, apart from the fact that references to existing rules will now have to be updated.

The qualification is s 893. This allows an order to be made whereby a 'charge' granted by a company which is registered in a 'special register' will not have to be separately registered in the Companies Register. What will happen is that the keeper of the special register will send details of the charge to the Registrar of Companies, who will insert that information in the Companies Register. But the parties to the charge do not need to concern themselves with this: as far as they are concerned, one registration suffices. Examples of 'special registers' would be the Land Register, the Sasine Register, the Patents Register, the Shipping Register etc.

Under current law, if a company grants a standard security, that security must be registered twice, first in the Land Register (or Sasine Register, as the case may be) and again in the Companies Register, the latter registration having to be within 21 days of the former: see Companies Act 1985 ss 410 ff. Failure to effect the second registration undermines the validity of the security. As and when a s 893 order is made with reference to the Land Register (and Sasine Register), double registration will be a thing of the past.

At present, floating charges have no special register of their own, but the Bankruptcy and Diligence (Scotland) Act 2007 creates such a register, the Register of Floating Charges. If the latter provisions were brought into force before a s 893 order were made, the result would be that floating charges would have to be registered twice. But it is expected that there will be synchronisation, so that a s 893 order will be in place for the Register of Floating Charges as soon as the provisions of the 2007 Act on that subject come into force. For the Register of Floating Charges see **Commentary** p 139.

Registers of Scotland

ARTL

The **Automated Registration of Title to Land (Electronic Communications) (Scotland) Order 2006, SSI 2006/491** paves the way for ARTL by amending (i) the Land Registration (Scotland) Act 1979 and (ii) the Requirements of Writing (Scotland) Act 1995. Provision for the mandates which will normally be needed in ARTL transactions is made by the Law Society in the Solicitors (Scotland) (ARTL Mandates) Rules 2006. See **Commentary** p 144.

New Land Registration Rules

The **Land Registration (Scotland) Rules 2006, SSI 2006/485** replaced the original Land Registration (Scotland) Rules 1980 with effect from 22 January 2007. See **Commentary** p 145. The new rules provide for ARTL, but make certain other changes as well including the provision of new application forms, for which see Registers of Scotland, *Update 21* (available on www.ros.gov.uk/updates). One important change is that, while land certificates will continue to be issued (in due course with the option of an electronic version), they will no longer be updated. See Registers of Scotland, *Update 9.1* (available on www.ros.gov.uk/updates).

New fees order

The primary order is the Fees in the Registers of Scotland Order 1995, SI 1995/1945. The **Fees in the Registers of Scotland (Amendment) Order 2006, SSI 2006/600** is the most recent amendment, and brings about major changes. It came into force on 22 January 2007. For details see www.ros.gov.uk/fees, and Registers of Scotland, *Update 18.1* (available on www.ros.gov.uk/updates). While some fees have gone up, the overall trend is down. Apparently the new rules will lead to a reduction in registration fee income of around 26%, or, to view it the other way round, a reduction in what the average client has to pay by about 26%. That is a welcome development, and credit must be given to Registers of Scotland for achieving it. Moreover the new system is simpler. For instance the standard scale goes down from 51 bands to 12 (or 24 including Table B). For heritable securities a single fee of £30 will apply, regardless of amount. This fee will also apply to discharges of securities. The same figure (£30) becomes the standard flat fee for a number of miscellaneous cases, such as deeds of conditions, minutes of waiver, tree preservation orders, rejections of applications and notings of overriding interests.

For dispositions there are two scales, A and B. Table B is for ARTL transactions:

Consideration or value not exceeding £	Table A fee £	Table B fee £
50,000	30	20
100,000	100	75
150,000	200	150
200,000	300	225
300,000	400	300
500,000	500	375
700,000	600	450
1,000,000	700	550
2,000,000	1000	800
3,000,000	3000	2500
5,000,000	5000	4500
Over 5000,000	7500	7000

There are numerous other changes, some important, others less so. All those potential clients who have found you in the Yellow Pages and who phone up to ask how much it will be to register a charter in the Register of the Great Seal can now be told that this will cost £250.

The Keeper is also introducing a direct debit system for payment of fees. This will be optional, except for ARTL transactions for which it will be mandatory.

New application forms for GRS

The Register of Sasines (Application Procedure) Rules 2004, SSI 2004/318 prescribe the application forms for GRS transactions. The **Register of Sasines (Application Procedure) Amendment Rules 2006, SSI 2006/568** amend the 2004 Rules with effect from 22 January 2007, substituting new forms.

GRS: recording in electronic form

Since 30 April 2006 deeds in the Register of Sasines are being recorded in electronic form. See the **Register of Sasines (Methods of Operating) (Scotland) Regulations 2006, SSI 2006/164**. This replaces microfiche, which in turn replaced photocopying, which itself replaced the copying of deeds by hand. The recording stamp will now give the sequential number of the deed within the relevant county and year, rather than the fiche and frame. Back conversion of existing records is also under way.

Private landlord registration

Part 8 of the Antisocial Behaviour etc (Scotland) Act 2004 came into force on 30 April 2006: see the **Antisocial Behaviour etc (Scotland) Act 2004 (Commencement and Savings) Amendment Order 2006, SSI 2006/104**. This was a month later than the intended commencement date, due to difficulties with the mechanism for transferring fees paid on internet-based applications.

With the provisions now in force, most private landlords require to be licensed by the local authority, although there are exemptions, most notably where the house is also the landlord's main residence. For details, see *Conveyancing 2004* pp 92–95 and *Conveyancing 2005* pp 33–35. The fee for registration is £50 for every landlord and an additional £11 for every property registered. Registration is possible online at www.landlordregistrationscotland.gov.uk, and the same website has a useful facility for searching the new register both by property and by person. Landlords who already have an HMO licence are put on the register automatically. We understand that in some areas there is a backlog in applications for registration.

New rural housing bodies

Rural housing bodies are bodies which are able to create and hold rural housing burdens under s 43 of the Title Conditions (Scotland) Act 2003. A rural housing burden is a personal right of pre-emption. The first list of rural housing bodies was prescribed by the Title Conditions (Scotland) Act 2003 (Rural Housing Bodies) Order 2004, SSI 2004/477. The names – 19 in all – are reproduced in *Conveyancing 2004* pp 39–40. The **Title Conditions (Scotland) Act 2003 (Rural Housing Bodies) Amendment Order 2006, SSI 2006/108** has now added a further four names:

Buidheann Tigheadas Loch Aillse Agus An Eilein Sgitheanaich Limited
Ekopia Resource Exchange Limited
Rural Stirling Housing Association Limited
West Highland Housing Association Limited.

Conservation bodies added and removed

Conservation bodies are bodies which are able to create and hold conservation burdens under s 38 of the Title Conditions (Scotland) Act 2003. A conservation burden is a personal real burden which preserves or protects the natural or built environment for the benefit of the public. The first list of conservation bodies was prescribed by the Title Conditions (Scotland) Act 2003 (Conservation Bodies) Order 2003, SSI 2003/453. The names, which include all local authorities, are reproduced in *Conveyancing 2003* pp 33–34. The **Title Conditions (Scotland) Act 2003 (Conservation Bodies) Amendment Order 2006, SSI 2006/110** adds Aberdeen City Heritage Trust to the list, while the **Title Conditions (Scotland) Act 2003 (Conservation Bodies) Amendment (No 2) Order 2006, SSI 2006/130** removes Glasgow Conservation Trust West (which has been wound up).

End of period of transitional validity for feudal burdens

Where a feudal superior could not satisfy the 100-metres rule but wished to preserve real burdens, s 20 of the Abolition of Feudal Tenure etc (Scotland) Act 2000 provided a complex procedure whereby the superior, having first registered a notice, could apply to the Lands Tribunal for reallotment of the burdens on the ground that extinction would cause material detriment to the land which the superior nominated as the potential benefited property. See K G C Reid, *Abolition of Feudal Tenure in Scotland* (2004) pp 56–62. If the application had not been disposed of by the Tribunal by the appointed day, the burdens continued to be enforceable after that day for a transitional period, ending on a day to be specified by Scottish Ministers. That day has now been specified as 31 March 2006: see the **Abolition of Feudal Tenure etc (Scotland) Act 2000 (Specified Day) Order 2006, SSI 2006/109**. In fact no applications under s 20 were ever made.

Occupancy rights

Written declarations replace affidavits

When s 6(3) of the Family Law (Scotland) Act 2006 provided that affidavits should be replaced by 'written declarations', the provision – no doubt unintentionally – extended only to sales and not to the grant of heritable securities. That had the odd result that, when the provision came into force on 4 May 2006, affidavits survived for heritable securities: see *Conveyancing 2005* pp 79–80. After a short delay, the omission was put right by the **Family Law (Scotland) Act 2006 (Consequential Amendments) Order 2006, SSI 2006/384**, which makes an appropriate amendment to s 8 of the Matrimonial Homes (Family Protection) (Scotland) Act 1981 and to s 108 of the Civil Partnership Act 2004. The amendments took effect on

30 June 2006 and means that written declarations must now be used for heritable securities as well. Since affidavits are themselves 'written declarations', it is not incompetent to continue to use them (see *Conveyancing 2005* p 81).

Form of consent to dealing by civil partners

The Civil Partnership Act 2004 gave to civil partners occupancy rights in the 'family home' which are virtually identical to those held by spouses under the Matrimonial Homes (Family Protection) (Scotland) Act 1981. See *Conveyancing 2004* pp 32–33. The **Civil Partnership Family Homes (Form of Consent) Regulations 2006, SSI 2006/115** now stipulate the form of consent which is to be used for dealings. For consents within a deed, such as a disposition or standard security, the wording is:

> … with the consent of AB (designation), civil partner of the said CD (designation), for the purposes of the Civil Partnership Act 2004. …

And when consent is given in a separate document, the wording is:

> I, AB (designation), civil partner of CD (designation), hereby consent for the purposes of the Civil Partnership Act 2004 to the undernoted dealing of the said CD relating to (here describe the family home or the part of it to which the dealing relates).

These are modelled on the equivalent styles prescribed for spouses by the Matrimonial Homes (Form of Consent) (Scotland) Regulations 1982, SI 1982/ 971.

Building regulations

Amendments to building regulations

The Building (Scotland) Act Regulations 2004, SSI 2004/406 are amended with effect from 1 May 2007 by the **Building (Scotland) Act Amendment Regulations 2006, SSI 2006/534**. This updates standards and guidance in relation to a number of topics including energy conservation.

New forms for building warrants etc

The forms for building warrants, completion certificates and numerous other forms and notices under the Building (Scotland) Act 2003, originally prescribed by the Building (Forms) (Scotland) Regulations 2005, SSI 2005/172, have now been replaced, with effect from 1 May 2006, by the modified forms contained in the **Building (Forms) (Scotland) Amendment Regulations 2006, SSI 2006/163**.

Fire safety

The **Fire Safety (Scotland) Regulations 2006, SSI 2006/456** came into force on 1 October 2006. Most of the regulations (4–23) are based on fire safety provisions in existing legislation, primarily the Fire Precautions (Workplace) Regulations

1997, SI 1997/1840 (as amended), the Management of Health and Safety at Work Regulations 1999, SI 1999/3242, and the Dangerous Substances and Explosive Atmospheres Regulations 2002, SI 2002/2776. These provisions were previously limited to workplaces, but part 3 of the Fire (Scotland) Act 2005 extends them to the majority of non-domestic premises and to houses in multiple occupation subject to licensing. In addition, regulation 24 extends certain controls to the common areas of private dwellings. For a discussion of part 3 of the 2005 Act, see an article by Donna Brown, Donna McGuffog and Linda Martin published in (2006) *Greens Property Law Bulletin* 3.

Community right to buy: revised definition of excluded land

Settlements of more than 10,000 people form 'excluded land' for the purposes of s 33 of the Land Reform (Scotland) Act 2003 and cannot be the subject of a community buy-out under part 2 of the Act. The **Community Right to Buy (Definition of Excluded Land) (Scotland) Order 2006, SSI 2006/486** gives a new list of such areas, reflecting population movement since the original list was enacted by the Community Right to Buy (Definition of Excluded Land) (Scotland) Order 2004, SSI 2004/296. The only additions are Stonehaven and Westhill in Aberdeenshire. The complete list is:

Aberdeen; Alloa; Arbroath; Ardrossan; Ayr; Bathgate; Bo'ness; Bonnybridge; Broxburn; Buckhaven; Carluke; Carnoustie; Cowdenbeath; Cumbernauld; Dalkeith; Dumbarton; Dumfries; Dundee; Dunfermline; East Kilbride; Edinburgh; Elgin; Erskine; Falkirk; Forfar; Fraserburgh; Galashiels; Glasgow; Glenrothes; Greenock; Hamilton; Hawick; Helensburgh; Inverness; Inverurie; Irvine; Kilmarnock; Kilwinning; Kirkcaldy; Kirkintilloch; Largs; Larkhall; Linlithgow; Livingston; Montrose; Penicuik; Perth; Peterhead; St Andrews; Stirling; Stonehaven; Stranraer; Troon; Westhill (Aberdeenshire); Whitburn.

PART III
OTHER MATERIAL

OTHER MATERIAL

Crofting Reform etc Act 2007 (asp 7)

This Act, which spent much of 2006 in the Scottish Parliament, was finally passed on 25 January 2007. It makes numerous changes to the legislation on crofting, including the possible extension of crofting tenure to land that is currently not subject to it and outwith the traditional crofting counties.

Consumers, Estate Agents and Redress Bill

This Bill, recently introduced to the Westminster Parliament, contains amendments to the Estate Agents Act 1979. It extends to the whole of the UK. The Scottish Ministers intend to introduce a Sewel Motion (technically a 'Legislative Consent Motion') to confirm the Bill's application to Scotland: www.scottish executive.gov.uk/News/Releases/2006/11/15081720.

The provisions are framework ones, so that details will depend on statutory orders. Schedule 6 para 2 will add a new s 23A to the Estate Agents Act 1979, as follows:

(1) The Secretary of State may by order require persons who engage in estate agency work in relation to residential property ('relevant estate agency work') to be members of an approved redress scheme for dealing with complaints in connection with that work.

(2) An order may provide for the duty to apply—
   (a) only to specified descriptions of persons who engage in estate agency work; and
   (b) in relation to any relevant estate agency work carried out by a person to whom the duty applies or only in relation to specified descriptions of work (which may be framed by reference to descriptions of residential property).

   ...

(8) For the purposes of this section—
   (a) a 'redress scheme' is a scheme which provides for complaints against members of the scheme to be investigated and determined by an independent person ('the ombudsman')....

The Bill is, naturally, framed in English style. For instance a seller is 'in relation to residential property a person who claims that he is or may become interested in disposing of an interest in land in respect of that property' (Sch 6 para 8(d)).

The CML Handbook

The *CML Handbook*, which was once a printed text, has for some time existed only in digital form, and is available at the website of the Council of Mortgage Lenders, www.cml.org.uk. It was last amended in 2004, but there has now been a further batch of amendments, effective as from 1 December 2006. A useful explanation of the changes is given by John Lunn at p 52 of the December issue of the *Journal of the Law Society of Scotland*.

To a considerable extent, the changes are caused by new legislation. For example, the impending introduction of ARTL has required the introduction of a whole new clause (clause 18). A new clause 6.5.3 makes additional provision for properties which are already let at settlement: the letting must be under a short assured tenancy, the landlord must be registered with the local authority under part 8 of the Antisocial Behaviour etc (Scotland) Act 2004, and an HMO licence must have been obtained where necessary. A matching change is made to clause 16.4 for properties let after settlement. Other, generally minor, changes reflect the introduction of SDLT, the prospective dematerialisation of land certificates, and the Tenements (Scotland) Act 2004 and the Civil Partnership Act 2004. Not all changes are in response to legislation: for example there is no longer a time limit on the age of coal mining reports (clause 5.2.3), while when a loan is paid off by cheque, the cheque should now bear the name of the borrower and the loan account number (clause 17.1.2).

Elderly person in care: voluntary deprivation of assets

If an old person goes into local authority care, a financial assessment is carried out to determine liability for fees. Assets which the person deliberately gave away can be brought into this calculation. This issue arises frequently, and in practice the asset in question is typically the house.

In the case with which this note is concerned, the local authority, East Dunbartonshire Council, brought into the reckoning a house which the old person had given to his son nine years before. The son complained to the Scottish Public Services Ombudsman, who on 19 December 2006 upheld the complaint. Details can be found at the ombudsman's website, www.spso.org.uk. The ombudsman recommended the Council to:

   (i) review their current practice for assessment of nominal capital to ensure that it complies with the spirit of the relevant regulations;

  (ii) reassess Mr A's financial means, excluding the nominal value of the property; and

 (iii) apologise to Mr C for the previous lack of formal procedures available to him to progress his complaint.

The report notes that 'the Council's correspondence file contains a number of comments from several members of staff expressing concern at the difficulties in operating under the current guidance and a need for a change in the law and/or regulations to bring clarity to this matter'. It adds: 'I am concerned that the current system is confused and inconsistent throughout Scotland and in particular that there is no recognised, independent appeals process for such financial assessments and decisions....'

Septic tanks and the Controlled Activities Regulations

The Water Environment (Controlled Activities) (Scotland) Regulations 2005, SSI 2005/348, came into force on 1 April 2006. The Regulations are made under the Water Environment and Water Services (Scotland) Act 2003, which transposes Directive 2000/60/EEC. An account of some of the implications for conveyancing is given at (2006) 51 *Journal of the Law Society of Scotland* April/52. See also the article by Donna Brown, Donna McGuffog and Linda Martin in (2006) 83 *Greens Property Law Bulletin* 3.

In principle, all 'controlled activities' require to be authorised by SEPA, and the carrying out of such an activity without authorisation is an offence. Discharges to the water environment, including all discharges from septic tanks, are 'controlled activities'.

Any septic tank which was previously authorised under the Control of Pollution Act 1974 is taken to be authorised under the Controlled Activities Regulations and no action need be taken. But, unlike the 1974 Act, the new Regulations extend to septic tanks with discharges to land via full soakaway. All existing such septic tanks – and there are many – will now require to be registered. In the case of domestic septic tanks, however, SEPA is content to wait until the property next changes hands. Registration costs £94, or £70 if done online: www.sepa.org.uk/wfd.

Conversion of ultra-long leases into ownership

In its Report on *Conversion of Long Leases*, published in December 2006 (Scot Law Com No 204; available on www.scotlawcom.gov.uk), the Scottish Law Commission put forward detailed proposals for the conversion of ultra-long leases into ownership. A draft Bill accompanies the proposals.

On the basis of quite extensive empirical research, the Scottish Law Commission discovered that long leases are almost always either (i) 'proper' leases, with a duration of anything from 20 to 125 years but with a concentration in the lower part of the range and (ii) ultra-long leases – in effect quasi-feus – with a duration of 700 years or more but typically for 999 years. The Commission considered, but rejected, the introduction of a conversion scheme for (i). Instead its proposals are confined to ultra-long leases.

As ultra-long leases are quasi-feus, the Commission modelled its conversion scheme on the scheme for conversion of *dominium utile* into outright ownership which was contained in the Abolition of Feudal Tenure etc (Scotland) Act 2000. Thus, much of the Commission's draft Bill has a familiar look about it. On a day to be appointed there would be automatic conversion of the tenant's interest in a qualifying lease into outright ownership. At the same time the landlord's interest would be extinguished against payment of compensation calculated as a multiplier of the rent. A lease would qualify for conversion if it had been granted for more than 175 years and had more than 100 years left to run. It would be possible for a tenant to opt out of conversion. Following conversion, certain leasehold conditions would become real burdens or servitudes.

Registers of Scotland

Scottish Statutory Instruments

Various SSIs passed during 2006 and relating to registration matters were described on pp 66–68.

Introduction of ARTL

ARTL (automated registration of title to land) is expected to be fully available throughout the country by 30 April 2007. See **Commentary** p 144.

First registrations on the decline

Applications for first registration reached their peak in 2003 and have been on the decline ever since. See (2006) 51 *Journal of the Law Society of Scotland* Feb/51.

Identifying flats in tenement properties on Registers Direct

Registers of Scotland, *Update 20* (available on www.ros.gov.uk/updates) gives information on a new system for identifying a particular flat in a tenement building on Registers Direct:

> Older flatted properties are invariably described by the street number of the tenement of which they form part, with a verbal description of the location of the flat within the tenement. This means that a typical address search will return a list of all of the flats within the tenement concerned, without any information that might enable the searcher to identify a specific flat. The only way to identify a specific flat would be to open up each of the listed entries individually until the required selection is displayed, incurring a fee each time.
>
> To resolve this issue, we have introduced a roll-over facility that allows users to read the first 300 characters of the A Property Section description without the need to open the full Title Sheet and incur unnecessary costs. Simply place the mouse pointer over the address in the Property Address Field in the rightmost column of the displayed list of entries.

Turnaround times and targets

A detailed explanation of ministerial targets for turnaround times in respect of first registrations is given in (2006) 51 *Journal of the Law Society of Scotland* Feb/50. For new 'domestic' first registrations, the target is 90 days, but there are further targets to deal with past arrears.

Electronic SDLT certificates

An electronic version of SDLT 5 has been available since 1 November 2006. This takes the form of the receipt received by online customers on successful completion of their application. On being printed, the certificate can be used in the same way as the paper version. But if there are multiple addresses, only the first is shown, and in submitting the certificate to Registers of Scotland it will be necessary to include a copy of any SDLT 3 or SDLT 4. Oddly, a paper certificate will also be issued, but should not be sent to the Registers if the electronic certificate has already been sent. A difficulty is that the online service remains unreliable, with too much system downtime. For information on the electronic SDLT 5 and on other recent developments in SDLT, see www.ros.gov.uk/registration/ stampdutylandtax.html.

'On the usual borrowing terms': charging for lending or delivering titles etc

The following Law Society guideline was reproduced in the December 2006 issue of the *Journal of the Law Society* (p 28):

Charging for lending or delivering files, titles and other papers

Where a solicitor is asked to lend titles or other documents to another solicitor, a fee may properly be charged for such lending to cover both the delivery and return of the documents. If more than three documents are lent, a fee for an inventory may be charged.

Delivering documents in response to client's mandate

Where files or documents are delivered by one solicitor to another in accordance with the client's written instructions or mandate, a fee may properly be charged. No charge should be made for delivering such papers direct to the client or former client, but any outlay incurred in posting or delivering by courier may properly be recovered from the client or former client.

Amount of fee which may be charged

The Society is not in a position to give guidance on the amount of fee which may be charged in either of the above situations, but in terms of article 6 of the Code of Conduct, the fees charged shall be fair and reasonable in all the circumstances having regard to the various factors set out in article 6.

It should be noted that where the Council are satisfied that a solicitor has issued an account for fees and outlays of an amount which is grossly excessive, whether or not the account has been paid, the Council may in terms of s 39A of the Solicitors (Scotland) Act 1980 withdraw the solicitor's practising certificate, but only after enquiry and after giving the solicitor an opportunity of being heard. What is grossly excessive is a matter to be determined by the Auditor of the Court of Session at taxation.

Books

Andrew Ferguson, *Common Good Law* (Avizandum Publishing Ltd 2006; ISBN 978-1-904968-09-2)

Roderick R M Paisley, *Access Rights and Rights of Way* (The Scottish Rights of Way and Access Society (Scotways) 2006; ISBN 978-0-954-6735-2-9)

Elspeth C Reid and John W G Blackie, *Personal Bar* (Thomson W Green 2006; ISBN 978-0-414-01464-0)

Kenneth G C Reid and George L Gretton, *Conveyancing 2005* (Avizandum Publishing Ltd 2006; ISBN 978-1-904968-12-2)

Articles

Craig Anderson, 'Possession by the tenant following the expiry of a seasonal let: *Bell v Inkersall Investments Ltd*' 2006 SLT (News) 221

Craig Anderson, 'Agricultural tenants and the right to buy: some thoughts on part 2 of the Agricultural Holdings (Scotland) Act 2003' 2006 SLT (News) 241

David Bartos, 'Double yellow or single yellow: the right to park after *Moncrieff v Jamieson*' 2006 SLT (News) 9

David Bell and Robert Rennie, 'Purchase options in leases' (2006) 51 *Journal of the Law Society of Scotland* May/49

Donna Brown, Donna McGuffog and Linda Martin, 'Fire and water – the new regimes' (2006) 83 *Greens Property Law Bulletin* 3

Stewart Brymer, 'The shape of conveyancing practice in 2007 and beyond' 2006 SLT (News) 105

Stewart Brymer, 'Opportunities in the conveyancing market place' (2006) 80 *Greens Property Law Bulletin* 1

Stewart Brymer, 'When is a notice to quit not a notice to quit?' (2006) 82 *Greens Property Law Bulletin* 3 (considering *Ben Cleuch Estates Ltd v Scottish Enterprise* [2006] CSOH 35)

Stewart Brymer, 'Property sale questionnaire: threat or opportunity?' (2007) 85 *Greens Property Law Bulletin* 5

Alistair S Burrow, 'Due diligence' (2006) 51 *Journal of the Law Society of Scotland* Jan/44 (discussing the Bankruptcy and Diligence etc (Scotland) Bill)

Alistair S Burrow, 'Fully charged' (2006) 51 *Journal of the Law Society of Scotland* April/48 (discussing part 2 of the Bankruptcy and Diligence etc (Scotland) Bill)

Bryan Clark, 'Water law in Scotland: the Water Environment and Water Services (Scotland) Act 2003 and the European Convention on Human Rights' (2006) 10 *Edinburgh Law Review* 60

Malcolm M Combe, 'Parts 2 and 3 of the Land Reform (Scotland) Act 2003: a definitive answer to the Scottish land question' 2006 *Juridical Review* 195

Malcolm M Combe, 'No place like *Holme*: community expectations and the right to buy' (2007) 11 *Edinburgh Law Review* 109 (discussing *Holmehill Ltd v The Scottish Ministers* 2006 SLT (Sh Ct) 79)

Alan W Eccles, '*Foster v Keeper of the Registers of Scotland*, 2006 SLT 513' 2006 SLT (News) 246

Robin Evans-Jones, 'Causes of action and remedies in unjustified enrichment' (2007) 11 *Edinburgh Law Review* 105 (discussing *Satchwell v McIntosh* 2006 SLT (Sh Ct) 117)

Alasdair G Fox, 'Victories for tenants?' (2006) 51 *Journal of the Law Society of Scotland* Sept/40 (discussing new case law on succession to joint agricultural tenancies)

Alasdair G Fox, 'A reprieve for landlords?' (2006) 51 *Journal of the Law Society of Scotland* Dec/42 (discussing *Bell v Inkersall Investments* 2006 SC 507)

Alasdair Fox and Allison Alcock, 'Clause for concern' (2006) 51 *Journal of the Law Society of Scotland* April/47 (discussing the provisions in the Antisocial Behaviour etc (Scotland) Act 2004 on registration of private landlords as they apply to agricultural holdings)

Alasdair G Fox and John A Mitchell, 'A debate to be resumed' (2006) 51 *Journal of the Law Society of Scotland* June/42 (discussing *Earl of Stair's 1970 Trs v Downie* 24 November 2005, Land Court)

David Johnston, '*J A Pye (Oxford) Limited v United Kingdom*: deprivation of property rights and prescription' (2006) 10 *Edinburgh Law Review* 277

Alistair Lauder, 'Note on affordable housing' (2006) 80 *Greens Property Law Bulletin* 3

Christopher Lindley, 'RCIL – the landowner's quandary' (2006) 84 *Greens Property Law Bulletin* 5

Angus McAllister, 'Leases and the requirement of writing' 2006 SLT (News) 254 (considering *Advice Centre for Mortgages v McNicoll* 2006 SLT 591)

Alan McMillan, 'Contractual irritancy for failure to repair – uphill all the way?' (2006) 81 *Greens Property Law Bulletin* 3

James Ness, 'Back to the future' (2006) 51 *Journal of the Law Society of Scotland* Jan/50 (discussing the introduction of ARTL)

James Ness, 'ARTL: your chance to be heard' (2006) 51 *Journal of the Law Society of Scotland* March/52

Roderick R M Paisley, 'Right to make roads and *res merae facultatis*' (2007) 11 *Edinburgh Law Review* 95 (discussing *Peart v Legge* 2006 GWD 18-377 affd 2007 SCLR 86)

Chris Rae, 'Compulsory purchase' (2006) 81 *Greens Property Law Bulletin* 1

Chris Rae, 'Landlord's hypothec: still surviving?' (2006) 84 *Greens Property Law Bulletin* 3

Donald B Reid, 'Land attachment and suspensive missives' (2006) 51 *Journal of the Law Society of Scotland* Aug/54

Emma Reid, 'Regulation of private landlords' (2006) 80 *Greens Property Law Bulletin* 3 (discussing part 8 of the Antisocial Behaviour etc (Scotland) Act 2004)

Kenneth Reid, 'In on the Act' (2006) 51 *Journal of the Law Society of Scotland* Feb/48 (discussing the Scottish Law Commission's discussion papers on land registration)

Robert Rennie, 'Standard missives and negligence' 2006 SLT (News) 65

Linda Ritson, 'Stamp duty land tax group relief' (2006) 81 *Greens Property Law Bulletin* 6

Linda Ritson, 'Limited liability partnership' (2006) 83 *Greens Property Law Bulletin* 5 (considering issues in lending, leasing and assigning to LLPs)

Alistair Sim, 'Certificates of title' (2007) 85 *Greens Property Law Bulletin* 3

Andrew J M Steven, 'Goodbye to sequestration for rent' 2006 SLT (News) 17 (discussing provisions of the Bankruptcy and Diligence etc (Scotland) Bill)

Andrew J M Steven, 'Options to purchase and successor landlords' (2006) 10 *Edinburgh Law Review* 432 (discussing *The Advice Centre for Mortgages Ltd v McNicoll* 2006 SLT 591)

Andrew Steven and Scott Wortley, 'Is that burden dead yet?' (2006) 51 *Journal of the Law Society of Scotland* June/46 and July/50.

John Sturrock and Pamela Lyall, 'Mediation in property matters' (2006) 84 *Greens Property Law Bulletin* 1

Robert Sutherland, 'Possession by the tenant following the expiry of a seasonal let: the continuing problem for landlords' 2006 SLT (News) 249 (considering *Bell v Inkersall Investments Ltd* 2006 SC 507)

Ken Swinton, '... And to the survivor of them' (2006) 74 *Scottish Law Gazette* 12

Ken Swinton, 'A selling creditor's duty of care – *Wilson v Dunbar Bank*' (2006) 74 *Scottish Law Gazette* 76

Ken Swinton, 'Interest clause – a case of *Black* and white' (2006) 74 *Scottish Law Gazette* 115

Ian Thornton-Kemsley, 'Sending the right signals' (2006) 51 *Journal of the Law Society of Scotland* Sept/52 (discussing leases of land for telecommunication installations)

C Wilson, 'Bankruptcy and Diligence etc (Scotland) Bill' 2006 SLT (News) 45

PART IV
COMMENTARY

COMMENTARY

MISSIVES OF SALE

From pro-buyer to pro-seller

Until not so long ago, residential missives were resolutely pro-buyer. In exchange for payment of the price the seller undertook a whole host of obligations which, in time, extended far beyond the traditional obligation to give a good and marketable title, so as to encompass matters such as property enquiry certificates, planning, building warrants, central heating, and so on. But slowly the balance of power has changed. On the one hand, the buyer's obligation to pay the price has been supplemented, in cases of breach, by an obligation to pay interest at premium rates for indeterminate periods. And on the other, the seller's obligations – although covering the same basic terrain as before – have tended to be reduced from a warranty to something less. The buyer is given the opportunity to examine certain things – the property enquiry certificates, the building warrants, even the titles. But fewer guarantees are given than previously. Buyers who do not like what they see can rescind, provided this is done promptly. But in the absence of a guarantee they cannot claim damages.

This change in the nature of missives is illustrated by some of the cases decided during 2006. But before turning to the cases it seems worth asking why the change has occurred. One reason, no doubt, is the normal swing of the pendulum: missives, having become too pro-buyer, began to move in the opposite direction. Another is that it can sometimes take so long to conclude missives that the buyer's concern with their actual terms is reduced; for if he is unhappy with the documentation which he is shown, he can either delay conclusion a little longer or simply walk away from the bargain. Yet this is only part of the story. Missives still matter. They are not always concluded at the eleventh hour, particularly in this new age of regional standard clauses. And, as the case law shows, missives may have to be enforced. If that unhappy event occurs, the buyer may have cause to regret that his legal adviser did not fight a little harder for a more even-handed contract.

Obligations on the buyer: paying the price

The buyer must pay the price on the date of entry.[1] In cases where this obligation is breached it is important to distinguish late payment from non-payment – the

---

1 Assuming, of course, that the seller performs in turn.

case where the buyer does eventually pay, albeit late, from the case where he never pays at all.

Late payment: interest clauses

We begin with late payment. For 30 years or more it has been standard practice to include in missives a provision saying that, in the event of late payment, the buyer must pay interest at a rate which is similar to the rate on bridging loans – for example, 4% above the base rate of a specified bank. Without this provision no interest would be due. (The law says that interest will be payable if the buyer takes entry, but of course that almost never happens.[1])

On one view, interest clauses are unnecessary, because a seller is by law entitled to damages for loss, and should not be compensated for more than that loss; and in any event, unless the seller has bought another property on the strength of the sale and faces the prospect of bridging finance,[2] the loss is likely to be small or non-existent. Nonetheless an interest clause can be justified as a spur to performance: faced with the prospect of daily interest, a buyer is likely to hurry to assemble the necessary funds.[3] Conversely, without the protection given by such a clause, the seller may be faced with long delay, and hence with substantial inconvenience. It seems worth adding that an interest clause would not seem to prevent a claim for damages in respect of *other* losses arising out of the breach.

Interest clauses in the strict sense – ie interest on a price that is eventually paid – do not seem to have given rise to difficulties in practice and are not discussed further here.

Non-payment: the 1993 clause

Naturally enough, the interest clause as originally drafted presupposed that the price would eventually be paid. Consequently, when, in *Lloyd's Bank plc v Bamberger*,[4] the seller brought the contract to an end by rescission, it was held that no interest was due. In other words, the clause dealt with late payment and not with non-payment.

Bamberger was decided in 1993. Immediately attempts were made to 'get round' it, and the attempt which quickly won favour was a clause which was published in the *Journal of the Law Society*.[5] This started with the existing interest clause and sought to extend its ambit to cases where payment was not merely late, but never happened at all. But although the clause talked of 'interest', the word was

---

1 G L Gretton and K G C Reid, *Conveyancing* (3rd edn 2004) para 5-20. However, the Scottish Law Commission has recommended legislation providing for interest on unpaid debts, including the unpaid price in the sale of heritable property: see Report on *Interest on Debt and Damages* (Scot Law Com No 203, 2006; available on www.scotlawcom.gov.uk) para 3.20.

2 For bridging finance to be recoverable, it may be necessary to have drawn the buyer's attention to the possibility that bridging might be necessary. See p 94 below.

3 Another device to enhance the probability that the buyer will settle is the deposit system. This is widely used in commercial property transactions, and in England it is used for residential ones as well.

4 1993 SC 570.

5 (1993) 38 *Journal of the Law Society of Scotland* 450.

being loosely used, for there can be no interest on a capital sum which, following rescission, has ceased to be due. In fact the clause was aiming at something quite different. In the normal course of events, a seller who rescinds for non-payment is entitled to damages for his loss. But the quantum of loss may be disputed, leading to delays and even to litigation. Although clothed in the language of interest, the real purpose of the new clause was to avoid such disputes by stipulating in advance what the buyer must pay in the event of default. In other words, it was a clause of liquidated damages.

Rescission without re-sale

The 1993 clause is familiar to all practitioners. It remains in widespread use today, and it has influenced the drafting of the corresponding provision in the standard clauses produced by local groups of solicitors. In the version used in a new case, *Black v McGregor,*[1] it read as follows (our lettering):

> [A] Payment of the purchase price in full on the date of entry is of the essence of the contract. [B] In the event of the purchase price or any part thereof remaining outstanding as at the date of entry, then notwithstanding consignation or the fact that entry has not been taken by your clients, your clients shall be deemed to be in material breach of contract [C] and further, interest will accrue at Five *per centum* (5%) *per annum* above the Clydesdale Bank plc base lending rate from time to time until full payment of the price is made or in the event of our clients exercising their option to rescind the contract until such time as our clients shall have completed a re-sale of the subjects and received the re-sale price [D] and further, interest shall run on any shortfall between the purchase price hereunder and the re-sale price until such time as the shortfall shall have been paid to our clients. [E] In the event that the said purchase price is not paid in full within fourteen days of the date of entry, our clients shall be entitled to treat your clients as being in material breach of contract and to rescind the missives on giving prior written notice to that effect to your clients [F] without prejudice to any rights or claims competent to our clients arising from the breach of contract by your clients including our clients' rights to claim all losses, damages and expenses sustained as a result of your clients' breach of contract including interest on the price calculated as set out in this clause. [G] For the purpose of computation of our clients' loss, the interest element of that loss shall be deemed to be a liquidate penalty provision exigible notwithstanding the exercise by our clients of their option to rescind the contract for non-payment of the price or any repudiation of the contract by your clients. [H] This clause shall have effect always provided that any unreasonable delay in settlement is not attributable to us or our clients.

As can be seen, this is really two clauses in one. There is the standard clause that, in the event of late payment, interest will run on the unpaid price;[2] but the same interest formula is then used in order to provide for liquidated damages in the event of non-payment and rescission.

In *Black v McGregor* missives were concluded for the sale of 'Rockmount', 150 East Clyde Street, Helensburgh at a price of £600,000 and with entry on 28

---

1 2006 GWD 17-351 affd [2006] CSIH 45, 2006 GWD 31-668.
2 This is an interest clause in the strict sense, as discussed above.

November 2002. The buyer having failed to pay the price, the seller rescinded on 16 December 2003 and sought 'interest' (really liquidated damages) of £60,928.79 in respect of the period from 28 November 2002 to the date on which the action was raised.

In the interest clause as it applies to *late* payment, interest is to run from the date when the price was due to the date on which it was actually paid. But where, as in the 1993 clause, payment of 'interest' is no more than a device for calculating liquidated damages after rescission, it is not so easy to know when 'interest' should cease (ie what should be the *terminus ad quem*).[1] In the 1993 clause the terminus for 'interest' is dealt with in part [C]: 'interest' is due either (i) until 'full payment of the price is made' or (ii), in the event of rescission, until 'such time as our clients shall have completed a re-sale of the subjects and received the re-sale price'. The difficulty in *Black* was that while the seller had rescinded, he had not, or not yet, re-sold. Could 'interest' still run under the clause? At first instance, the sheriff found for the seller, but both the sheriff principal[2] and, on further appeal, an Extra Division of the Court of Session[3] took a different view. In the Court of Session the issue was treated as a simple matter of construction:[4]

> It [ie the clause] provides that interest will continue to accrue after rescission by the seller, but that provision applies only in the situation in which the property is then resold and the seller receives the resale price. The clause makes no provision for the situation in which no resale of the subjects takes place.... As the court held in *Bamberger*, the phrase 'interest will accrue' means no more than 'interest will run' and carries no implication that accrued rights to payment of interest are continuously created. Accordingly the events specified in the passage require to occur before the seller is entitled to payment of interest.

No 'interest', therefore, was due.

Of course, it will usually be within the power of a seller to make the event specified in the 1993 clause occur: all he has to do is resell the property and then interest will be due. But sometimes the seller may have changed his mind and want to retain the property; or resale may be slow or has to be done in lots. An example of the second situation arose in another new case, *Wipfel Ltd v Auchlochan Developments Ltd*.[5] Here the seller rescinded on 22 July 2004, sold a part of the property quite quickly, but, by the time of the action, had not managed to dispose of the rest, although from 1 September 2005 this was subject to a resale contract which was contingent on the granting of planning permission. With some reluctance,[6] the Lord Ordinary (Lord Clarke) concluded that he was bound by the decision in *Black v McGregor*, and dismissed the claim for 'interest'.

---

1 W W McBryde, *Law of Contract in Scotland* (2nd edn 2001) para 22-143(2).
2 2006 GWD 17-351.
3 [2006] CSIH 45, 2006 GWD 31-668.
4 At para 10 *per* Lord Philip.
5 [2006] CSOH 183, 2006 GWD 39-763.
6 Paragraph 24.

Time for a re-think?

The decisions in *Black v McGregor* and *Wipfel Ltd v Auchlochan Developments Ltd* are merely the latest in a series of cases which have chipped away at the 1993 clause.[1] As Lord Clarke put it in *Wipfel*:[2]

> If, as one might reasonably suppose, the draughtsmen of this provision had intended to produce clarity and certainty into the matter which would not necessitate litigation, their intentions, in that respect, have not been fulfilled.

While, therefore, the 1993 clause has proved a doughty survivor, the time has probably arrived for it to be re-thought. Certainly, the clause in its current form has been shown to suffer from a number of difficulties.

(1) *Liquidated damages not interest.* Although couched in the language of interest, the clause is actually intended to provide for liquidated damages. By confusing juridical categories it tends to mislead. It is true that the clause says that

> For the purpose of computation of our clients' loss, the interest element of that loss shall be deemed to be a liquidate penalty provision exigible notwithstanding the exercise by our clients of their option to rescind the contract for non-payment of the price or any repudiation of the contract by your clients.

But as Lord Philip pointed out in *Black v McGregor*,[3] the meaning and effect of this provision

> are not entirely clear. In the context of a claim for damages for breach of contract the phrase 'liquidate penalty', used in former times in feu contracts and similar writs in relation to delayed payment of feu duty, or other periodical payment, sits a little unhappily with the distinction between liquidated damages and penalty provisions. However, we think the effect of the clause to be that in the event of the contract being rescinded by the seller and a resale thereafter taking place, any financial loss suffered by the seller by reason of the seller's not having received the original sale price, and subsequently the 'shortfall', is liquidated in the contractually stipulated rate of interest and the seller does not need to establish actual loss in the shape of lost investment returns or the incurring of finance charges.

(2) *Time for rescission.* In a third new case, *McPhee v Black*,[4] the sheriff principal observed that:[5]

> This contract is difficult to follow. Condition 25 [ie the 1993 clause] provides that payment by 1.00 pm on the date of entry is of the essence of the contract and that failure to pay by then is a material breach of contract. It is *implicit* that the seller would on

---

1 For some previous cases in which the clause has been judicially considered, see D J Cusine and R Rennie, *Missives* (2nd edn 1999) paras 8.21–8.31. See also *Conveyancing 2005* pp 59–62.
2 Paragraph 7.
3 [2006] CSIH 45 at para 11.
4 31 July 2006, Ayr Sheriff Court. The sheriff principal was James A Taylor.
5 Paragraph 8.

such an occurrence be entitled to accept the material breach and rescind the contract. However, rather than allow the common law to operate, the sellers complicate matters. Later in Condition 25 they provide that if the purchase price is not paid within 14 days of the date of entry the sellers can treat the purchasers as being in material breach of contract and *explicitly* provide that the sellers can rescind the contract. Thus it is a material breach if payment is not made on the date of entry. It is also a material breach if payment is not made within 14 days of the date of entry.

The first declaration as to material breach seems to make the second unnecessary, indeed puzzling, for if the buyers can already rescind on the date of entry there is no reason to provide that they can also rescind 14 days later. Yet it is unlikely that this is what was really intended. The aim, one suspects, was to allow rescission *only* after 14 days, and no doubt it is possible to read the clause in that way.[1] But if that is correct, the opening declaration that payment is of the essence seems to have wandered in from a different style undetected. Doing no good it may instead do harm.

(3) *Prior written notice.* The 1993 clause provides, in part [E], that rescission requires the giving of *'prior* written notice'. Prior to what? At first blush this suggests that the rescission cannot be immediate but that there must instead be a two-stage process: first, the sending of the notice, and then, after the elapse of a reasonable time, the actual act of rescission. Yet this is presumably not what is intended. Fortunately, in *Charisma Properties Ltd v Grayling (1994) Ltd*[2] an Extra Division of the Court of Session, by a majority, took the indulgent view that the word 'prior' was mere surplusage and that the notice could itself effect rescission. But such indulgence is not to be relied on, and the surplusage needs to be removed.[3] Indeed there is much to be said for removing *all* references to the method of rescission on the basis that, in the heat of the moment, parties have an unfortunate tendency to disregard their own provisions. That would restore the rule of the common law by which rescission is effected by intimation to the other party, whether formal or informal.[4]

(4) *End-point for 'interest'.* Both *Black v McGregor* and *Wipfel Ltd v Auchlochan Developments Ltd* show the shortcomings of the 1993 clause in respect of the point at which 'interest' is to end. As Professor McBryde points out, however, these are just examples of a more fundamental difficulty – the difficulty of predicting a seller's future behaviour and needs:[5]

---

1 As was done in *obiter* remarks in *Charisma Properties Ltd v Grayling (1994) Ltd* 1996 SC 556.
2 1996 SC 556.
3 In *McPhee v Black* 31 July 2006, Ayr Sheriff Court, *Charisma Properties* was not cited to the sheriff principal, who, having found it in the course of his own researches, allowed counsel the opportunity to address him on it, with results which are not (or not yet) recorded. The sheriff principal's personal preference was for the minority view in *Charisma Properties* (see para 10 of his Opinion).
4 W W McBryde, *Law of Contract in Scotland* (2nd edn 2001) para 20-107.
5 W W McBryde, 'A question of interest' (2007) 11 *Edinburgh Law Review* (forthcoming).

The seller might resell only part of the subjects. The seller might, or might not, sell other parts at a later date. The seller might combine the subjects originally sold with other neighbouring subjects owned by the seller and dispose of a larger parcel of land. The property might become part of an asset sale by a company with a price which includes moveables. The seller might resell, but subject to conditions which are not purified, or not purified at the time of claiming interest. The seller might not resell, but transfer the property to a subsidiary company or, as appropriate, gift it to a relative. The seller might become insolvent and the property be dealt with in insolvency proceedings. And so on and so on. It is easy enough to provide when the 'interest' starts to run. But when does the 'interest' cease to run? Is it possible, after all, to draft a clause which will deal with all the infinite varieties of human behaviour? If it is, no one has yet succeeded and probably never will.

It will be seen that this is an argument, not just against the 1993 clause, but against any clause which provides for a daily penalty. The argument can be met by providing a fixed date as a cut-off point, for example six months after the date of entry.

(5) *Time when payment is due.* The 1993 clause has no provision as to when payment of 'interest' is due. Must the seller wait until the end-point or can a claim be made at any time? In both *Black v McGregor* and *Wipfel Ltd v Auchlochan Developments Ltd* it was taken for granted that the end-point must have arrived. The clause, however, is simply unclear.

Doing without liquidated damages?

A radical way of solving the drafting problems would be to abandon the clause altogether. Is a clause of liquidated damages really necessary? What is wrong with the ordinary common law rules about damages for breach of contract? In an article in the *Edinburgh Law Review*,[1] Professor McBryde argues strongly and persuasively that matters are indeed best left to the common law. In his view, '[t]he common law of rescission, its methods and timing, and the common law of damages, seem far superior to ill-judged attempts at improvement'.

There are, of course, things to be said in favour of a clause of liquidated damages. It provides a ready method of calculating the amount due.[2] And by showing what might have to be paid, it encourages prompt performance, thus making contractual failure less likely. Further, if there is to be an interest clause in respect of late payment – which, as we have seen, is probably necessary – it may be difficult to avoid a comparable provision in respect of non-payment. For if the financial consequences of rescission were to be less serious than those of late payment, a buyer who could not pay on time would have a strong incentive not to pay at all.

The case against liquidated damages clauses is, however, stronger still. It has four strands. In the first place, and depending on the circumstances, such clauses

---

1 W W McBryde, 'A question of interest' (2007) 11 *Edinburgh Law Review* (forthcoming).
2 Although, as we will see, this particular virtue is not much in evidence in the 1993 clause.

are often strikingly unfair to the buyer. As the recent cases confirm, the seller's entitlement need bear no relation to his loss.[1] On the contrary, the whole point of such a clause is to agree the damages in advance. Often, of course, the seller loses a great deal if the buyer fails to pay, or pays late, particularly if the seller is already committed to another purchase. But not always. He might make a profit by reselling the property for a higher price.

So long as the seller makes a loss, even a small one, it seems clear that he is entitled to liquidated damages as provided for by the clause. Arguably the position is the same even where the seller makes a profit, although there would then be a question as to whether the profit falls to be deducted from the liquidated damages. In *Black v McGregor* an Extra Division of the Court of Session would not be drawn on this point:[2]

> We would add that before the sheriff principal, and to a limited extent before us, there was discussion whether, in the event of a resale producing a higher price than that contracted for in the contract between the parties, that gain required to be brought into account. It is however not necessary for us to express any view on that question.

Furthermore, if loss is irrelevant, it can be argued that there can be no duty to mitigate that loss. The consequence is spelled out by Lord Clarke in *Wipfel Ltd v Auchlochan*,[3] in commenting on *Black v McGregor*:

> The decision in *Black*[4] is not necessarily all good news for the buyer in breach, since it would seem to mean that (subject to questions of prescription) the seller can delay as long as he wishes to resell (there being no duty to mitigate if the clause is truly a liquidate damages provision) and then sue for interest, after resale, which by that time might be a very considerable sum indeed. In that situation, the buyer, in breach, would then only be left with arguing that the provision was not truly a liquidate damages provision but a penalty, but that matter would, of course, require to be judged by reference to the circumstances pertaining at the time the missives were concluded.

If this *obiter* view is correct, the result is alarming for buyers. Given the favourable rate of 'interest' prescribed in the clause – and, in many cases, a rising market – there is a financial incentive for the seller to delay for as long as possible. In another new case, *Kenmore Homes (UK) Ltd v Cumming*,[5] interest on the unpaid price amounted to £67.45 per day. That is £24, 619.25 for one year, or £123,096.25 for five. The purchase price in that case was £254,000. A higher price would produce

---

1 *Black v McGregor* [2006] CSIH 45 at para 11 *per* Lord Philip ('the seller does not need to establish actual loss in the shape of lost investment returns or the incurring of finance charges'); *Wipfel Ltd v Auchlochan Developments Ltd* [2006] CSOH 183 at para 24 *per* Lord Clarke ('not conditional on the seller averring and proving actual loss').
2 [2006] CSIH 45 at para 11.
3 [2006] CSOH 183 at para 24.
4 Ie that no interest was due because, although the seller had rescinded the contract, she had not resold the house.
5 [2006] CSOH 72, 2006 GWD 17-334.

a correspondingly higher daily charge. This potentially ruinous liability needs to be explained to clients before agreeing to accept a liquidated damages clause on their behalf. We do not think they should be advised to accept it.

But if liquidated damages clauses are bad for buyers they may also, sometimes, be bad for sellers. This is the second strand. There is a fine line between a clause of liquidated damages (which is enforceable) and a penalty clause (which is not). Although the point has not yet been pled in any case, there must be a serious risk that the 1993 clause, or anything which resembles it, would be struck down as a penalty clause. If so, the seller, having lost an expensive litigation, would have to begin again with a claim for ordinary damages based on loss.[1]

Thirdly, given that the 1993 clause, in part [F], is said to be 'without prejudice to any rights or claims competent to our clients arising from the breach of contract by your clients including our clients' rights to claim all losses, damages and expenses sustained as a result of your clients' breach of contract', it seems to lack the traditional virtue of liquidated damages provisions of removing the need to calculate loss. At the least it suggests that the liquidated damages do not cover the whole ground of anticipated loss.[2]

Finally, liquidated damages clauses are difficult to get right. In *Wipfel Ltd v Auchlochan Developments Ltd*,[3] Lord Clarke's unflattering verdict on the current clause was this:

> I cannot forbear from remarking, in my view, that the difficulties and disputes that this case and others have thrown up have, perhaps, been at least, in part, caused by somewhat over-elaborate drafts contained in the style clauses ... in what seems to me also to have been perhaps an over-reaction to what was decided in the case of *Lloyd's Bank*.

But any replacement clause is also likely to be long, unwieldy and – very likely – accident-prone.

Option A

We doubt whether it is sensible to continue to use the 1993 clause – or the provisions in regional missives which derive from that clause. But what should take its place?

In our view, it is difficult or impossible to produce a liquidated damages clause which is clear, trouble-free, and which fairly balances the interests of both parties to the contract. If that is correct, the attempt should be abandoned. This approach we may term Option A. Of course an interest clause in the strict sense (ie where payment of the price does happen, albeit late) will still be needed, and it will also be necessary to give the seller the right to rescind. A possible style is the following:

1 Unless of course there were alternative conclusions for ordinary damages.
2 See *Kerr v McCormack* 12 January 2005, Glasgow Sheriff Court, discussed in *Conveyancing 2005* pp 59–62.
3 [2006] CSOH 183 at para 24.

Option A

(1) If the price remains unpaid in whole or in part after the due date, the Seller is entitled to interest on the amount outstanding at the rate of 4% *per annum* above the Royal Bank of Scotland plc base rate from the due date until the date when payment is made.

(2) If the price remains unpaid in whole or in part at any time more than two weeks after the due date, the Seller is entitled to rescind the contract, and to damages in respect of all loss arising out of the Buyer's failure to pay the price (which may include the cost of a bridging or other loan to enable the Seller to complete a purchase of heritable property).

(3) In this clause the 'due date' means whichever is the later of –

　　(i)　the date of entry;[1]

　　(ii)　the date on which payment of the price was due, having regard to the circumstances of the case including any entitlement to withhold payment owing to non-performance by the Seller.

Much of this style is familiar from existing practice, but two special features should be mentioned. First, we have used 'due date' – defined in subclause (3) – rather than the traditional 'date of entry'. This is to accommodate possible changes in the contractual date of entry, whether by agreement or due to the seller's default. This means, for example, that if the seller fails to produce documentation, and settlement is delayed, the 'due date' will be the first date on which the documentation is made available to the buyer and settlement is offered. Interest would then be due only if the buyer delayed in turn.

Secondly, subclause (2) mentions bridging finance. Having regard to the decision in *Tiffney v Bachurzewski*,[2] it is important to put the buyer on notice that the seller may be relying on the price to buy another property and will have to take a bridging loan if the price is not paid.

Option B

Option B is to re-write the 1993 clause in the light of the case law and other criticisms but to leave the policy unchanged. This is the *status quo* option. For reasons already mentioned we do not recommend this approach. Nor are we confident that our drafting will overcome all problems.

A revised clause might look like this:

Option B

(1) If the price remains unpaid in whole or in part after the due date, the Seller is entitled to interest on the amount outstanding at the rate of 4% *per annum* above the Royal Bank of Scotland plc base rate from the due date until the date when payment is made.

---

1 Strictly speaking, (i) could be omitted, as being already included in (ii). The same point applies to Options B and C.

2 1985 SLT 165. It was held by the Second Division that the possibility of the seller having to bridge was not within the reasonable contemplation of the parties at the date of the contract and so too remote to be allowable in damages under the rules in *Hadley v Baxendale* (1854) 9 Ex 341.

(2) If the price remains unpaid in whole or in part at any time more than two weeks after the due date, the Seller is entitled to rescind the contract, and to payment from the Buyer, on the end date, of damages calculated as the amount of interest which would have run on the amount of the price outstanding at the rate of 4% *per annum* above the Royal Bank of Scotland plc base rate from the due date until the end date.

(3) Subclause (2) provides for liquidated damages for non-receipt of the price and is without prejudice to damages in respect of other losses arising out of the failure of the contract.

(4) In this clause –

    (a) the 'due date' means whichever is the later of –

        (i) the date of entry;

        (ii) the date on which payment of the price was due, having regard to the circumstances of the case including any entitlement to withhold payment owing to non-performance by the Seller.

    (b) the 'end date' means whichever is the earlier of –

        (i) the date falling 6 months after the due date;

        (ii) where the Property is resold following rescission, the date of entry under the contract of resale.

A number of comments may be made about this clause:

(a) Subclause (1) is a standard provision for interest for late payment.

(b) Subclause (2) omits both the normal, but contradictory provision, that payment on the date of entry is of the essence of the contract, and also the requirement that rescission be by 'prior notice'.

(c) Although the concept of interest is retained in subclause (2), it is used only in the context of a convenient formula for calculating a sum which, as subclause (3) makes clear, is intended as liquidated damages. Subclause (2) also makes clear that payment is due only at the end of the period during which the notional interest runs (the 'end date').

(d) Subclause (3) makes clear what is, perhaps, not clear enough in the current clause,[1] namely that the interest payments are merely to make up for the loss of use of the unpaid money. So it remains open for the seller to claim damages in the normal way,[2] eg in respect of legal fees[3] or any shortfall in the resale price.[4]

---

1 See *Kerr v McCormack* 12 January 2005, Glasgow Sheriff Court, discussed in *Conveyancing 2005* pp 59–62, approved in *Wipfel Ltd v Auchlochan Developments Ltd* [2006] CSOH 183 at para 24 *per* Lord Clarke.

2 For possible heads of damages, see K G C Reid and G L Gretton, *Conveyancing* (3rd edn 2004) para 5-14.

3 But of which sale? In *Black v McGregor* 2006 GWD 17-351 the sheriff principal drew attention (at para 15) to a conflict of authority: 'In *Johnston's Exrs v Harris* 1977 SC 365 Lord Ross expressed the view (at 374) that it was fees in respect of the abortive transaction which were recoverable. However in *Grant v Ullah* 1987 SLT 639 Lord Davidson had taken the view, applying the principle of *restitutio in integrum*, that the first set of fees would have had to be paid if the transaction had proceeded and accordingly that what was recoverable was the fee incurred for the second transaction.' We would agree with the sheriff principal's preference for the second view.

4 However, the clause in current use provides for contractual 'interest' on any shortfall in the resale price.

(e) As already mentioned in the context of Option A, subclause (4)(a) accommodates possible changes in the contractual date of entry, whether by agreement or due to the seller's default.

(f) In subclause (4)(b) the only innovation – other than the drafting device of using the words 'end date' – is the additional *terminus ad quem* of six months after the date of entry. Not only is this fairer to the buyer, but it avoids the difficulties – exposed in *Black v McGregor*[1] and *Wipfel Ltd v Auchlochan Developments Ltd*[2] – if there is no resale. In some situations, and for some types of property, six months may be too short. Regional standard clauses already include a cut-off point for 'interest' but this applies only after a year.

Option C

There is also a third possibility. Option C takes its inspiration from the Highland Standard Clauses.[3] In the Highland clause there are two different measures of damages. The seller can either have interest at 5% above base or he can have damages which reflect his actual loss. He cannot have both. In the Highland clause the choice is determined by whichever of the two measures produces the higher amount,[4] but as this means that actual loss must always be assessed – the very thing which liquidated damages clauses are designed to avoid – it seems easier to leave a free choice with the seller. A possible Option C, modelled loosely on the Highland clause, would be:

Option C

(1) If the price remains unpaid in whole or in part after the due date, the Seller is entitled to interest on the amount outstanding at the rate of 4% *per annum* above the Royal Bank of Scotland plc base rate from the due date until the date when payment is made.

(2) If the price remains unpaid in whole or in part at any time more than two weeks after the due date, the Seller is entitled to rescind the contract, and to payment from the Buyer, at the Seller's option, of one (but not both of) –

    (a) ordinary damages in respect of all loss arising out of non-payment of the price and the failure of the contract (which may include the cost of a bridging or other loan to enable the Seller to complete a purchase of heritable property); or

    (b) liquidated damages, payable on the end date, calculated as the amount of interest which would have run on the amount of the price outstanding at the rate of 4% *per annum* above the Royal Bank of Scotland plc base rate from the due date until the end date.

(3) In this clause –

    (a) the 'due date' means whichever is the later of –

        (i) the date of entry;

---

1 [2006] CSIH 45, discussed above.
2 [2006] CSOH 183, discussed above.
3 Available eg on www.lawscot.org.uk/Members_Information/convey_essens/stdmissives/. The relevant clause is clause 1.2.
4 'The Purchaser shall pay to the seller whichever is the greater amount of the following….'

> (ii) the date on which payment of the price was due, having regard to the circumstances of the case including any entitlement to withhold payment owing to non-performance by the Seller.
>
> (b) the 'end date' means whichever is the earlier of –
>
> (i) the date falling four months after the due date;
>
> (ii) where the Property is resold following rescission, the date of entry under the contract of resale.

An important difference from Option B is that the liquidated damages cover *all* seller's losses, including for example expenditure on legal fees. In other words, if the seller opts for liquidated damages, he can claim nothing else.[1] For that reason, and others, Option C strikes a better balance between the interests of the parties. On the one hand, the buyer's liability in liquidated damages is properly limited – in our version to 'interest' for only four months.[2] But on the other hand, the seller is protected by the fact that he can always recover in full for his losses by opting for ordinary damages. In one sense, therefore, Option C is a compromise between Option A (which we recommend) and Option B (which we do not).

Obligations on the seller

We now pass from obligations on the buyer to those on the seller. A convenient way of assessing the current state of seller's obligations, in residential conveyancing, is to look at the standard clauses prepared by regional solicitors. Take for instance the Edinburgh and Lothians Standard Clauses.[3] Clause 16 shows the pattern. It begins with a series of warranties relating to title conditions, for example:

> The existing use of the Property is in conformity with the title deeds. There are no unusual, unduly onerous or restrictive burdens, conditions, servitudes or overriding interests (within the meaning of Section 28(1) of the Land Registration (Scotland) Act 1979) affecting the Property.

At one time, the clause would have stopped here: the seller, having issued the warranty, would stick with it so that, in the event that things were not as promised, the buyer could rescind or claim damages (or both), provided always that he did so within the two years for which missives are typically in force. In the event the clause continues:

> If the title deeds disclose a position other than as stated above the Purchaser will be entitled to resile from the Missives without penalty to either party but only provided (i) the Purchaser intimates his intention to exercise this right within five working days of receipt of the Seller's titles; and (ii) such matters intimated as prejudicial are not rectified or clarified to the Purchaser's satisfaction (acting reasonably) by the Date of Entry or within ten weeks from the date of such intimation whichever is earlier. The Purchaser's right to resile shall be his sole option in terms of the Missives.

---

1 W W McBryde, *The Law of Contract in Scotland* (2nd edn 2001) para 22-176.
2 In the Highland clause it is 12 months, which strikes us as too long.
3 Accessible eg on www.lawscot.org.uk/Members_Information/convey_essens/stdmissives/.

This provision removes most of the value from the initial warranty. The seller declines to put his money where his mouth is, for if the warranty is broken, nothing whatsoever is due. The buyer who finds a problem[1] in the titles is left with an unpalatable choice. Either he continues with the purchase, in which case he has no remedy for the breach. Or he takes the nuclear option of rescission, but with no prospect of recovering the costs of the abortive transaction. And he must make his choice within five working days, assuming of course that he manages to spot the problem in the first place.

This is not an isolated provision. The same formula is used in the Edinburgh and Lothians Standard Clauses in relation to property enquiry certificates and to coal authority reports.[2] Other sets of standard clauses, for example those for Glasgow, exhibit a similar pattern. We do not criticise. So long as it is confined to ancillary matters, the formula can be justified as avoiding last-minute ambushes on the part of the buyer. But as it represents a deterioration in the buyer's position, it seems important that further deterioration should be avoided. Viewed in this light, the recent decision in *McPhee v Black*[3] is a step in the wrong direction.

One of the clauses at issue in *McPhee* was the following:

> The whole Title Deeds relative to the subjects, or copies thereof, will be exhibited within four weeks from the date of conclusion of Missives to follow hereon. In the event of the Title Deeds disclosing any matter materially prejudicial to the purchasers' interests then they will be entitled to resile from the bargain without expense but only by giving notice of the intention to do so in writing and that within ten working days from the date of receipt by you of the Title Deeds. In the event of the purchasers' failure to resile in writing within the stated period then thereafter they will have no recourse against the seller with regard to any matter disclosed by the Title Deeds and will not thereafter be entitled to resile.

The buyers were unhappy with the titles and intimated accordingly. The sellers, however, alleged that the matters founded on were already known to the buyers before conclusion of missives and so could not be said to have been 'disclosed' by the titles. No remedy, therefore, was available to the buyers. The sheriff principal agreed:[4]

> Collins English Dictionary gives as a meaning for disclose 'to make (information) known'. It seems to me therefore that if the purchasers were aware of certain issues with regard to the titles before the titles were delivered it could not be an examination of the titles which made this information 'known' to the purchasers. Thus they cannot now rely upon such matters to get out of their bargain.

Whether this is the correct interpretation of the provision is arguable. 'Disclose' could be construed subjectively (what is made known to a particular buyer at a

---

1 In relation to title conditions. The provision quoted does not deal with other matters such as good and marketable title.
2 Respectively clauses 21 and 22.
3 31 July 2006, Ayr Sheriff Court.
4 Sheriff Principal James A Taylor at para 15.

particular time) or objectively (what the titles actually say, without reference to the particular person who happens to be reading them at a particular time). The latter seems a more natural construction, taking the sentence as a whole. The subjective approach also has the problem that it leaves dangling the question of precisely who is supposed to be reading the deeds and when they are supposed to be doing the reading. What is the position, for example, if there are two buyers, and one of them has pre-knowledge of the defect but the other does not? Do the titles then 'disclose' to one buyer but not to the other, leaving one with a remedy and the other without?

Although this is a decision on a particular clause in a particular contract, it is likely to have wider ramifications, for the word 'disclose' is commonly used in provisions of this kind, and indeed is used in the provisions in the Edinburgh and Lothians Standard Clauses discussed above. On one view, of course, the result may be perfectly acceptable. It prevents a buyer from complaining about something which he knew about all along, and hence from using the later 'disclosure' as an excuse for rescission when his real motivation for withdrawal is different. The result indeed resembles the rule for warrandice, at least as it applies to ancillary matters such as title conditions.[1] On the other hand, the decision in *McPhee* weakens an already weak hand. A buyer seeking to rescind may be met with the argument that he knew of the defect at least in outline. How much prior knowledge is needed before rescission is barred? And is constructive knowledge sufficient? There is legal uncertainty here and, with the collapse into subjectivity, the possibility of factual uncertainty as well. From the buyer's point of view this gives more room for argument than is desirable or, perhaps, reasonable.

If desired, the decision in *McPhee v Black* could be avoided by appropriate amendment to the clause in question. For example, in the case of clause 18 of the Edinburgh and Lothians Standard Clauses, one possibility among many would be to add a few extra words as follows:

> If the title deeds disclose a position other than as stated above the Purchaser, *regardless of his previous state of knowledge*, will be entitled to resile from the Missives without penalty....

One further comment may be made. Hitherto the device of requiring prompt rescission has tended to be confined to ancillary matters. But in *McPhee* it seems to apply to the central obligation of the seller – the obligation to give a good and marketable title.[2] We do not think that that is acceptable, at least in the ordinary case. If the buyer must pay the price, so the seller must guarantee the title, and the guarantee must both extend into the future (for not all title defects are immediately obvious) and also allow a claim in damages. In short it must be an ordinary warranty. After all, if the seller were to incur no liability for failure to produce a title then, in fairness, the buyer should incur no liability for failure to pay the

---

1 K G C Reid, *Law of Property in Scotland* (1996) para 705.
2 We have not, however, seen the full missives, and it may be that good and marketable title was warranted after all, although it would be hard to reconcile such a warranty with the clause quoted.

price; but of course the buyer's liability in that regard has never been greater, as we have seen. We have heard the refusal of a title guarantee justified on the basis that the seller's solicitor may not be familiar with the title and so not in a position to advise the seller as to whether to take the risk; but one might equally say that no buyer should accept liability for failure to pay the price unless his solicitor has first investigated his solvency and liquidity. As it happens, the denial of a title guarantee may be less effective than the parties suppose. If missives are silent, the law will imply a warranty of good and marketable title,[1] and this implied term is not displaced even by the deletion of an express clause to the same effect.[2] Furthermore, a seller who grants warrandice in the disposition does much to undermine any reticence in the missives.

Naturally, parties are free to make whatever bargain they want. It is not illegitimate for a person to offer a property for sale on an 'as is' basis, the buyer accepting the title simply as it is held by the seller. Contracts on such terms are nothing new, and indeed in sales by roup they have always been the norm. But the terms of such a contract should be reflected in the price.

So, what *are* the missives?

The conclusion of missives may involve an unpleasantly large number of letters. Which letters – and which terms within which letters – constitute the legally binding contract? Since, in orthodox analysis, a qualified acceptance is both a rejection of the previous offer and also a fresh offer in itself,[3] it follows that the key letters are the last two: the final qualified acceptance, which contains the terms of the final offer, and its *de plano* acceptance. But in practice the last qualified acceptance is likely to be no more than an ungainly tailpiece to a long series of prior negotiations. Usually it is short and uninformative, and a person hoping to find the substance of the contract from its terms is likely to be disappointed.

So where, then, is the substance to be found? The uncontroversial answer given by Lord Drummond Young in *Middlebank Ltd v University of Dundee*[4] is that:

> [T]he terms of the parties' contract must be sought in the final qualified acceptance that is itself accepted by the other party; it is that qualified acceptance that is the effective offer. If any provision in earlier correspondence is to be included in the missives, there must be sufficiently clear reference to it in that final qualified acceptance.

And again:[5]

> The operative letters are the offer of 10 March 2004 and the acceptance of 11 March 2004 [ie the final two letters in the sequence]. All earlier correspondence merely forms part of the negotiations, and regard may be had to that correspondence only to the extent that it is incorporated into the offer and acceptance and is not inconsistent with those two letters.

---

1 G L Gretton and K G C Reid, *Conveyancing* (3rd edn 2004) ch 6.
2 *Baird v Drumpellier & Mount Vernon Estates Ltd* 2000 SC 103.
3 G L Gretton and K G C Reid, *Conveyancing* (3rd edn 2004) para 3-13.
4 [2006] CSOH 202 at para 14.
5 Paragraph 20.

In this second passage two requirements are made in respect of earlier correspondence: positively, it must be incorporated into the final offer and acceptance, and, negatively, it must not be inconsistent with them.

It might be supposed that there could be no difficulty in complying with the first requirement, for it is usually taken for granted that all terms of all prior letters are part of the missives except insofar as they have been expressly deleted. But in *Middlebank* all was not well in this regard. The final qualified acceptance (and, therefore, offer) was a letter of 10 March 2004. So far as relevant it was in the following terms (our lettering):

> [A] we ... offer on behalf of the said Importa Limited and Middlebank Limited to amend the terms of our formal letter, dated 17 February 2004, [B] relative to your formal letter, dated 9 February 2004, on behalf of your clients, The University of Dundee, relative to our formal letter, dated 3 February 2004, relative to your formal letter, dated 27 January 2004, being a Qualified Acceptance of our [C] Offer, dated 21 January 2004, on behalf of Century 21 (Homes) Limited or their Nominees to purchase from your said clients the subjects at 6–12 Perth Road, Dundee, at the price of FIVE HUNDRED THOUSAND POUNDS (£500,000) STERLING [D] and on the other terms and conditions stated in said Missives, as follows, [E] and make the following further qualifications....[1]

In *Middlebank* it was important to know whether the previous formal letters had been incorporated into the final contract because there was a dispute as to what had been sold. The letter of 10 March referred to 'the subjects at 6–12 Perth Road, Dundee', which Lord Drummond Young interpreted, no doubt correctly, to mean (i) those upper flats entering by the common passage and stair at 6 Perth Road and (ii) those upper flats entering by the common passage and stair at 12 Perth Road. But the seller (Dundee University) also owned the shops and offices (numbered 2, 2A, 4 and 8) on the ground and basement underneath the flats at number 6, and the buyer argued that these too were included in the sale due to clause 3 of an earlier formal letter, that of 3 February. This sought to amplify the description of the subjects as follows:

> It is understood that the property comprises (1) the subjects described in the Disposition by Millpark Limited in favour of The University of Dundee recorded GRS (Angus) on 9 February 1968....

The 1968 Disposition was a conveyance of the whole tenement, 2–8 Perth Road, and so included the shops and offices.

It was held by Lord Drummond Young that the letter of 10 March, although referring to the letter of 3 February, did not incorporate its terms. Hence the only description of the property was that contained in the letter of 10 March. Hence the shops and offices were not included in the sale.

This result gives cause for reflection. Although the narration of previous letters in the letter of 10 March was clumsily done, the conclusion that they were not duly

---

1 At the risk of stating the obvious, when missive letters take such convoluted form, the risk of confusion grows. It can be better to scrap the existing open missives and start again with a clean offer. This approach became easier when word processing was invented.

incorporated is perhaps surprising. Admittedly the structure of the narration is difficult to penetrate. But if our bracketed lettering correctly indicates the breaks,[1] then the narration could be read, in part, as follows:

> [A] we ... offer on behalf of the said Importa Limited and Middlebank Limited to amend the terms of our formal letter, dated 17 February 2004 ... [D] and on the other terms and conditions stated in said Missives, as follows....

This looks very much like an express incorporation of the earlier missives letters, ie those already enumerated in the letter.

Whether one agrees with the decision or not, it usefully emphasises the need to take care. For every qualified acceptance might be the last, and so must properly incorporate the previous formal letters. In the normal course of events this would be done merely by the words of acceptance of the immediately previous letter, provided that that letter itself incorporated the previous letters. One of the difficulties with the letter in *Middlebank* is that there were no words of acceptance.

An oddity of *Middlebank* is that the criticism which was levelled at the letter of 3 February, and was said to prevent its use, could equally well be levelled at the description of the property in the letter of 10 March (at part [C]), on which Lord Drummond Young relied. This is because, far from being a new and independent description, it was merely part of an earlier letter, of 21 January.

All this is not to say that the decision in *Middlebank* is wrong. In fact there were good reasons for supposing that only the flats were included in the sale – not least the evidence of the sales particulars. These, of course, were only surrounding circumstances; but, as Lord Drummond Young rightly emphasised, in construing a description in missives, it is impossible not to take such circumstances into account.[2]

LEASES

Advice Centre for Mortgages Ltd v McNicoll,[3] a dispute about premises at 4/5 Crighton Place, Edinburgh, is important for the law of leases, and especially for purchase options in leases. It is also an important case on personal bar, and on the offside goals rule. The opinion of the Lord Ordinary[4] does not hesitate to probe into difficult issues and is of great value. Not surprisingly, given its importance,

---

1 Part [D] cannot be read as belonging to part [C] because there were no 'said Missives' at the time of the original offer of 21 January.
2 Paragraph 12. For the weight given to the sales particulars, see paras 23–26. Lord Drummond Young relied in particular on *Houldsworth v Gordon Cumming* 1910 SC (HL) 49. On the whole question of extrinsic evidence, see further G L Gretton and K G C Reid, *Conveyancing* (3rd edn 2004) para 4-03.
3 [2006] CSOH 58, 2006 SLT 591, 2006 SCLR 602, 2006 Hous LR 22.
4 Lord Drummond Young.

the case has already generated a considerable amount of discussion.[1] It is not an easy case, partly because it is so rich in legal issues, and partly because of the messy facts. Angus McAllister puts it well: 'incomplete missives, two lost drafts (one revised, one not), an unsigned engrossment (also lost), and substantial delays between each of these stages'.[2]

There were two main issues: whether the lease (which was supposed to be for ten years) had come into existence at all, and, if it had, whether a purchase option contained in it bound the successor landlord. Since the pursuer (the alleged tenant) failed on the first point, the second did not have to be decided, but the Lord Ordinary (Drummond Young) nevertheless considered both branches of the case in great detail.

Purchase options

We begin with the second issue. Purchase options in commercial leases are quite common. More than one motivation is possible. For instance, a business finds premises attractive but is not sure if it wishes to commit to a purchase. A lease with an option to buy can be a good solution. If the property proves a success, the option can be exercised. If it is not so successful, matters will remain on the basis of the lease. Indeed, there may be a break option which will enable the tenant to get out early. Another motivation is tax planning: an owner wishes to realise heritable property but at the same time wishes to retain ownership for the sake of capital allowances.

Will such an option bind a successor?

The common law of leases is based on Roman law, and under Roman law a lease did not bind a successor owner. To the tenant's argument that he held a contract allowing use of the property, a new owner could reply: 'you have a contract, but not with me'. The law was changed by the Leases Act 1449. Provided that certain conditions are satisfied – and usually they are – a lease will bind a successor owner. The contract of lease is transferred. If Eve owns land and lets it to Fergus, and then disposes it to Graham, Graham is substituted for Eve in the contract. He acquires her rights (especially to receive rent) and her obligations (chiefly to allow Fergus to possess). This is what is meant by saying that a lease is a real right. The same happens if the lease is a registrable one and is registered.

But whilst the contract will normally transfer in this way, not every clause in it will necessarily be included. If the contract binds the landlord to brush his teeth twice a day, that will not bind Graham. Only those clauses which are 'leasey' will transfer – or, to put it in the terminology used in the authorities, only such provisions as are *inter naturalia* of the lease. Is a purchase option *inter naturalia*? In

---

1 A Steven (2006) 10 *Edinburgh Law Review* 432; E Reid (2006) 10 *Edinburgh Law Review* 437; D Bell and R Rennie (2006) 51 *Journal of the Law Society of Scotland* May/49; A McAllister 2006 SLT (News) 254; E C Reid and J W G Blackie, *Personal Bar* (2006) paras 10-01 ff.
2 2006 SLT (News) 254 at pp 255–256.

Advice Centre for Mortgages the Lord Ordinary held, following *Bisset v Magistrates of Aberdeen*,[1] that it is not. In principle a new owner is not bound.[2]

The offside goals rule

But the pursuer had another argument. It invoked what is sometimes called the 'offside goals rule', a rule of some antiquity, the best-known modern illustration being *Rodger (Builders) Ltd v Fawdry*.[3] The defender had, the pursuer argued, acquired the property in bad faith and so was bound by the option.

The Lord Ordinary rejected this argument. Even if a valid lease could have been established, the offside goals rule can apply only where the buyer has acquired in such a manner as to involve a breach of the seller's obligations. And the seller (Thomas H Peck Ltd) had been under no obligation which prevented the property being sold:[4]

> What the purchaser must know, actually or constructively, to bring it [the offside goals rule] into operation is that the implement of the contract in his favour will render the seller in breach of a legal obligation that he has undertaken to a third party. If there is no breach of any existing obligation, it is difficult to see that any question of dealing in good faith arises, because the seller is merely doing what he has a legal right to do.[5] ... The result in the present case is very clear. The sale of property by Thomas H Peck Ltd to the defender did not involve the seller in any breach of its existing obligations.

Accordingly, *Davidson v Zani*,[6] a sheriff court case which held that the offside goals rule does apply to purchase options, was wrongly decided.[7]

Possible solutions: the Lord Ordinary's suggestions

The Lord Ordinary went on to offer two suggestions as to how a purchase option could be made binding on a singular successor. These are helpful even if they do not exhaust the issues:[8]

> The simplest is to insert a term in the lease obliging the landlord to bind any disponee of the property to the terms of the option. In that event, if the landlord sold the property without imposing such a term, he would be in breach of the lease, and the rule in *Rodger*

---

1 (1898) 1 F 87.
2 Is a break option *inter naturalia*? This issue did not arise in the case but it is an important one. In our view it is *inter naturalia*. It is part of the machinery for determining the ish, and so is central to the whole contract. However, there does not seem to be clear authority, although see *Murray v Brodie* (1806) Hume 825 and *Ross v McFinlay* (1807) Hume 832.
3 1950 SC 483.
4 Paragraph 46.
5 Paragraph 45. He cites various authorities, and in the next paragraph quotes at length from K G C Reid, *Law of Property in Scotland* (1996) para 695, adding 'I agree with that formulation of the law.'
6 1992 SCLR 1001.
7 For the same view of *Davidson v Zani*, based on the same reasons, see *Conveyancing 2004* pp 105–107.
8 Paragraph 48. In the passage that follows, the Lord Ordinary is not using the term 'real burden' in the sense of a title condition, but rather as meaning a subordinate real right.

(Builders) Ltd v Fawdry [ie the offside goals rule] would apply. Another possibility is to secure the option by means of a standard security (which can secure an obligation *ad factum praestandum*: Conveyancing and Feudal Reform (Scotland) Act 1970 s 9(8)(c)). In that way the option is made a real burden over the subjects.

Whom do the contracting parties seek to bind?

A preliminary question that the draftsman must ask is: whom is the option clause *intended* to bind? Of course, mere intention may not succeed, but it is the starting point. For instance if the lease does not seek to bind a successor, then presumably a successor will not be bound.[1] Clarity on these issues would be a necessary first step before either of the Lord Ordinary's suggestions could be taken forward.

There is more than one possibility as to whom the option is to bind:

(1) Only the original landlord, and only for so long as he continues as landlord.
(2) Only the original landlord. If he later sells, the new landlord is not intended to be bound. But the original landlord remains liable to ensure that the option will continue to be effective. Thus if the option is exercised and refused by the new landlord, the original landlord is in breach.[2]
(3) Only the landlord for the time being. Once the original landlord has transferred ownership to someone else, he is off the hook.
(4) The landlord for the time being, but with the original landlord liable jointly and severally (ie in practice liable for damages in the event of breach).

Again, the clause needs to be clear not only as to the identity of the debtor in the option, but also as to the creditor, ie who is the option holder. This might be intended to be (a) the original tenant so long as he remains the tenant, or (b) the original tenant, even if he later assigns the lease, or (c) the tenant for the time being.

In fact these multiple possibilities potentially apply to other terms of leases as well. Our law of leases is reasonably well developed as far as the relationship of lessor and lessee is concerned, but as soon as the possibility of third parties arises, such as a successor to the landlord or a successor to the tenant, the law starts to look less impressive.

The Lord Ordinary's first suggestion

Now back to the Lord Ordinary's first suggestion. This may indeed work. But we have some doubts. The first is a practical one. Even if it works in relation to

---

1 Thus it is arguable that one reason why in *Bisset* (above) the successor was not bound is that the terms of the original agreement did not purport to bind successors.
2 At para 49 the Lord Ordinary says that if a lease is not a real right then it would create only 'personal rights that would necessarily terminate on a sale because they were not valid against singular successors'. With respect, this may be questioned. The fact that a personal right is not valid against a singular successor does not necessarily mean that it disappears on a transfer. In *Ashford & Thistle Securities v Kerr* 1 December 2005 (digested above as Case (56)) the sheriff, after holding that a rent remission agreement did not bind a successor landlord, commented at p 14 that in principle it would still bind the original landlord.

the first transferee, would the suggestion work in relation to subsequent ones?[1] The second concerns the basic logic of the offside goals rule. The rule potentially applies where Eve and Fergus make a contract, and then Eve transfers to Graham, who knows of the contract. The rule is that Graham is affected if, but only if, the Eve/Graham transfer was in breach of the Eve/Fergus contract. Does a contract of lease implicitly forbid the landlord to transfer the property? Surely not. If the first suggestion is adopted, Eve (the original landlord) would be in breach of her contract with Fergus in not imposing a certain obligation on Graham. *That* would be the breach, and *not* the transfer itself. Hence it is by no means clear that the offside goals rule would be engaged.

The Lord Ordinary's second suggestion

A standard security can, as the Lord Ordinary observes, be granted for an obligation *ad factum praestandum*. What that means is that it enforces the damages due in the event that such an obligation is breached. It thus does not make it possible for the option to be enforced directly. Nevertheless, it could be a useful tool.

As an accessory right, a standard security is of assistance only if the option clause is drafted in such a way as to survive the transfer of the land. It cannot secure a dead option.[2]

Statutory personal bar

The first branch of *Advice Centre for Mortgages Ltd v McNicoll*[3] was whether there was a lease at all, and we return to that issue now. The facts concerning the formation of the alleged lease were complex. Thomas H Peck Ltd (THP) was the owner of the property. In 1999 it entered into negotiations with Advice Centre for Mortgages Ltd (ACM) for the latter to take a lease. On 29 November 1999 there was a formal offer from THP of a lease for ten years. Two days later, ACM was given the keys and took possession. Rent was paid and work to the premises carried out. About six months later, on 22 May 2000, a qualified acceptance was sent to THP's agents. No further missive was sent, and the missives thus remained unconcluded. A deed of lease was adjusted but was never executed. In 2004 THP transferred ownership of the property to Frances McNicoll.[4] ACM now wished to exercise the purchase option contained in the unsigned lease. But the new owner was not willing to sell. ACM then raised this action seeking declarator that it held (a) a valid ten-year lease and (b) an option to purchase which was binding on the new landlord. The action failed.

The pursuer's pleadings for declarator of the existence of a lease are not easy to follow. In the first place, it pled that the lease came into being when

---

1 Cf A McAllister, *Scottish Law of Leases* (3rd edn 2002) para 2.38(2).
2 See eg *Trotter v Trotter* 2001 SLT (Sh Ct) 42.
3 [2006] CSOH 58, 2006 SLT 591, 2006 SCLR 602, 2006 Hous LR 22.
4 Presumably by way of sale. Some of the background to the dispute is unclear. The pursuer averred that the defender had been one of its employees and that her husband had been one of its directors.

possession was taken on 1 December 1999.[1] In the second place, it pled that the lease was constituted by the offer and qualified acceptance of November 1999 and May 2000.[2] In the third place, it pled that the lease was constituted by the unsigned lease of October 2000.[3] Yet each of these would have resulted in different contractual terms. Possibly the pursuer was asserting them in the alternative: this is unclear.

The pursuer had two hurdles to leap. One was to show that there had been an agreement at all, given that the missives had never been concluded and that the lease had never been signed. The second was the problem that a lease for more than a year needs not merely agreement, but agreement in writing.[4] In the event, it was held that the pursuer's averments were insufficient to establish consensus. As for the second hurdle, the pursuer's case was that the contract could be set up by 'statutory personal bar'.

Section 1 of the Requirements of Writing (Scotland) Act 1995, while saying that a lease for more than a year must be in writing, also says that a contract can dispense with writing if it can be shown that there was agreement and that there had been actings in reliance on the agreement: this is 'statutory personal bar'. But the pursuer faced two difficulties, each of which was insurmountable. In the first place, the timing was wrong. The pursuer's pleadings, as interpreted by the Lord Ordinary, were that the agreement came into existence in or after May 2000, by which time the actings in question had already taken place. Hence the actings could not be said to have been 'in reliance' on the agreement.

In the second place, and more importantly, the Lord Ordinary came to the conclusion that the statutory personal bar provisions cannot rescue a lease at all. Section 1(2) draws a distinction between (a) 'a contract ... for the creation, transfer, variation or extinction of a real right in land' and (b) the actual 'creation, transfer, variation or extinction of a real right in land'.[5] Personal bar applies in relation to the former but not to the latter. The distinction is in general easy to draw, but the Lord Ordinary points out, as others have done,[6] that when it comes to leases the distinction does not work well. Nevertheless, it has to be applied. He says:[7]

---

1 'The pursuers assert that on taking entry and actual occupation of the subjects on 1 December 1999 they acquired a real right of lease in terms of the Leases Act 1449' (para 5 of the Lord Ordinary's opinion). Or was this perhaps a claim that a real right of lease arose without a contract of lease? (But that would be unstateable.)

2 'They seek a declarator that the terms of a valid contract of lease are set out in a formal offer dated 29 November 1999 from agents acting on behalf of Thomas H Peck Ltd to the pursuers' agents and a formal letter dated 22 May 2000 from the pursuers' agents to Thomas H Peck Ltd's agents' (para 2 of the Lord Ordinary's opinion).

3 'They seek a declarator that a valid contract of lease, containing an option to purchase the subjects, is found in an unsigned lease together with schedules and a draft offer to purchase ... those documents having been agreed, it is said, between the pursuers and Thomas H Peck Ltd on 13 October 2000' (para 2 of the Lord Ordinary's opinion).

4 Requirements of Writing (Scotland) Act 1995 s 1. This was not a new rule in 1995.

5 Requirements of Writing (Scotland) Act 1995 s 1(a)(i), (b). We quote it in its current form: in the case it is referred to in its older form, applicable to the events in question, but the differences are not material for present purposes.

6 McAllister 2006 SLT (News) 254 makes this point well.

7 Paragraphs 19–20.

On one hand, a lease is itself a contract for the creation of an interest in land. On the other hand, it creates an interest in land, which will give rise to real rights when possession is taken or the lease is registered. For present purposes it is not necessary to determine any general criteria for allocating leases to one or other of the two categories. It is sufficient to hold that, where it can be inferred that the intention of the parties to a lease is that possession should be taken by the tenant on the faith of the lease document, or the lease document should be registered, thus creating real rights in the tenant, that document will create an interest in land and will accordingly fall within subsection (2)(c)[1] of s 1. In that event the personal bar provisions contained in subsections (3) and (4) will not apply. In my view that is the clear intention of subsection (2). That subsection draws a fundamental distinction between documents that create property rights on one hand and mere contracts on the other hand. That distinction must be given effect in the case of leases. While that task may in some cases be difficult, if the document in question is one that is clearly intended, objectively speaking, to create a right of property in the tenant, it must be treated as falling within paragraph (b) of the subsection and not paragraph (a)(i).

In the present case the Lease is a formal document. Moreover, it was clearly designed to follow antecedent missives. In the circumstances I am of opinion that it must be inferred that the parties' intention was that possession should be taken on the faith of the Lease. It follows that the Lease is a document intended to create an interest in land, falling within s 1(2)(b), and not a mere contract for the creation of an interest in land, which would fall within s 1(2)(a)(ii). The consequence is that the personal bar provisions contained in subsections (3) and (4) do not apply.

This is a convincing interpretation of the words of the statute. As we read the passage, the basis of this approach is not that the relation of missives of let to a 'formal lease' is the same as that of missives of sale to a disposition, with the former being the 'contract' document and the latter being the 'property' document. The Lord Ordinary does not say that. Rather he says that if the document is one which is intended to be the basis of possession (or of registration), then it is a property document for the purposes of s 1, and therefore comes under paragraph (b) of s 1(2), so that personal bar does not apply. The truth is that a formal lease is just as much a bilateral contract as missives of let. The question, therefore, that must be asked is not 'is this document a contract?', for the answer to that must be affirmative, but rather 'is this document the basis for the creation of a real right?'

The Lord Ordinary leaves open the difficult question of the relationship of missives to a formal lease. Both are bilateral contracts. Either is capable of having real effect. As Paton and Cameron observe, 'an agreement to lease is as effective as a lease'.[2] So what is happening if missives of let are followed by a formal lease? The missives/lease relationship is different from the missives/disposition relationship. When ownership of land is transferred, what the buyer gets at first (a contractual right) is different and separate from what he gets at the end (the real right of ownership). Indeed, the contract can fall away, and usually does so. But when a lease is granted, and the lessee obtains a real right, that real right is

---

1 This seems to be a typing slip: the relevant provision is subsection 2(b).
2 G C H Paton and J G S Cameron, The Law of Landlord and Tenant in Scotland (1967) p 17.

not something separate from or independent of the contract. It is a product of the contract and stands or falls with it. A 'lease' and a 'contract of lease' are the same thing. A lease is an unusual real right, because it is a real right that is a contract. It is a contract that in itself can have real effect.

Whilst (i) the relationship of missives to disposition is different from (ii) the relationship of missives to lease, the former is much the same as (iii) the relationship of missives to an assignation of an existing lease. In both (i) and (iii) there is first an agreement to transfer an existing right, and then there is the transfer itself.

Suppose that missives of lease are concluded, and provide for a formal lease to be signed subsequently. Is that a contract to contract? If so then it is, on standard views of contract law, unenforceable: an agreement to agree cannot be enforced. So that cannot be the right analysis. But the right analysis is important. Take two cases. (1) There are unsigned missives of lease, for a term of more than a year. The missives do not provide for the signing of a subsequent 'formal lease'. The missives are acted on. Section 1 of the 1995 Act cannot be invoked to 'set up' the lease, for the reasons given by the Lord Ordinary. (2) The same, but the unsigned missives provide for a 'formal lease' to be signed. Could it now be argued that the latter is the 'property' document, so that s 1 *can* be invoked to set up the unsigned missives? There seem to be insuperable objections to either way of answering this question.

The technical interpretation of s 1 is one thing. There remains the question of whether it is a satisfactory result in policy terms. The Lord Ordinary thinks so, and questions the contrary view expressed by McAllister in his book on leases.[1] McAllister however continues to stick to his guns.[2] We offer no view on this issue. But one point may be worth noting. If an unwritten contract of lease for a term of ten years could, on being set up by personal bar, come within the provisions of the Leases Act 1449, then what about an unwritten lease contract for a term of twenty-five years? The difficulty here is that a lease for more than twenty years cannot be a real right unless it is registered in the Land Register.[3] Could an unwritten lease be so registered? That is a debatable question.

REAL BURDENS

References to 'superiors'

As is now becoming apparent, the bonfire of burdens which feudal abolition had at one time seemed to promise has not taken place. Of course, many burdens were consumed in flames on the appointed day,[4] but many others are with us still, and often subject to more enforcers than previously. The main

---

1 'I do not share the author's misgivings about such a result' (para 21 of the Opinion). The passage in question is A McAllister, *Scottish Law of Leases* (3rd edn 2002) para 2.5.
2 2006 SLT (News) 254.
3 Land Registration (Scotland) Act 1979 s 3(3).
4 28 November 2004.

cases of survival are in developments, or 'communities' to use the language of the Title Conditions (Scotland) Act 2003. Housing estates and tenements are examples. Where, in such 'communities', burdens were previously enforceable by the superior, the effect of ss 52 and 53 of the Title Conditions Act is usually to confer enforcement rights on neighbours. Sometimes this is nothing new, because the neighbours had enforcement rights already by virtue of the doctrine known as *jus quaesitum tertio*.[1] But in cases where previously only the superior could enforce, the legislation transfers enforcement rights from superior to neighbours. The effect of feudal abolition, it sometimes seems, is that we are all superiors now.

A practical difficulty is that burdens which were created under the feudal system often make reference to 'the superior' or, more commonly, 'the superiors'. How are such references to be read after the appointed day?[2] A partial answer can be found in s 73(2) of the Abolition of Feudal Tenure (Scotland) Act, which provides that:

> On or after the appointed day, any reference
>
> (a) in any document executed before that day or
> (b) in the Land Register of Scotland or any certificate or copy such as is mentioned in subsection (1)(d) above (whenever issued),
>
> to a superior shall, where that reference requires to be construed in relation to a real burden which a person is entitled, by virtue of section 18, 18A, 18B, 18C, 19, 20, 28, 28A or 60 of this Act or section 56 of the Title Conditions (Scotland) Act 2003 (asp 9) (facility burdens and service burdens) to enforce on and after that day, be construed as a reference to that person.

At first sight s 73(2) seems to say, for 'superiors' read 'the new enforcers', and so it does – but only in respect of those new enforcers who acquired rights under the provisions which are listed. These are less important than their number suggests. Virtually all of the provisions listed from the 2000 Act concern parties who obtained enforcement rights by the registration of notices before the appointed day – that is to say, very few. The only other provision mentioned is s 56 of the 2003 Act, which concerns facility and service burdens, the main example being burdens concerned with maintenance. But in practice maintenance burdens rarely made any reference to 'superiors'.

More important than what s 73(2) does say is what it does not. There is no reference to ss 52 and 53 of the Title Conditions Act, so that for neighbours who acquire enforcement rights under these provisions – for, in other words, the main case of reallocation of rights – there is, quite simply, no provision. The silence is eloquent. Because s 73(2) does not apply, no translation is available for the word 'superiors'. And because no translation is available, the word falls to be disregarded.

---

1 If rather inaccurately.
2 For discussion, see K G C Reid, *The Abolition of Feudal Tenure in Scotland* (2003) para 7.18; A Steven and S Wortley, 'Is that burden dead yet?' (2006) 51 *Journal of the Law Society of Scotland* July/50.

As it happens, s 73(2) of the 2000 Act has now been supplemented by s 73(2)(A), which was added by the Title Conditions (Scotland) Act 2003. It is the close companion of s 3(8) of the 2003 Act which, in respect of new real burdens, prevents provision being made for outsiders – those who do not hold a benefited property – to waive compliance with, mitigate or vary real burdens. Its purpose is to stop developers from retaining control once all units in a development have been sold; and, being post-feudal, it is not aimed at feudal superiors as such. Section 73(2A) of the 2000 Act is likewise not aimed at feudal superiors as such, but because it applies to deeds registered before the appointed day, it is capable of including superiors within is ambit. Its terms are similar to those of s 3(8) of the 2003 Act: any provision in a deed

> to the effect that a person other than the person entitled to enforce the burden may waive compliance with, or mitigate or otherwise vary a condition of, the burden shall be disregarded.

So far as references to 'superiors' are concerned, this provision makes explicit what is left implicit in s 73(2): references are to be disregarded. But as the provision is restricted to cases where the superior is entitled to waive, mitigate or vary, it does not cover the full range of possible references to 'superiors', leaving s 73(2) to fill the gap. Whichever provision applies,[1] however, the effect is the same: the word 'superiors' is disregarded.

The result is to cut a hole in the real burdens in question, for the word 'superior' or 'superiors' must be excised. What then? In our view the answer turns on whether the word is or is not severable from the rest of the provision. Where the word – together, often, with the words which immediately surround it – can be severed without loss of meaning in the words that remain, the provision survives in its lightly mutilated form and can be enforced in the normal way.[2] But where the whole provision depends on the word 'superiors', the provision, inevitably, will fall.

In 2006 ss 73(2) and 73(2A) were judicially considered for the first time, by the Lands Tribunal in *At.Home Nationwide Ltd v Morris*;[3] and both the result and the reasoning seem to confirm, if only by implication, the approach which was suggested above. The facts were these. A retirement housing development comprising 19 flats was subject to a deed of conditions which dated from 1993. Clause 3(j) provided that:

> In the event of any Proprietor desiring to sell or otherwise dispose of his Flat or to make any change in the use or occupancy thereof he shall be bound to notify the Superiors of his intention. Such notification must be in writing sent by registered post or recorded delivery to the Factor on behalf of the Superiors. No Proprietor shall be entitled to sell or otherwise dispose of his Flat or to make any change in the use or

---

1 Or, more accurately – since *both* s 73(2) *and* s 73(2A) will often apply – whether one provision applies or two.
2 This result is more or less presupposed by s 73(2A). And see *Conveyancing 2001* pp 89–90.
3 11 December 2006, Lands Tribunal. The Tribunal comprised J N Wright QC.

occupancy thereof unless the Superiors are satisfied and have given their approval in writing to the Proprietor that on such sale or disposal or change the Flat will be used and occupied in accordance with the provisions contained in Sub-Clause (d) hereof.

Clause 3(d) in turn imposed a number of use restrictions including the following:

Each of the Flats shall be used and occupied by not more than two persons each of whom shall be capable of leading an independent life and one of whom shall have attained the age of sixty years or be eligible to receive a Government Pension in respect of disablement provided always that the Superiors on cause shown may agree to relax this condition, either wholly or partially for such period or periods and on such conditions as they may determine.

It will be seen that, while both provisions make reference to the 'superiors', they do so in rather different ways.

The applicants, who owned nine of the flats, applied to the Lands Tribunal under its new jurisdiction to determine the validity and enforceability of real burdens.[1] The applicant was content with the restrictions in clause 3(d) and the application was restricted to clause 3(j), which was seen as interfering with the sale of the flats. Quite correctly, the Tribunal was satisfied that the conditions in the deed, formerly enforceable by superiors, were now mutually enforceable by the flat-owners by virtue of ss 53 and 54 of the Title Conditions Act.[2] In other words, the conditions were community burdens. The Tribunal was also satisfied that clause 3(j) did not so impair transfer as to be void as repugnant with ownership.[3]

Having reached these conclusions, the Tribunal was reluctant to hold clause 3(j) to be unenforceable:[4]

We have not found this an easy question, and have reached our view with a degree of reluctance having regard to the importance which the legislation clearly gives to community burdens: when the burden, as it were, passes the Act's other tests, it might seem strange that it falls down just because there is no longer a superior. Further, we note in this particular case that this is a burden imposed recently and in quite modern form, apart from the feudal clothing. Although only ancillary, it must have been considered a worthwhile administrative provision, and of course holding it now unenforceable means depriving the co-proprietors of its benefit.

But in the end the legislation left no choice:[5]

---

1 Title Conditions (Scotland) Act 2003 s 90(1)(a)(ii). An application was also made for a discharge in the normal way although, in the event, that proved unnecessary.
2 Section 54 is a special provision which applies only to sheltered or retirement housing.
3 Title Conditions (Scotland) Act 2003 s 3(6). This is the first ruling on that provision. In the Tribunal's view (p 10), clause 3(j) 'is merely an administrative provision, not designed to restrain sales (except in so far as the sales would be for use in contravention of clause 3(d), a type of restraint of which the Parliament has expressly approved – see section 54(5)(c). It may now create a problem, but that is one of practicality, not substantial restraint.'
4 Page 11 of the transcript.
5 Page 12 of the transcript.

However, we are satisfied that this decision follows the discriminating intention revealed by the statutory provisions in relation to burdens previously enforceable by superiors. In particular, the inclusion of only facility burdens and service burdens, and not community burdens generally, in section 73(2), seems to make the matter clear.[1] Moreover, although it seems unfortunate to deprive the co-proprietors of this protection, it is very clear that to require sellers of flats in a property community to obtain the consent of every co-proprietor (or apply to the Tribunal) would also be highly unsatisfactory.

The Tribunal's conclusion was that, following the abolition of the feudal system, and of feudal superiors, clause 3(j) was no longer valid or enforceable.

The treatment of clause 3(j) can be contrasted with the treatment of clause 3(d) (quoted above):[2]

The Tribunal has already had cases in which there has been a prohibition on a certain use or action without the superior's consent. Typically, a proprietor who previously held under a superior, with a real burden prohibiting any extension or alteration except with the consent of the superior, seeks to extend or alter. If there is a common scheme and related properties, section 53 may apply even where there was no previous right of co-proprietors to enforce. In that situation it seems to be accepted that section 73(2A) has the effect of simply excising the reference to the superior's consent, leaving a prohibition, enforceable at least by neighbours who can show an interest.... Clause 3(d), the substantive obligation to use these flats as retirement homes, would appear to be such a clause, because it had a proviso allowing some relaxation by the superior on cause shown.

Clause 3(j), however, was 'a different type of provision'.[3] Following feudal abolition 'there is no superior to carry out the certification procedure'.[4] The whole provision therefore must fall.

Real burdens in minutes of waiver

Most waivers are qualified. Often this amounts to allowing a particular breach (such as a new building) while reaffirming the burden in all other respects. In such cases there is no difficulty. But sometimes a new burden is imposed. Is that competent? The answer is that it depends.

Under the Title Conditions (Scotland) Act 2003 s 4(2)(b) a deed creating a real burden – a so-called constitutive deed – must be 'granted by or on behalf of the owner of the land which is to be the burdened property'. A minute of waiver, however, is normally a unilateral deed, granted only by the owner of the *benefited* property.[5] In order for it to be eligible to create real burdens, it would have to be bilateral in form, and granted by both owners. That of course could easily be done. The normal name for the resulting deed would be 'minute of agreement' rather than 'minute of waiver'.

---

1 In the Tribunal's view this was not a case to which s 73(2A) could apply.
2 Page 9 of the transcript.
3 Page 9 of the transcript.
4 Page 11 of the transcript.
5 Title Conditions (Scotland) Act 2003 s 15(1).

The position under the old law was less accommodating, as *Faeley v Clark*[1] shows. In that case a real burden imposed by disposition prohibited further building without the consent of an immediate neighbour. In 1990 this consent was given in the form of a minute of agreement between the two sets of owners. But the consent was conditional: a further house was to be allowed 'provided always that external additions shall not be made to the said dwellinghouse and no other erections shall be constructed upon 7A Rockland Park without our prior written consent'.[2] Under the law before the Title Conditions Act, real burdens could only be created in (i) a conveyance of the property which was being burdened or (ii) a deed of conditions.[3] Plainly the minute of agreement was not a conveyance. And while there is a reported case in which a court was willing to treat a bilateral deed as a deed of conditions,[4] the Lands Tribunal took the view that the minute of agreement:[5]

> does not in fact go beyond its main purpose of exercising the power under the existing condition to grant consent, subject to a proviso which may create a personal obligation but does not itself create a further real burden.[6]

RIGHT-TO-BUY ARRANGEMENTS

Hutchison v Graham's Exrx[7] is a fact-specific case which illustrates how easy it is for problems to arise when drafting a non-standard contract. Mrs Graham was a local authority tenant. She exercised her right to buy with the help of a loan from a building society. At the same time she entered into a written agreement with her granddaughter, Mrs Hutchison, and the latter's husband (the pursuers in this action). The deed, dated 7 and 9 December 1998, began with a narrative[8] that Mrs Graham was granting to the Hutchisons a third-ranking standard security (after the security to the building society and the discount standard security) and continued:[9]

> THEREFORE the parties hereby agree as follows:
>
> FIRST The security constituted by the said Standard Security shall be intended to secure

---

1 2006 GWD 28-626, Lands Tribunal. The Tribunal comprised J N Wright QC and I M Darling FRICS.
2 As this example shows, there is sometimes a fine line between the partial discharge of an existing burden and the creation of a new one.
3 K G C Reid, *Law of Property in Scotland* (1996) para 388.
4 *Gorrie and Banks Ltd v Burgh of Musselburgh* 1973 SC 33.
5 Page 15 of the transcript.
6 The Tribunal added that, in the event that the minute of agreement had qualified as a deed of conditions, it would not have mattered that the deed was not referred to in a subsequent conveyance of the burdened property. Section 17 of the Land Registration (Scotland) Act 1979 (now repealed) made such a reference unnecessary. We would agree with that view.
7 [2006] CSOH 15, 2006 SCLR 587.
8 Or so it seems. The narrative, however, is not quoted in the court's opinion.
9 The text is taken from the court's opinion. The 'pursuers' are the Hutchisons.

(One) repayment to the [pursuers] of the aggregate amount of those monthly payments made by the [pursuers] to the … Dunfermline Building Society …

(Two) payment of interest thereon at the rate of Two per centum per annum above the base lending rate of the Royal Bank of Scotland plc applicable from time to time

(Three) repayment of all fees and outlays incurred by the [pursuers] … in connection with the purchase of the said subjects,

(Four) repayment of all premiums paid by the [pursuers] in respect of the insurance of the said subjects. …

(Five) repayment of all sums expended by the [pursuers] in connection with the upgrading repair or maintenance of the subjects. …

SECOND It is understood that [Mrs Graham] shall have the right to reside in the subjects during the whole of her lifetime without payment of any rent or interest (except in the circumstances above mentioned).

THIRD [Mrs Graham] … binds and obliges herself not to dispose of the subjects by either *inter vivos* or *mortis causa* deed or otherwise to any individual except the [pursuers] or without the agreement of the [pursuers] and [Mrs Graham] hereby confirms that she has made a Will leaving the subjects to the [pursuers] and that she will not make any subsequent Will altering this particular provision; In the event of [Mrs Graham] disposing of the subjects to any individual without the agreement of the [pursuers] or otherwise contravening conditions of this agreement then she binds and obliges herself to instantly repay all sums due to the [pursuers] and the [pursuers] … bind and oblige themselves not to require payment of any of the sums secured hereunder unless [Mrs Graham] shall dispose of the subjects to any individual as before mentioned without their consent or the [pursuers] are disinherited as before mentioned. …

FIFTH [Mrs Graham] as agreed undertakes that as soon as practically possible after the day of Ninth September Two Thousand and One to convey the subjects to the [pursuers] without any consideration being paid but subject to the [pursuers] granting a Right of Occupancy/Licence to Occupy/Liferent in favour of [Mrs Graham].

SIXTH In construing these presents [Mrs Graham] shall include her executors and representatives whomsoever; and [the pursuers] shall include their executors and representatives whomsoever. …

Mrs Graham did make a will in favour of the pursuers. But later she revoked it and left the house to her daughter, Dawn Stoehrer, whom she also made her executor: this daughter was thus the defender in the present action. Despite the obligation to convey the property in September 2001 (presumably the end of the discount clawback period), Mrs Graham died, in August 2002, still the owner. After her death the Hutchisons raised an action for declarator that the legacy to them in the original will was incapable of revocation, or, in the alternative, for reduction of the revocation.[1]

---

1 It is not easy to see the difference between these alternative conclusions.

At first sight the Hutchisons' claim seems a strong one. The agreement says that Mrs Graham is not to change her will. Such an agreement is valid in our law. Though Lord Stair is not quoted, he puts the matter with authority and economy:[1]

> All is ambulatory during the defunct's life, and may be taken away expressly or implicitly, by posterior or derogatory deeds, unless the defunct be obliged by contract *inter vivos*, not to alter the same.

Nevertheless the Lord Ordinary (Carloway) found for the defender. The reason is simple. The deed says that the legacy is not to be revoked. But it then also says what the consequence is to be if Mrs Graham does revoke it. The consequence is that the sums due to the Hutchisons are to be repaid:

> In the event of [Mrs Graham] disposing of the subjects to any individual without the agreement of the [pursuers] or otherwise contravening conditions of this agreement then she binds and obliges herself to instantly repay all sums due to the [pursuers].

So the agreement, far from making the will irrevocable, makes it conditionally revocable. Mrs Graham was free to change her will provided she paid back the money that the Hutchisons had paid. Since this obligation was binding on the executor and secured on the property, the Hutchisons will presumably be paid.

Could the Hutchisons, while Mrs Graham was alive, have enforced against her the obligation to convey? The Lord Ordinary comments, albeit only by way of *obiter dictum*, that 'even if the pursuers had attempted to enforce it, Mrs Graham could have declined to transfer the property in terms of clause FIFTH, electing instead to terminate the Agreement and to suffer the stipulated consequences for doing so'.[2] This is on the basis that the consequences of breach spelled out in clause third apply equally to breaches of clause fifth. Was this what the parties intended? Indeed, can we be sure that they intended the same thing? Probing more deeply, can we be sure that there were clear intentions at all?

It is not uncommon to add to an agreement a provision for what is to happen in the event of breach, but such provisions have to be considered carefully. For instance, in offers to buy one often sees something like this:

> It is an essential condition of this offer that there are no outstanding local authority notices. Any such notices will be the responsibility of the seller.

These two sentences do not fit together. If there are to be no notices, how can the offer also accept that there may be? If there is a notice and if the buyers want to withdraw, after missives have been concluded, can they? Can they at least decline to settle until the notice has been dealt with? Or does the second sentence limit their freedom of action? As the Lord Ordinary observes:[3]

---

1 Stair III.8.33.
2 Paragraph 7.
3 Paragraph 7.

In some cases, contractually stipulated remedies can be seen as supplementing those at common law. In others, they can be seen as a substitute for them. Which situation applies will depend upon ascertaining the intention of the parties at the time of contracting by looking at the meaning of the words they employed in the context of the contract as a whole. Where a particular breach averred is anticipated by an Agreement and a specific remedy is provided in that event, the contractual remedy must be seen as being intended as a substitute for, and not as a supplement to, those at common law.

In drafting agreements there is a tendency to feel that every provision has to be backed up by further provision as to what is to happen in the event of breach. This is dangerous. Often such further provisions are simply unnecessary because the law will imply the consequences anyway and will generally do so in a satisfactory manner. And they can all too easily make matters worse.

Three other difficulties about this document may be mentioned, though none of them came up in the litigation. (i) The fifth clause provides that Mrs Graham is to convey the property in exchange for a 'Right of Occupancy/Licence to Occupy/Liferent'. This is not easy to understand. An offer to purchase for a price of '£250,000/£260,000/£270,000' would provoke puzzlement. 'Well, which do you mean?' would be the likely response. If the fifth clause had been litigated one can only speculate what would have happened. Arguably it is uninterpretable.[1] (ii) The third clause makes provision about Mrs Graham disposing of the property to an 'individual'. This term would not include, for instance, a charity. Was that really the intention? (iii) The same clause says: 'she will not make any subsequent will altering this particular provision'. What if she had revoked the will by tearing it up, without making a new one?

A contract of this general type is not easy to draft. As far as we know there are no styles in print, and we have none to offer. Are the family members who finance the purchase to get their money back, or are they to get the property? If they are to get the property, is this to be by a legacy or by an *inter vivos* transfer? Should a trust be used? If there is to be an *inter vivos* transfer, how is the elderly person's right to reside in the property to be protected? Can matters be left on a contractual basis, or should steps be taken to guard against the possibility of future insolvency? What about the risk that discount clawback might be triggered? What about separate legal representation of the parties? And so on.

RESIDENTIAL PROPERTY AND ENRICHMENT CLAIMS

The law of unjustified enrichment seems far removed from conveyancing law and practice. It resembles the law of delict in that it involves a minute dissection of case law and judicial dicta. But whilst the Roman roots of the law of delict, though deep, are not always obvious, the Roman roots of the law of unjustified enrichment are conspicuous, and sometimes it seems that the Latin words

---

1 One also wonders why the second and the second part of the fifth clauses are separate.

outnumber the English ones. And it is a field of high and pure academic debate. But conveyancers should not dismiss it, any more than they can dismiss the law of delict. Like the law of delict, enrichment law copes with the consequences of things going wrong. The task of conveyancing is to make things go right, and it is difficult to know how to make things go right unless you know how they can go wrong. Conveyancers practise preventive medicine, while litigators practise curative medicine. Prevention is better than cure, but prevention presupposes knowledge of what is to be prevented.

Suppose that X owns a house but Y has made some contribution. The contribution might be to the price, or it might be to the loan repayments, or it might be to maintaining or improving the property. No contract is made – or at any rate no express contract is made. Nothing is done to make the title reflect the financial contribution. Later the relationship between X and Y goes sour. Y visits his solicitor and asks what can be done.

The key words here are 'the relationship between X and Y goes sour', not only because of what they say but because of what they presuppose. For the contribution of Y can only have happened in the context of a close relationship. Outwith such a context, contributions are done on a contractual basis. The typical close relationship is marriage, and within that relationship the spouses are likely to make contributions that are not grounded in contract. Who pays for the house or for its maintenance may bear no relationship to the way in which title is taken. Everything is done on the footing of mutual trust. Usually this works well enough. If the marriage lasts, the economic interests of the parties remain substantially the same, and so disputes are unlikely, and if they do arise they are resolved within the framework of the relationship. If the marriage does not last, disputes can be handled by the law of divorce, which can bring to bear a reasonably sophisticated and flexible method of dealing with such matters.

So in practice the major problems tend to arise where X and Y are not married (and are not civil partners). The standard case is where they are cohabitants, though problems can also arise in other cases, as one of 2006's cases illustrates.[1] This is an area which has only begun to develop in recent years, ie since cohabitation became widespread.

What are the possible lines of argument which are available to Y?

(1) *Contract.* Y may seek to show that there was an agreement whereby the money would be returned, or that title to the property would be adjusted to reflect the financial input. The problem here is that it can be difficult to establish any definite agreement. Moreover, since any agreement would typically have been oral, there may be legal problems about whether it could be binding.

(2) *Delict.* The basis of delict is *damnum injuria datum*. Unless Y can prove (i) a wrongful act or omission which has (ii) caused (iii) loss, there is no claim in delict.

---

1 *Satchwell v McIntosh* 2006 SLT (Sh Ct) 117.

(3) *Constructive trust.* This is the road that has been taken in England. The possibility has also been urged here,[1] but remains untried, in our view rightly so.[2] The court practitioner may be conscious that the Scottish judiciary regards constructive trusts with something less than enthusiasm.[3] The English position may in part be attributed to the under-development of enrichment law in that country.

(4) *Unjustified enrichment.* The idea is simple. X has been enriched at Y's expense. The enrichment is without a valid legal basis. So it is unjustified Therefore it ought to be returned.

The idea of bringing the law of unjustified enrichment to bear on this matter really starts with the 1986 case of *Grieve v Morrison,*[4] though earlier examples can be found.[5] There X and Y were co-owning cohabitants. They broke up and one of them raised an action of division or sale. The other argued that she should receive more than half the net proceeds because she had contributed more than half, basing her case on the law of unjustified enrichment. Her argument failed. The *ratio* of the decision is open to debate. Though never overruled, *Grieve* is looking increasingly isolated, as successive decisions have distinguished it or declined to follow it. The breakthrough decision was the 1998 Inner House case, *Shilliday v Smith.*[6] Here a house was owned solely by X, but Y paid for improvements. When the relationship broke up, Y sued for payment of what she had contributed. The argument was that she had made the payments in the expectation of marriage and that, since the marriage never happened, she had the right to her money back. This argument was upheld.

2006 saw no fewer than three more cases of this general type, in all of which Y's claim was held to be relevantly pled: *Satchwell v McIntosh,*[7] *Smith v Barclay,*[8] and *McKenzie v Nutter.*[9] In *Satchwell* title was in the name of X alone, and the case was rather like *Shilliday,* with one important qualification. In *Shilliday* Y's payments had been made in the expectation of wedding bells, while in *Satchwell* Y conceded that the parties were not engaged, but argued that the payments had been made in the expectation of continued cohabitation. This was a step beyond *Shilliday,* but it was upheld. There is some tension here with the principle (not mentioned in the case) that money given to obtain sexual intercourse cannot be recovered.[10]

Smith v Barclay[11] was a more unusual case. Pamela Smith and William Barclay were cohabitants. They bought a house near Linlithgow, called 'the Den', at a price

---

1 See eg K McK Norrie, 'Proprietary rights of cohabitants' 1995 *Juridical Review* 209.

2 See G L Gretton, 'Constructive trusts' (1997) 1 *Edinburgh Law Review* 281 and 408.

3 *Mortgage Corporation v Mitchells Roberton* 1997 SLT 1305 at 1310 *per* Lord Johnston: 'I confess an almost instinctive abhorrence of the notion of constructive trusts in the law of Scotland.'

4 1993 SLT 852. The case dates from 1986.

5 Such as *Newton v Newton* 1925 SC 715.

6 1998 SC 725.

7 2006 SLT (Sh Ct) 117. For discussion see R Evans-Jones, 'Causes of action and remedies in unjustified enrichment' (2007) 11 *Edinburgh Law Review* 105.

8 27 August 2006, Dundee Sheriff Court, A 1459/04.

9 2007 SLT (Sh Ct) 17, 2007 SCLR 115.

10 See eg R Evans-Jones, *Unjustified Enrichment* vol 1 (2003) para 5.59.

11 27 August 2006, Dundee Sheriff Court, A 1459/04.

of £525,000. They took title in joint names. It was agreed that Pamela's mother, Phyllis Smith, should come to live with them. But for this to happen it was felt that a substantial extension would be needed. Until it was built she would continue to live in her own house. The extension was built. It is not clear just how much this cost, but it seems to have been at least £115,000 and possibly more. Phyllis paid £106,315 to Pamela and William, and the balance was met by William. But by the time the extension was complete, Pamela and William had broken up. Phyllis never moved in. 'The Den' was sold, for £700,000. At this point Pamela paid her mother £50,000. The latter asked William to pay her the balance of the £106,315, ie £56,315. He was prepared to pay her £25,000. At this point she contacted 'a nephew who had studied law' and he suggested that she make a claim based on unjustified enrichment. This she did, as a party litigant, aged 78. She was successful. Her claim was for £56,315, being the amount she had contributed, less what she had already recovered.

In fact the court went so far as to hold that if she had so claimed, she would have been entitled to more. It was held that the extension had enhanced the value of the property by £132,000, and the court expressed the view that she would have been entitled to the whole of this amount minus the £50,000 she had already recovered. This *obiter dictum* raises difficult questions. It does not seem to have a basis in *Shilliday*. If one divides the law of enrichment into the *condictiones*, a claim for the value of the extension could hardly be the *condictio causa data causa non secuta*, which was the basis of the pursuer's case. Moreover, what if the value of the extension had been less than her financial input? Would she be limited to the lower sum? The sheriff does not enter into these questions.[1] There is also the puzzle that, if we have understood the facts of the case correctly, the extension had not been erected solely at the pursuer's expense.

The third case is *McKenzie v Nutter*.[2] The parties bought a house in Quothquan for £105,000, taking title in joint names. The purchase was to be financed by both. But when one party was slow in coming up with her share of the money, which was to be obtained by the sale of another property, the other party contributed £76,000 from his own resources. The balance of £29,000 they contributed together, raising the money by means of a joint loan. But at this point the relationship ended, and in fact the first party never moved into the house. Instead she raised an action of division or sale. The question for the court was what should happen to the proceeds of sale, after the £29,000 (which was secured over the property) had been paid off. The defender argued that the pursuer had made no contribution and that he should receive the whole net proceeds of the sale. This argument was successful before the sheriff, and, on appeal, before the sheriff principal as well. The result seems reasonable, but the case leaves some loose ends. One of them is why it was taken as an enrichment rather than as a contract case.[3] The sheriff held that there had been an 'understanding between the parties that should things not

---

1 For the same issue, see *Moggach v Milne*, 22 October 2004, Elgin Sheriff Court, A451/01, discussed in *Conveyancing 2004* p 64.
2 2007 SLT (Sh Ct) 17, 2007 SCLR 115.
3 Another is why it was held that she made no financial contribution at all. She did: £14,500.

work out and the house required to be sold, each would recover proportionately what they put in'.[1] Perhaps that was regarded as too indefinite to be a contract.

What matters from the conveyancer's standpoint is not the law of enrichment but the sort of problem that the law of enrichment has to be employed to resolve. Cases like these arise only because the original transaction was not entered into on a proper contractual basis. In a marriage that does not matter so much, because the law of marriage[2] itself – which includes the law of divorce – will usually provide a solution if the relationship breaks down. But if there is no marriage, then there is no ready-made solution. Conveyancers who are involved in buying property for cohabitants should think about offering a co-purchase agreement.[3]

SERVITUDES

Servitudes 'for all necessary purposes'

In drafting servitudes it is possible to say too little. But it is also possible to say too much. The servitude under consideration in *Skiggs v Adam*[4] was an example of the latter. In that case a disposition recorded in 1979 granted a servitude in the following terms:

> a heritable and irredeemable servitude right of access to the subjects hereby disponed for all necessary purposes over the private roadway leading from Simpson Avenue, Tillicoultry and lying to the north of the subjects hereby disponed.

It is not clear why the words 'for all necessary purposes' were included. Possibly they were intended to facilitate the use of the servitude in the event of future development and subdivision of the dominant tenement – a common reason for adding words – but if so the words were not well-chosen.[5] There were two difficulties. First, the words were in danger of being so vague as to have no meaning at all. In that case they might invalidate the servitude. Secondly, and assuming a meaning could be found, that meaning might have the effect of restricting the servitude rather than – as was surely the intention – of extending it. Both difficulties were discussed in the case.

In relation to the first there was prior if *obiter* authority. In *Lord Burton v Anderson*,[6] Lord MacLean had said that:

> [I]f the access were to be used solely for 'all necessary purposes', one would be entitled to ask the question, 'Necessary for what?' The phrase would be so wide in its application as almost to be meaningless.

---

1 See paragraph 34 of the sheriff principal's opinion.
2 Or civil partnership.
3 For our suggestions about co-purchase agreements, including styles, see *Conveyancing 2004* pp 66-71. See also G Jamieson, *Family Law Agreements* (2005).
4 [2006] CSOH 73, 2006 GWD 17-352.
5 D J Cusine and R R M Paisley, *Servitudes and Rights of Way* (1998) para 14.51. By contrast, 'for all purposes' may have the effect of extending the servitude: see *Grant v Cameron* 1991 GWD 6-328.
6 1994 GWD 32-1918.

In *Skiggs*, however, Lady Clark was willing to accept that a meaning could be found. But that meaning – and this is the second difficulty – would be a restrictive one. In Lady Clark's view, the additional words meant that:[1]

> The servitude right of access does not automatically extend to all lawful purposes but is to be construed as covering all necessary purposes which may in this case be something less than all lawful purposes. To give a hypothetical example, if the dispute related to access to remove minerals from the dominant tenement, it might be claimed that this was not a necessary purpose if in fact no disposition of the mineral rights had been made.

No doubt that hypothetical example will not disturb many readers. But the principle which underlies it – that additional words can be read restrictively – should give pause for thought.

Prescriptive possession 'as of right'

A servitude is created by 'possession' – in effect by exercise – for the 20 years of positive prescription. But although the legislation does not say so,[2] the possession must be 'adverse' or, as it is sometimes expressed, 'as of right'. Possession which can be explained in some other way – possession by permission, by tolerance, or in the exercise of some *different* right (such as lease) – does not count for the purposes of prescription, however long it has continued in existence. The policy basis of this rule is notice. If possession is to be sufficient to create a new right, the owner of the land thus possessed must be in no doubt as to what is going on – and as to the legal consequences of allowing it to continue.

Decisions on adverse possession are few and far between. In 2006, however, there were two. Neither is satisfactory. In one, there was a finding for a prescriptive servitude where the possession was attributable to a different right altogether. In the other, a servitude was denied in circumstances where one might reasonably expect it to have been allowed.

Possession on a *different* right

The first case is *Aberdeen City Council v Wanchoo*.[3] Here the owner of a warehouse carried out substantial alterations so that lorries could be loaded and unloaded at a particular place. But this work presupposed that access could be taken over certain land belonging to the council, which the owner had been given to understand would be available. In the event the owner proceeded to take access for more than 20 years but without formal agreement.[4] When, subsequently, the access position was disputed, it was held that a servitude had been created by prescription.

---

1 Paragraph 10.
2 Prescription and Limitation (Scotland) Act 1973 s 3.
3 [2006] CSOH 196, 2007 SLT 289.
4 In fact the owner took a lease over the land in question; but as the use was restricted to car-parking, it was held that this had no bearing on the question of access.

The result in this case is of some interest and importance. Although there was no proper agreement, it was accepted that the council could not have prevented access, even at the time when it was first taken. This is because the council had led the owner to believe that access would be available, and on the basis of that belief the owner had spent significant sums of money. The council was therefore personally barred from refusing access. The difficulty, though, is that personal bar is personal to the person who is barred. There is no real right. So it seems that a servitude cannot be created by personal bar.[1] The right is therefore precarious: if, in the present case, the council had sold the land to someone else, the new owner would not have been bound to give access. The significance of the decision in *Wanchoo* is to present the hope of something better; for in the fullness of time a right which is born of personal bar may, after 20 years, mature into a fully-fledged servitude.

The idea is attractive. Nonetheless we do not think that it can be correct. In order to qualify for prescription, possession must be adverse or *as of right*. In *Wanchoo* that hurdle was surmounted by saying that the presence of personal bar gave the necessary 'right'. As Lord Glennie put it:[2]

> Clearly they [the owner of the warehouse] would not have carried out the considerable work in raising the roof of the garage building and installing the large double doors in the gable end of that building unless they had received an assurance that they could take access across the site. It matters not that the assurance or agreement in principle was not reduced to writing. It would have been sufficient to entitle Duthies [the owner] to succeed in a plea of personal bar in answer to any attempt by the council to prevent them using the access across the site. To that extent, it is clear that the access taken by Duthies was taken 'as of right' and not simply by tolerance on the part of the council.

But this mistakes the meaning of 'as of right'. It is not the case that possession which is not by tolerance is necessarily possession 'as of right' in the special sense meant here. To qualify as being as of right – to qualify, in other words, for the purposes of the acquisition of a servitude by prescription – the possession must be attributable *only to the alleged servitude* and not to some other cause.[3] Of course that other cause could be, and often is, tolerance on the part of the owner of the putative servient tenement. But it can also be the existence of some *other* right, such as lease or licence or, as in this case, a personal right founded on personal bar.[4] In other words, as the owner already had a right to possess, in a question with the council, possession based on that right could not be used to set up a different right, ie a right of servitude.

---

1 *Moncreiff v Jamieson* [2005] CSIH 14, 2005 SC 281, discussed in *Conveyancing 2005* pp 92–93.
2 Paragraph 24.
3 In fact, it appears that Lord Glennie accepted this point, but for some reason did not apply it to the facts in front of him. Thus at para 23 he records that counsel for the pursuer 'argued that the use of the site for access was not unequivocally referable to the right claimed; and, further, that the access across the site was not taken "as of right". In this case, and I suspect in many cases, these points merge into one'. We would agree that there is no real distinction between the two points. At the same time, it is clear that the possession was referable to the right constituted by personal bar, and hence *not* unequivocally referable to the right claimed.
4 *Houstoun v Barr* 1911 SC 134.

A good way of testing the argument is to consider the question of interruption. An important reason for insisting that possession be as of right is to alert the owner of the 'servient' tenement to the claim that is being made against him, and hence to allow the opportunity of blocking it by an interruption of the possession. But the council could not have interrupted access in the present case. It was personally barred. If, therefore, the decision is correct, the council would have had to sit helplessly by while, with the passing of the years, a servitude was constituted by prescription. We do not think that this is the law.

At root the confusion in *Wanchoo* is linguistic. If possession must be 'as of right' it is a natural mistake to suppose that any possession founded on a 'right' must qualify. That, however, is not the law. The best way to avoid the confusion is to drop the term.[1] An accepted alternative is to say that the possession must be 'adverse'. No one in *Wanchoo* could have supposed that the possession in that case would have qualified as adverse.

Disproving tolerance

The tale disclosed by *Neumann v Hutchinson*[2] was as unhappy as neighbour disputes usually are. The sheriff[3] captured the mood in his opening remarks:[4]

> Peaceable relations with neighbours extending even to friendships are part of the true assets which give quality of life. Because they have no cash value some will disregard them. That is their loss. Sadly in this case at the cost of probably irreparable damage to neighbour relations the Pursuer (and his wife) and the Defenders have a major dispute which is mostly about money in the value of their respective properties with or without a servitude right of access. It is to some extent for the Pursuer and his wife also about the quality of living in their house and using it as they have done ordinarily for many years. The parties were urged no doubt by others before me but certainly at the commencement of the Proof to contemplate even at that late stage mediation or some other compromise but declined that opportunity.

And so the proof went ahead. The result is a decision of some importance for practitioners.

The facts were these. Since 1976 the pursuer had owned a mid-terrace house, 146 Main Street, Callander, and more or less from the start he had taken access by car to the rear of the house by means of a private road and yard at one end of the terrace. The road and yard were part of what was originally a bus depot belonging to Walter Alexander & Son Ltd. The bus depot closed in 1992 and today, after one intermediate owner, it is a vehicle service and repair workshop known as MAC Burnside Garage and owned by the defenders.

---

1 Although the term is the subject of a vigorous defence in *McGregor v Crieff Co-operative Society Ltd* 1915 SC (HL) 93 at 103–104 *per* Lord Dunedin, 107 *per* Lord Sumner.
2 2006 GWD 28-628.
3 M P Anderson.
4 At p 10 of the transcript.

In 2004 the defenders applied for planning permission to build flats in the yard. Under the plans the area directly in front of the pursuer's access would be either garden ground or parking spaces. Either way access to the pursuer's property would cease to be possible from the yard. At about the same time the defenders began to park vehicles in the yard in such a way as to block the pursuer's access. The pursuer responded by raising this action, in which he sought to establish a servitude by prescription over the yard and to interdict the defenders from interfering with it.

After a proof the sheriff was satisfied that there had been possession for 20 years, and that its volume was sufficient for the purposes of prescription. Admittedly, the use in the early years – at which time the pursuer's property was tenanted – was limited to access for occasional deliveries and for visits by friends. But in later years possession was regular and sustained, with the pursuer adding hard standing (which encroached on the yard) in 1984, and building a carport ten years later. Whether that possession was 'adverse' or 'as of right' was, however, a different matter.

The opposite of adverse possession is possession which is consensual or based on some other right such as lease. And in determining whether possession is consensual, the key factor is the attitude, not of the possessor,[1] but of the owner of the land which is being possessed. The question to be answered is: did the owner give permission? If the answer is no, the possession is adverse and as of right. But if the answer is yes, the possession is attributed to that permission and cannot be used to set up a right against the owner.

The law, then, is reasonably clear. But in its application there are serious evidential difficulties. Where possession is begun on the basis of a putative servitude, it is possible to imagine a whole range of responses by the person who owns the land which is being possessed, including:

(i)   express permission for the possession, whether in writing or by word of mouth;
(ii) tolerance;
(iii) indifference;
(iv) intolerance;
(v)   active opposition.

In practice the extremes – (i) and (v) – are uncommon. Faced with possessory acts, the owner will generally do nothing and say nothing. He puts up with the intrusion but without saying why. How is such silence to be interpreted? Is it tolerance, in which case the possession is not as of right? Or is it intolerance, albeit unsupported by active interruption, in which case the possession, if it continues for 20 years, will result in a servitude? And what is the legal effect of indifference, perhaps the most common reaction of all? As *Neumann v Hutchison* shows, the way these questions are answered in practice depends crucially on the burden of proof.

---

1 The question of whether any significance attaches to the attitude of the possessor is discussed below, in the context of *Webster v Chadburn* 2003 GWD 18-562.

In *Neumann*, as so often, the evidence was equivocal and unsatisfactory.[1] Certainly there had been no words of express permission on the part of the owner of the yard, but equally – one isolated incident apart – there had been no active opposition. For as long as the yard was still a bus depot, the response of the bus drivers, and presumably of their employers, was one of indifference. On the evidence, the next person to own the yard – who also lived in the end-terrace house – was more obviously supportive of the access needs of his neighbour and at one stage even helped him to build the carport. The final owner, the defender, was initially indifferent and ultimately hostile. But none of the owners gave expression to their views.

In the light of this evidence the sheriff concluded that the defender had failed to show that the pursuer's possession was attributable to tolerance. But that, the sheriff said, was not enough for the pursuer to succeed, for in an earlier case, *Nationwide Building Society v Walter D Allan Ltd*,[2] Lady Smith had placed a heavy evidential burden on the pursuer:

> It is well established that it is for the party claiming the prescriptive acquisition of servitude to prove that the usage relied on occurred by means of assertion of right rather than by the tolerance or licence of the landowner. Further, if the approach of the Court of Appeal in England is to be followed, it seems that that party must exclude tolerance as an explanation of the use founded upon. If their use of the other party's land is as consistent with toleration or licence on the part of that landowner as it is with user as of right, that is not enough (*Patel & Ors v W H Smith (Eziot) Ltd* [[1987] 1 WLR 853]). Such an approach seems logical and would accord with the principle clearly recognised in Scots law to the effect that the use relied upon requires to be shown by the proprietor relying on it to have been as of right.

These *obiter* remarks, founded on English authority, went considerably beyond the (Scottish) authorities which are discussed in the succeeding paragraphs of Lady Smith's opinion.[3] Nonetheless they were adopted by the sheriff in *Neumann*. The result, as he acknowledged:[4]

> gives the Pursuer real difficulties. Can I be satisfied that tolerance is excluded? It does seem to me that the use of the land is as consistent with tolerance or licence ... as it is with assertion of an adverse right. On the approach of the Court of Appeal in England which Lady Smith approved as being logical and in accordance with Scots principles, the Pursuer fails. Let me explain further. The logic is in my view that no

---

1 Often but not always. For a case in which there was ample evidence, and in which burden of proof was therefore unimportant, see *Aberdeen City Council v Wanchoo* [2006] CSOH 196, discussed above.

2 2004 GWD 25-539 at para 31. See *Conveyancing 2004* pp 89–90.

3 *Grierson v School Board of Sandsting and Aithsting* (1882) 9 R 437; *McInroy v Duke of Athole* (1890) 17 R 456, (1891) 18 R (HL) 46; *McGregor v Crieff Co-operative Society Ltd* 1915 SC (HL) 93. Both the first (as she acknowledged) and the last of these contain passages which are incompatible with the view adopted by Lady Smith. In the other case, *McInroy*, the servitude was refused because there had been only minimal possession in a location so remote that the owner of the putative servient tenement was unlikely to have known of it. It seems worth adding that Lady Smith's statement (para 35), based on a passage by Lord Young in *Grierson* (at 442), that 'servitudes emanate from grants' was doubted by Lord Glennie in *Aberdeen City Council v Wanchoo* 2007 SLT 289 at para 31.

4 At p 89.

one should have an adverse right set up against them unless they are proved to have been agreeing to it.

Later he expanded on the question of onus:[1]

The Defenders have not made out their positive case for permission or tolerance but that doesn't get the Pursuer home. It is for the Pursuer to prove the negative in this case – ie to prove the use did not result from permission or tolerance.

Onus of proof, so often unimportant, becomes crucial in cases where evidence is scant; and in determining the nature of prescriptive possession, the evidence will often be scant indeed.

The established view on prescriptive possession – insofar as such a view can be said to exist – is that, if the pursuer establishes a sufficient volume of possession for 20 years, that possession is presumed to be as of right, and it is for the defender to show the contrary.[2] As Lord Sumner expressed the position in *McGregor v Crieff Co-operative Society Ltd*,[3] one of the cases relied on by Lady Smith:

Open unqualified user in ordinary course may well be deemed to be in fact adverse user as of right, and no more appears; but if the evidence suggests that it was after all due to tacit permission, the question must then be whether the user does, upon the whole case, establish the growing acquisition of a servitude right.

The words 'and no more appears' are important, suggesting that if the evidence is equivocal, the pursuer will win. The rule for public rights of way is the same and more clearly established by case law, although in *Nationwide Building Society* Lady Smith dismissed these cases as involving 'different considerations'.[4] *Neumann* turns the established rule on its head. The pursuer must prove not only possession but also an absence of tolerance. As the sheriff said, in the passage quoted above, he must 'prove the negative'. *Neumann* is an eloquent illustration of the consequences. The defender could not prove tolerance; but, equally, the pursuer could not prove its absence. The result of this impasse was defeat for the pursuer.

So what must a pursuer now prove if he is to succeed in establishing a servitude by prescription? Plainly, a history of intolerance or active opposition by the defender – categories (iv) and (v) above – would be sufficient. But that will be rare. In its absence, the pursuer's task, according to *Neumann*, is to show that the defender was 'allowing the Pursuer to go ahead asserting a right and building the prescriptive period'.[5] This is assent, not to the possession as such (for that

---

1 At p 91.
2 D J Cusine and R R M Paisley, *Servitudes and Rights of Way* (1998) pp 349–350: 'A practical difficulty arises where activity continues without any indication of the "servient" proprietor's attitude. He may simply do nothing. How can it be determined that the possession is "adverse" and "of right"? In such a case ... what matters is the volume of possession. Where the volume is reasonably substantial, taking account of the nature of the right claimed, this will be regarded as adverse and as the assertion of a right.'
3 1915 SC (HL) 93 at 108.
4 Paragraph 39.
5 At p 85. Likewise at p 89, in a passage already quoted: 'no one should have an adverse right set up against them unless they are proved to have been agreeing to it'.

would be tolerance) but to using the possession to establish an adverse right. In effect the defender must have been saying or implying to the pursuer something along the lines of: 'I'm quite content that you are building up a right against me. Only seven more years to go and we can open the champagne.' Unsurprisingly, such generous sentiments only rarely occur and can still more rarely be proved. They could not be proved in *Neumann*.

Neumann is persuasively argued. But it offers a view of the law which is neither founded on the authorities nor workable in practice. If the decision is followed, it will become much harder to establish a servitude by prescription. In our view, it should not be followed.

In one respect, however, the decision may ease the task of a pursuer. In a previous case, *Webster v Chadburn*,[1] the sheriff principal had seemed to impose as an additional requirement that, in the course of possessing, the pursuer must normally believe that he *already* had a right. Absent such a belief, the possession was not as of right and so could not found prescription. The sheriff in *Neumann* did not think that this was consistent with views expressed by Lord Sumner in *McGregor v Crieff Co-operative Society Ltd*.[2] We would agree. As the sheriff put it, 'as of right' in this context really means 'as if having a right'.[3]

Extinction by prescription: *res merae facultatis*

Just as servitudes are born, so do they die. Twenty years' exercise creates a servitude, but twenty years' non-exercise leads to its extinction.[4] And in principle negative prescription is universal, that is to say, it operates on any servitude without regard to how that servitude was originally created. This, of course, is familiar law; but in recent years it has become apparent that it may be subject to exceptions.

In *Bowers v Kennedy*[5] it was held by the First Division that, where property is otherwise landlocked, a right of access is not lost by prescription, at least provided that the access is exercisable over other land from which the property was originally broken off. Strictly, this is not an exception at all: in *Bowers* the original servitude was indeed lost by prescription, but the court held that, following that loss, a new access right came into existence which was an incident of ownership and so not itself subject to prescription.[6] In *Bowers* the immunity from prescription thus affected, not the servitude, but the right which had come into existence in its place.

A new case, *Peart v Legge*,[7] identifies a genuine exception. And just as in *Bowers* the result was achieved by excavating old law (in that case the institutional

---

1 2003 GWD 18-562, discussed in *Conveyancing 2003* pp 65–68.
2 1915 SC (HL) 93 at 108.
3 At p 97.
4 Prescription and Limitation (Scotland) Act 1973 s 8.
5 2000 SC 555. See *Conveyancing 2000* pp 52–54.
6 For ownership of land is imprescriptible: see PL(S)A 1973 sch 3 para (a).
7 2006 GWD 18-377 affd 2007 SCLR 86. For a discussion, see R R M Paisley, 'Right to make roads and *res merae facultatis*' (2007) 11 *Edinburgh Law Review* 95.

writers), so in *Peart* the decision turned on a decision of 1884, *Smith v Stewart*,[1] which had rather been forgotten.

The starting point, however, is with the Prescription Act itself. Schedule 3 to that Act lists a small number of rights and obligations which are exempt from prescription, and at para (c) one finds 'any right exercisable as a *res merae facultatis*'. The lapse into Latin is both unusual[2] and also instructive. On the one hand, rights *res merae facultatis* were exempt from prescription under the law which the 1973 Act replaced. On the other hand, no one was – or is – sure what, precisely, is encompassed within the term. Leaving the term untranslated was thus a convenient way of leaving the law unchanged without confronting the problem of what that law actually was.

In his important book on *Prescription and Limitation* (1999), David Johnston QC gives a detailed analysis of the authorities on rights *res merae facultatis* before concluding that:[3]

> a *res merae facultatis* is a property right which cannot be lost by negative prescription either (1) because it is a right whose exercise implies no claim on anyone else or against their rights or (2) because it is a (normal) incident of ownership which can be lost only as a consequence of the fortification in some other person of a right inconsistent with it.

A servitude does not fall into either of these categories.

Now to the case itself. *Peart v Legge* concerned land at Newbattle in Midlothian. By a disposition recorded in 1981 the Marquis of Lothian conveyed a plot of land together with

> a right of access to said piece of ground by the lane or track leading from the Eskbank/ Newtongrange road to the northwest side of the said piece of ground as the same is shown coloured blue on said plan but subject to the provisions that the disponee shall be entitled to breach the existing wall on the northwest boundary of the said piece of ground only subject to the approval of me and my successors as adjoining proprietors of making good the wall where necessary and inserting gates or doors of a form and type satisfactory to me or my foresaids all of which and the maintenance of the said[4] shall be done at the sole expense of the disponee and his foresaids.

Subsequently this plot came to belong to the defender. By a disposition recorded in 1997 the Marquis of Lothian disponed a different plot to the pursuers. Included in that plot was the lane over which access rights had been created in 1981. As the 1981 deed implies, the defender's plot was separated from the lane by a wall so that the lane could not be used for access unless or until a gap in the wall had been created. No gap was made, and the right over the lane went unexercised for

---

1 (1884) 11 R 921.
2 Though not unique. The very next paragraph in schedule 3 refers to 'any right to recover property *extra commercium*'. Perhaps the draftsman had a classical bent. Another familiar phrase is *pari passu*: see eg Conveyancing and Feudal Reform (Scotland) Act 1970 s 27(1)(c).
3 Paragraph 3.16.
4 There is a word missing here, at least in the transcription in the sheriff principal's opinion.

a period which exceeded 20 years. In these circumstances the pursuers sought a declarator that the servitude over the lane had been extinguished by negative prescription.

The difficulty facing the pursuers was the decision of the First Division in *Smith v Stewart*.[1] Insofar as this case had not been forgotten about altogether, it was usually thought of as having been wrongly decided or, to say the same thing more politely, special on its facts. Rankine, for example, describes *Smith* as 'a narrow case',[2] while Johnston states bluntly that servitudes 'clearly prescribe and so cannot be *res merae facultatis*, although sometimes the borderline between a servitude right and a right *res merae facultatis* may be difficult to draw'.[3] Johnston adds, in a footnote, that *Smith* is 'better regarded as a servitude since it relates to another's property', thus implying that the case is mis-classified and wrongly decided.

But if *Smith* was special on its facts, it was the misfortune of the pursuers in *Peart v Legge* that the facts were almost identical to those in *Peart*. And as a decision of the First Division, *Smith* was binding on the court. Thus it was held both by the sheriff and, on appeal, by the sheriff principal that the access right was *res merae facultatis* and so had not prescribed. The view of the sheriff principal,[4] reached 'not without hesitation',[5] was that, following *Smith*:[6]

> it cannot therefore be said that *res merae facultatis* can be confined to rights which arise as incidents of ownership. In my judgment the term must be said to cover a category of servitude, created by express grant, which is not intended to be exercised until the occurrence of a particular event over which only the owner of the dominant tenement has control.

We understand that there is to be a further appeal, and it may be that the Inner House will decide that *Smith* should be overruled.[7]

Peart v Legge is an important decision. It revives a case which was widely thought to be of little authority; and it expands that unsatisfactory case into a general rule, namely that a servitude is exempt from prescription where it is not intended to be exercised until the occurrence of an event over which the dominant owner has control. In Victorian times there was sheriff court authority for applying the doctrine of *res merae facultatis* to servitudes involving the making of a road on the servient tenement,[8] and in the light of *Peart* these now appear as particular examples of a more general rule. A common, and it may be a defining, feature is that in all cases decided so far, including *Smith* and *Peart*, the delaying event has been the need to perform some building work before it was physically possible

---

1 (1884) 11 R 921.
2 J Rankine, *Landownership* (4th edn 1909) p 440.
3 D Johnston, *Prescription and Limitation* (1999) para 3.18(3).
4 Edward F Bowen QC.
5 Paragraph 21.
6 Paragraph 20.
7 But in that case it will be necessary to convene a larger court.
8 *Mitchell v Brown* (1888) 5 Sh Ct Rep 9; *Crumley v Lawson* (1892) 8 Sh Ct Rep 307.

to exercise the servitude – to construct a road, for example, or to demolish a wall. Whether the rule is wider than this is, at the moment, impossible to say.

There is no ready justification for exempting a servitude from prescription merely on the ground that the dominant owner must first carry out some work. Nonetheless, the decision in *Peart* is likely to be welcome to developers who, faced with planning or other delays, or simply not wishing to proceed to immediate development, can have the assurance that the servitude, if appropriately worded, is likely to qualify as *res merae facultatis* and so not be at risk of loss by prescription. Conversely, it will be less welcome to those whose property is affected by the servitude.

The rule, however, has its limits. It applies, probably, where the exercise of a servitude is triggered by some building activity on the part of the dominant owner – at least where that activity is provided for expressly in the grant. But it probably does not apply to other trigger events. For example, it would not apply to a servitude granted now but expressed to be exercisable only from 1 January 2017.[1] Admittedly, it is arguable that there is still a suspension of prescription. The legal basis, however, would not be *res merae facultatis* but rather the fact that, under the statute, prescription starts to run only from the point when the servitude 'has become exercisable or enforceable'.[2] Even if prescription could be evaded in this way, however, it is less clear that the dominant owner would have an immediate real right which could be pled against successors.[3] Thus a right which survived prescription might turn out to be lost by transfer of the servient tenement.

BANKRUPTCY AND DILIGENCE (SCOTLAND) ACT 2007

The Bankruptcy and Diligence (Scotland) Act 2007 (asp 3) is a blockbuster, with more than 200 sections. Only parts are of interest to conveyancers, but even those parts are so extensive that here we can only discuss them in outline. The Act is not yet in force[4] and we have no information as to commencement dates.

As affecting conveyancers, the Act's provisions come under four main heads:

- bankruptcy law
- abolition of adjudication and its replacement by land attachment

---

1 Such an event is not, of course, within the control of the dominant owner, as the sheriff principal requires.
2 PL(S)A 1973 s 8(1). So the servitude would not be extinguished until 1 January 2037.
3 R R M Paisley, 'Right to make roads and *res merae facultatis*' (2007) 11 *Edinburgh Law Review* 95 at 98. See *Millar v McRobbie* 1949 SC 1. It can, however, be strongly argued that the effect of registration is to create an immediate real right notwithstanding that exercise of the servitude is suspended: see Land Registration (Scotland) Act 1979 s 3(4). Indeed, *Peart v Legge* – which involved successors – would be authority for that view if (i) only the right to breach the wall (and not the servitude) had been *res merae facultatis* with the result that (ii) the servitude was suspended. But the sheriff principal (paras 18-20) regarded the servitude itself as *res merae facultatis*.
4 Other than s 222, which allows the registration in the Books of Council and Session and sheriff court books of an office copy of electronic standard securities. See s 227.

- law of inhibition
- floating charges[1]

As will be seen, several provisions have been deliberately crafted with the needs of conveyancing practice in mind. For example, there is more than one provision ensuring that a good faith buyer is protected in circumstances where under current law there is no protection.

Bankruptcy law

Shortening of standard discharge period

The normal period for automatic discharge from sequestration is reduced from three years to one.[2] This change, and certain others connected with bankruptcy, track recent changes south of the border.

Protection to purchasers against the seller's sequestration

Following *Sharp v Thomson*,[3] the Justice Department asked the Scottish Law Commission to examine the law and make recommendations. In 2001 the Commission published a discussion paper on the issue.[4] Subsequent developments, including the decision of the House of Lords in *Burnett's Tr v Grainger*,[5] superseded some of the Commission's proposals, but proposal 4 has now been implemented by the 2007 Act.[6] This is aimed at protecting good faith buyers who act with reasonable diligence. There are two aspects to this protection. The first is that in the 'race to the register' the trustee in sequestration has a handicap of 28 days. The second concerns the rule that a post-sequestration dealing by the debtor is void, unless consented to by the trustee.[7] Under current law there are certain exceptions, and the 2007 Act adds another. If a person who has been sequestrated grants a disposition (or other deed) to a good faith grantee, the sequestration does not invalidate that deed, provided that it is delivered not later than seven days after the sequestration has been registered in the Register of Inhibitions.

What are the practical implications? Suppose that you are acting for a buyer. On Tuesday you know that the Register of Inhibitions showed no entry against the seller. On Friday you settle the transaction, and your client gets a registration date from the Keeper three weeks later, after you have won your battle with HM Revenue & Customs over SDLT. Is your client safe from the possible sequestration of the seller? The answer is affirmative. Take two examples:

---

1 For floating charges, see p 139.
2 Bankruptcy and Diligence (Scotland) Act 2007 s 1, amending the Bankruptcy (Scotland) Act 1985 s 54.
3 1997 SC (HL) 66.
4 Scottish Law Commission, Discussion Paper on *Sharp v Thomson* (Scot Law Com DP No 114 (2001); available on www.scotlawcom.gov.uk).
5 2004 SC (HL) 19.
6 Bankruptcy and Diligence (Scotland) Act 2007 s 17, amending the Bankruptcy (Scotland) Act 1985 ss 31 and 32.
7 Bankruptcy (Scotland) Act 1985 s 32(8).

(1) Suppose that the seller was sequestrated on the Monday, with the entry in the Register of Inhibitions being made on the Thursday, ie the eve of settlement. The disposition is in principle void (because granted by a bankrupt after the date of sequestration). But the 2007 Act protects the buyer, assuming that he was in good faith, because the disposition was delivered within seven days of the entry in the Register of Inhibitions.

(2) Suppose that the seller's trustee in sequestration decides to complete title in his own name, ie to race your client to the Register. This could happen regardless of whether the disposition was delivered before or after the date of sequestration. The trustee will in future have a 28-day handicap. That period starts to run with the making of the relevant entry in the Register of Inhibitions. So long as your client applies for registration in the Land Register with reasonable speed, there should be nothing to fear.

Trust clauses and letters of obligation

These new provisions will not, alas, make letters of obligation altogether unnecessary. But, once they are in force, they will reduce the risks. As for trust clauses, our view is that (i) it is doubtful whether they work and (ii) if they do work they can cause dangers for the seller.[1] Whatever view is taken, the 2007 Act reduces the need (if there is a need) for such clauses. As will be seen below, the 2007 Act also has new protections for a buyer against the danger of diligence, so the overall picture is considerably brighter. And with the advent of ARTL there will be a further decline in the role of the letter of obligation and in the (alleged) need for trust clauses.

Debtor's home

If the trustee has done nothing with the family home within three years, it ceases to be part of the sequestrated estate.[2] Various steps can be taken by the trustee which will prevent this outcome, including sale, and also completing title in his own name. Incidentally, the older practice was that trustees would not often complete a title in their own name. Nowadays that is not uncommon.

Land attachment

A judicial heritable security, like adjudication

Under current law the attachment of land is done – if indeed it is done at all – by means of adjudication. The 2007 Act, when the relevant provisions come into force, will abolish adjudication and replace it with 'land attachment'. The Act implements, with some changes, recommendations made by the Scottish Law Commission in 2001.[3]

---

1 See *Conveyancing 2004* pp 79–85.
2 Bankruptcy and Diligence (Scotland) Act 2007 s 19.
3 Scottish Law Commission, Report on *Diligence* (Scot Law Com No 183 (2001); available on scotlawcom.gov.uk).

Land attachment is adjudication by another name (just as 'attachment' is poinding by another name).[1] In property law terms, the old law and the new law have a fundamental similarity. The creditor registers his right in the Land Register (or Sasine Register), and the result is to give him a type of subordinate real right,[2] a heritable security created by judicial authority rather than the voluntary act of the debtor. The major differences between old adjudication and new land attachment do not lie in the property basics, but in the procedural details.

Creation

A creditor who has obtained decree for payment for at least £3000, and who has served a charge to pay which has expired, can register a notice of land attachment. This must identify the land in question. A *pro indiviso* share can be attached.[3] In the case of residential property there are special protections, discussed below. The notice must be doubly registered: both (i) in the Land Register (or Sasine Register) and (ii) in the Register of Inhibitions. That having been done, the notice is then served on the debtor (and on any co-owner) by a 'judicial officer'.[4] The attachment takes effect 28 days after registration. That rule is to ensure that the new diligence does not cause problems for ordinary conveyancing practice. Take the example given earlier. Suppose that you are acting for a buyer. On Tuesday you know that the registers were clear. On Friday you settle the transaction, and your client gets a registration date from the Keeper three weeks later. Suppose that on the day before settlement, a land attachment was registered against the seller. It does not affect your client, because your client completed title less than 28 days later. On the date when your client completed title, the land attachment was not yet a real right.

Special rules for residential property

Whether residential property should be attachable was a matter of sharp political controversy. The Act as finally passed represents a compromise, but whether that compromise will prove a lasting one remains to be seen: s 92 allows for the possibility of a statutory instrument being made which would take residential property out of the Act altogether, while s 127 provides that 'the Scottish Ministers must, within 15 months of the commencement of this Chapter, prepare, publish and lay before the Scottish Parliament a statement setting out the impact of land attachment on debt recovery and homelessness'.

Section 98 provides that, in considering whether to grant a sale warrant for residential property, the court must have regard to these factors:

---

1 Debt Arrangement and Attachment (Scotland) Act 2002.
2 Bankruptcy and Diligence (Scotland) Act 2007 s 81(5): 'A land attachment confers on the creditor a subordinate real right.'
3 See in particular BAD(S)A 2007 s 102.
4 This is the new name the 2007 Act gives to those old friends, sheriff officers and messengers at arms.

(a) the nature of and reasons for the debt secured by the land attachment;
(b) the debtor's ability to pay ...;
(c) any action taken by the creditor to assist the debtor in paying that debt;
(d) the ability of those occupying the dwellinghouse as their sole or main residence to secure reasonable alternative accommodation.

Sale

If six months pass and the debt has still not been paid, the creditor may apply to the sheriff court for a warrant to sell.[1] The debtor can pay off the debt at any time until missives of sale have been concluded.[2] There are extensive procedural provisions which are far more complex than for adjudication and may deter creditors.

If warrant is granted – and the sheriff has a discretion to refuse it if it would be 'unduly harsh'[3] – the creditor can remove the debtor[4] and sell. Although the creditor is then in substantially the same position as a standard security holder in possession, the sale is not carried out by him but by a person appointed by the court, called 'the appointed person'.[5] This has to be a solicitor, who 'must act independently of the creditor'[6] and so presumably cannot be anyone in the law firm which is used by the creditor. How easy it will be to find persons willing to act remains to be seen. The sale can be done in the ordinary way or by roup. The Act does not say who signs the disposition,[7] but presumably the appointed person signs, and nothing else (apart from a witness) is needed. On sale, substantially the same rules apply as in the case of a sale by a standard security holder in respect of (i) disencumbering the property from other securities[8] and (ii) disbursing the proceeds of sale.[9] There is some post-sale procedure to be gone through,[10] but this does not affect the buyer.

To sell or not to sell

The procedure for sale is complex, and there is no guarantee that at the end of the day the court will grant the warrant. So some creditors may be deterred. There is the alternative of not seeking a sale warrant, but waiting instead. A land attachment is a heritable security. So suppose the debtor wishes to sell: in practice the buyer will insist that the land attachment be discharged. Or suppose

---

1 BAD(S)A 2007 s 92.
2 BAD(S)A 2007 s 121(3).
3 BAD(S)A 2007 s 97(3).
4 BAD(S)A 2007 ss 106 and 107.
5 BAD(S)A 2007 s 97(2).
6 BAD(S)A 2007 s 108 (1).
7 The Act says that the appointed person is to sell. A narrow reading would limit his power to concluding the contract of sale. But the absence of a provision for anyone else to sign the disposition strongly suggests that the appointed person has that power. It would be awkward if the debtor had to sign, or for the clerk of court to have to sign for him.
8 BAD(S)A 2007 s 112.
9 BAD(S)A 2007 s 116.
10 This procedure, together with parts of the pre-sale procedure, is to a considerable extent based on the equivalent procedure for poindings (attachments).

the debtor dies: again, it can be expected that the land attachment will be paid off. And so on. So the creditor who is prepared to be patient is likely to receive a cheque eventually.

Post-missives attachments

Section 91 provides:

> (1) This section applies where –
>   (a) a person has entered into a contract to purchase land from a debtor; and
>   (b) ownership has not been transferred to that person.
> (2) The person may, for the purpose of receiving intimation of any application ... for a warrant for sale of the land, register in the Register of Inhibitions a notice in ... the form prescribed by Act of Sederunt.

Such a person can lodge objections to the granting of a sale warrant.[1] Section 100 then provides that:

> The sheriff may, on the application of the prospective purchaser ... make an order –
> (a) suspending the warrant for sale for a period not exceeding 1 year from the day on which the order is made;
> (b) requiring the prospective purchaser to pay the price under the contract to the appointed person....

These provisions seem to have their origins in concerns expressed by the Law Society of Scotland.[2] However, the Society remains concerned that these provisions do not go far enough, because the sheriff only 'may' make such an order, rather than 'shall'.[3] An alternative view would be that these provisions are unnecessary. It is an implied term of a contract of sale of heritable property that encumbrances be discharged. That is as true of a land attachment as of a standard security. A buyer who sees that there is a land attachment will do precisely what he does when he sees that there is a standard security: insist on its discharge. This does not seem to raise any new points of conveyancing practice.

With standard securities there is always the danger of a new security granted on the eve of settlement. Conveyancing practice copes with that danger. It is not a danger that exists for land attachments, because they do not become real rights until four weeks after registration. Take two examples:

> (1) X is selling to Y. Z registers a land attachment against X on 1 May. Settlement of the sale is due on 3 May. Y may settle without knowing about the land attachment. But that does not matter. So long as Y completes title within 28 days from 1 May, he is safe.

---

1 BAD(S)A 2007 s 92.
2 See Scottish Law Commission, Report on *Diligence* (Scot Law Com No 181 (2001); available on www.scotlawcom.gov.uk) paras 3.15 and 3.130–3.132.
3 See D B Reid, 'Land attachment and suspensive missives' (2006) 51 *Journal of the Law Society of Scotland* Aug/54.

(2) The same, but settlement happens on 30 May, by which time the land attachment has become a real right. Again, Y should be safe, because by 30 May he can hardly fail to be aware of the existence of the land attachment.

Of course, the concern may not be so much that the buyer (Y) runs actual risks, but rather that if there is a land attachment against the seller, and if the seller would be unable to pay off the attaching creditor out of the proceeds of sale (ie negative equity), then the sale would abort, and that would be inconvenient for the buyer. Yet it is arguable that there is no significant problem here that needs to be solved. In the first place, the danger, such as it is, already exists where there is a negative-equity standard security. In the second place, if there is negative equity, a rational creditor (whether a standard security holder or a land attacher) will normally be happy to see the sale go ahead, because that is an easier and quicker way of being paid than enforcing the security. If there is negative equity it will not be full payment, but enforcing the security would not have that result either.

Inhibitions

The 2007 Act makes a large number of miscellaneous reforms to the law of inhibition, not all of which are of particular interest to conveyancers.[1] Some which are of interest are summarised here.

Name of register changed

The current official name is the 'Register of Inhibitions and Adjudications'. That is changed to the 'Register of Inhibitions'.

Acquirenda

At common law, inhibition affected not only such heritable property as the debtor had at the time, but also heritable property he might acquire after the inhibition (*acquirenda*). The rule was changed by s 157 of the Titles to Land Consolidation (Scotland) Act 1868: inhibition now has no effect against *acquirenda*. Thus if Tom inhibits Jane and later Jane acquires land, the inhibition has no effect against that land, and Jane is free to sell it or grant a heritable security over it. But uncertainty exists as to the moment when land is deemed to be 'acquired' for the purposes of s 157. Is it (i) when Jane concludes missives to buy, or (ii) when the disposition is delivered to her, or (iii) when she completes title? In *Leeds Permanent Building Society v Aitken, Malone and Mackay*[2] it was held (in the Outer House) that it is (ii). But there have always been doubts about the soundness of that decision, and the opportunity has been taken to make the law clear, the decision being in favour of (ii).[3]

1 Again these substantially implement recommendations of the Scottish Law Commission: see Report on *Diligence* (Scot Law Com No 183 (2001)).
2 1986 SLT 338.
3 BAD(S)A 2007 s 150 .

The good faith disponee

It is of the ABC of conveyancing practice that a buyer will check the Register of Inhibitions to see whether there is an entry against the seller. Very occasionally the result can be a false negative – ie it appears that there is no entry but in fact there is. In those circumstances the Act provides that a disponee who has acted in good faith and without negligence is protected.[1]

Prescription of inhibitions

Under current law an inhibition last five years. The Act does not change that. But it resolves a doubt which exists in the current law about an inhibitor's right to challenge a breach of inhibition. Suppose that in year 0 W inhibits X. In year 4 X dispones to Y. That disposition is reducible. Does W's right to reduce it come to an end (i) when the inhibition comes to an end, ie in year 5, or (ii) in year 20, ie 20 years after the breach? The Act provides that (ii) is the answer.[2] This means that the search period of five years which is stated in form 10 and form 12 is, strictly speaking, not adequate. Thus suppose that in year 10 Y sells to Z. A search is done backwards for five years. This will not disclose the inhibition. And yet the inhibition is still live.

Inhibitions and the Land Register

Under current law there exist some difficulties with what the Land Registration (Scotland) Act 1979 says about how the Keeper is to deal with inhibitions.[3] Section 167 of the 2007 Act amends the 1979 Act by adding to s 6 a new subsection (1A):

> The Keeper shall enter an inhibition registered in the Register of Inhibitions in the title sheet only when completing registration of an interest in land where the interest has been transferred or created in breach of the inhibition.

This is a welcome improvement.

COMPANY SECURITY RIGHTS

The Bankruptcy and Diligence (Scotland) Act 2007 makes changes to the law of floating charges. It also consolidates it, for it repeals the whole of Part XVIII of the Companies Act 1985.[4] The changes implement, with modifications, proposals put forward by the Scottish Law Commission in 2004.[5] In addition, the Companies

---

1 BAD(S)A 2007 s 159. For the current law see *Atlas Appointments Ltd v Tinsley* 1997 SC 200.
2 BAD(S)A 2007 s 161. For the current law see G L Gretton, *Law of Inhibition and Adjudication* (2nd edn 1996) pp 67–69.
3 See Scottish Law Commission, Discussion Paper on *Land Registration: Miscellaneous Issues* (Scot Law Com DP No 130 (2005); available on www.scotlawcom.gov.uk) part 8.
4 The Companies Act 2006 prospectively repeals the Companies Act 1985 but leaves Part XVIII untouched, on the basis that the Scottish Parliament would be dealing with it.
5 Scottish Law Commission, Report on *Registration of Rights in Security by Companies* (Scot Law Com No 197 (2004); available on www.scotlawcom.gov.uk).

Act 2006 makes important changes to the law about the registration of company security rights, notably floating charges and standard securities.

An end to dual registration

The current law is that a security right granted by a company must be registered in the Companies Register within 21 days of its creation.[1] Thus a standard security must be registered twice: first in the Land Register (or Sasine Register) and again in the Companies Register. A floating charge is created without registration, but still needs to be registered in the Companies Register within 21 days of its creation. Section 893 of the Companies Act 2006 will change all this. It provides that if a security right granted by a company is registered in what it calls a 'special register' (such as the Land Register) then a second registration in the Companies Register is unnecessary. What will happen is that the registrar of the special register (eg the Keeper in respect of standard securities) will send information about the security to the Registrar of Companies, who will enter it in the Companies Register. Thus anyone inspecting the latter will continue to find the information that they find at the moment. But the process will be internal to the civil service. The parties to the security – the creditor and the debtor – will need to concern themselves only with one registration. Section 893 will come into operation only as and when orders are made under it. These will specify particular 'special registers'. Thus the first order could (for example) specify the Land Register but not the Shipping Register, or vice versa.

Register of Floating Charges

As just mentioned, floating charges are created without registration. That will change. The Bankruptcy and Diligence (Scotland) Act 2007 sets up a new Register of Floating Charges, to be kept by the Keeper (not by the Registrar of Companies). Once the relevant provisions are in force, a floating charge will be created by registration in the new Register. If these provisions were to be brought into force immediately, the result would be a requirement of dual registration (as for standard securities). But it is understood that that is not what will happen. Rather the Register of Floating Charges will be activated in synchronisation with a s 893 order. As a result, a floating charge will have to be registered only once, in the new Register.

When a security right is registered in the Companies Register, what is registered is not the deed itself but only selected 'particulars'.[2] This can cause various problems in connection with floating charges, which are not registered in any other register.[3] In the Register of Floating Charges the whole deed will be registered.[4] In practice parties will, no doubt, use short floating charges, rather

---

1 Companies Act 1985 s 410.
2 Companies Act 1985 s 410(2).
3 Though they can of course be registered in the Books of Council and Session. This is sometimes done.
4 Bankruptcy and Diligence (Scotland) Act 2007 s 38(3).

like form B standard securities, in which the loan contract is contained in separate documentation.

Creation and ranking

Another change concerns the date of creation. Under current law a floating charge is created without registration but has to be registered within 21 days,[1] although this period can be, and often is, extended by the court.[2] This was widely regarded as unacceptable, and in the new law a floating charge is created on registration, not before.[3] There will be no deadline for registration. For instance, a floating charge could be delivered in February but not registered until November.[4]

Suppose a company grants a floating charge to X and later a standard security to Y. Under current law,[5] the standard security, though later, will rank before the floating charge. But, says current law, the floating charge can contain a special clause that will prevent that result.[6] Unsurprisingly, almost all floating charges contain such a clause. The 2007 Act now says that a floating charge ranks ahead of a subsequent standard security (unless otherwise agreed).[7] Hence these special ranking clauses will no longer be necessary.

Floating charges by English companies

Under current law, if an English company grants a floating charge, the charge is fully effectual against assets in Scotland so long as it has been duly registered in England and Wales. The 2007 Act changes this rule, but only partially: for full effectiveness against Scottish assets, the charge must be registered in the Register of Floating Charges. The Act does not say this in terms, but it is implicit in its unqualified statement that a floating charge must be registered in the Register of Floating Charges.[8] The subject is a large and complex one, but two examples may be offered which give an indication of how the law will probably look in the future.

> *Example (i).* In 2011 an English company, ABC Ltd, grants a floating charge to Bank DEF plc. The charge is validly created in England but is not registered in Scotland. ABC Ltd goes into liquidation. ABC Ltd owns heritable property in Scotland. The liquidator can sell the property, because Scots private international law recognises the power of an English liquidator to realise assets in Scotland. English law will then direct the liquidator to apply the proceeds as if the charge extended to the property.[9]

---

1 Companies Act 1985 s 410.
2 Companies Act 1985 s 420.
3 Bankruptcy and Diligence (Scotland) Act 2007 s 38(3).
4 What has just been said presupposes that a s 893 order will be made for the Register of Floating Charges.
5 Companies Act 1985 s 464, a section of considerable complexity and obscurity.
6 Companies Act 1985 s 464(1).
7 Bankruptcy and Diligence (Scotland) Act 2007 ss 40 and 41.
8 For discussion see Scottish Law Commission, Report on *Registration of Rights in Security by Companies* (Scot Law Com No 197 (2004)) paras 5.8 ff.
9 See *Re Anchor Lines* [1937] Ch 483, still a leading case. On this whole area of law see C Bispeng, 'The classification of floating charges in international private law' 2002 *Juridical Review* 195.

Example (ii). The same example, except that after granting the floating charge, ABC Ltd granted a standard security to Bank GHI plc. This standard security was duly registered in the Land Register. Although the liquidator can still sell the property, he cannot do so free of the standard security. Because the floating charge was never registered in Scotland, the standard security ranks (according to internal Scots law) as if the prior floating charge did not exist. So although the standard security is later than the floating charge, it ranks first. Thus the floating charge suffers from the fact that it was not registered in Scotland.

Will English floating charges be registered in Scotland in practice? That depends. If the company has no Scottish assets and is unlikely to acquire them, such registration would be a waste of time and money. But if circumstances change, and the company acquires Scottish assets, registration in Edinburgh can be effected at that stage, because there is no deadline for registration in the Register of Floating Charges.

WARRANDICE

What price car-parking? £31,000 for a space in Edinburgh's West End, according to evidence led in *Holms v Ashford Estates Ltd.*[1]

The facts in *Holms* were these. The defender converted a former office at 24 Manor Place, Edinburgh into five flats. In 1999 one of those flats was sold to the pursuers. In terms of the disposition there were conveyed to the pursuers (i) the flat itself (ii) car parking space number 42 at the rear of the building, and (iii) a servitude right of access for pedestrian and vehicular traffic over a lane, called Bishops Lane, which led from Manor Place to the car parking area, and also over the car parking area itself. It seems that by 'car parking area' was meant not only the unallocated part which was needed for access but also the individual parking spaces themselves. The development as a whole was subject to a deed of conditions which reserved

> to the proprietors having an interest in the car parking area ... all necessary rights of access and egress to and from the car parking area for all necessary purposes whenever reasonably required.

At the time of purchase, the pursuers were under the impression that there were only to be three car parking spaces at the rear of the building (numbers 40, 41 and 42). However, in addition to these three spaces, which were in a row, the defender added a fourth (number 43) which was at right angles to number 42 and separated from it by a small unallocated area. Evidence given at the proof showed that, when spaces 41 and 43 were being used, it was still possible to park a Smart Car in space 42. Unfortunately, the pursuers owned a Mercedes estate. In effect, therefore, their parking space was unusable.

---

1 2006 SLT (Sh Ct) 70 affd 2006 SLT (Sh Ct) 161.

Quid juris? The obvious route might have been to explore a case based on misrepresentation. Instead the pursuers sued in warrandice. In order to reach space 42, they said, they needed access over space 43. Such access had been granted by the servitude which was included in their disposition (and the deed of conditions), and that grant was underwritten by the disposition's warrandice clause. But the servitude was excluded by the competing title to space 43, which was held by the owner of one of the other flats at 24 Manor Place. As a result, space 42 could not be used, and damages were due.

A difficulty facing claims in warrandice is the need, in most cases at least, to show 'eviction'.[1] For far from being an absolute guarantee of title, warrandice merely guarantees that the property will not be taken away from the grantee/purchaser by eviction. Eviction has two elements, both of which must be present. In the first place, a rival title must exist in the hands of a third party which is sufficient to exclude the title granted to the purchaser. And in the second place, the third party must actually assert that title against the purchaser. In the absence of such assertion, no warrandice claim can arise – a long-established rule which was confirmed and applied by the First Division in the leading case of *Clark v Lindale Homes Ltd*.[2]

What kind of assertion counts as eviction? That issue was discussed in some detail in *Clark*. The case, however, must be read with some care because, for most of his opinion, Lord President Hope advanced a view which he proceeded to discard in the final page,[3] and it is only in Lord Morison's judgment – with which Lord Hope ultimately agreed[4] – that the discussion can be regarded as authoritative.

Warrandice is a doctrine of the civil law. Lord Morison's starting point was with the French eighteenth-century jurist, Robert Pothier. In his *Contract of Sale*,[5] Pothier wrote that:

> The term eviction is applicable, strictly speaking, to those cases only in which the buyer is deprived of the thing sold by a sentence. It is used, however, though in a sense less proper, to include cases in which the buyer is deprived, without any sentence, of the power to retain the thing, in virtue of sale.

In other words, although eviction normally meant that the third party must raise an action against the purchaser and proceed to decree, it was also possible to have eviction without court process. Stair, too, recognised the possibility of extra-judicial eviction, but added the rider that the third party's claim must be based on 'an unquestionable ground'.[6] The idea, presumably, was to avoid unnecessary litigation. On the basis of these and other authorities, Lord Morison summarised the law in the following words:[7]

---

1 K G C Reid, *Law of Property in Scotland* (1996) para 707.
2 1994 SC 210.
3 The discarded view came close to saying that eviction was *not* required and that a remedy in warrandice was available merely on the ground that the purchaser's title was defective.
4 See p 220.
5 R Pothier, *Contract of Sale* (transl L S Cushing 1839) para 86.
6 Stair II.3.46.
7 At p 224.

It is of course obvious that 'eviction' does not mean physical removal. But it is in my view equally clear on these authorities … that it does involve the emergence of a real or threatened burden on the property. The word itself in any event clearly indicates this to be the case. If such a burden has been judicially established, the position is clear. If it has not been judicially established, the warrandice clause may still be invoked if eviction in the strict sense is threatened, providing that the threat is based on an unquestionable right. Such a threat could only come as a result of a demand from the competing title-holder, for no one else has any right, let alone an unquestionable right, to make it.

In *Holms v Ashford Estates Ltd* the question of eviction was not always focused with ideal clarity, partly because there was a tendency to rely on parts of Lord Hope's judgment in *Clark v Lindale Homes* from which he later departed. There had, of course, been no judicial eviction, because the owner of space 43 had shown no interest in vindicating her rights in court. The case therefore turned on whether there was extra-judicial eviction. So far as we are aware, it is the first reported case to do so.

As Lord Morison said in the penultimate sentence of the passage just quoted, two requirements must be met if extra-judicial eviction is to be established: first, eviction in the strict sense must be threatened; and secondly, the threat must be based on an unquestionable right. In *Holms* it was touch-and-go as to whether these requirements could be met, and the case could indeed have been decided either way.

Both requirements caused difficulty. It is not clear on the evidence whether the owner of space 43 could be said to have threatened eviction in the strict (ie judicial) sense. Certainly she parked her car in her space and allowed others to do so, and so in that sense asserted her right of ownership. But there was no overt challenge to the pursuers' servitude, and even the parking was sporadic and infrequent. Nothing, however, was made in *Holms* of these shortcomings.

The second requirement was more obviously met. It is a principle of servitudes, now enshrined in statute,[1] that they must not be repugnant with ownership, ie so extensive in character as to leave nothing to the servient owner. In an earlier case, *Nationwide Building Society v Walter D Allan*,[2] Lady Smith had held that the right to park two cars in an area which could take only six was unduly burdensome and could not be created as a servitude. In the present case the supposed servitude was more intrusive still: a right of access at all times which, if insisted on, would prevent the owner of space 43 from using the space for parking or indeed for much else. That being the case, it seems clear that the servitude, insofar as it affected space 43, was void as repugnant with ownership, or in other words that, notwithstanding the terms of their disposition (and the deed of conditions), the pursuers had no right to take access over space 43.[3] And the defect in their title was plain and 'unquestionable'.[4]

---

1 Title Conditions (Scotland) Act 2003 s 76(2).
2 2004 GWD 25-539. See *Conveyancing 2004* pp 87–89.
3 There is, however, a possible argument that the servitude granted was only exercisable over those parts of the car-parking area which had not been individually allocated.
4 2006 SLT (Sh Ct) 161 at para 19 *per* Sheriff Principal E F Bowen QC: 'I accept the submission on behalf of the pursuers that imposition of the servitude upon Ms Mason would amount to eviction and would be regarded as unenforceable.'

In the event, both the sheriff and the sheriff principal found for the pursuers and awarded £15,000 in damages. And if the decision is short on legal analysis, it has the merit of reaching an apparently just result.

ARTL

ARTL stands for automated registration of title to land. On this matter Registers of Scotland have made impressive progress. By way of comparison, in England the legislative foundation for digital conveyancing was put in place by the Land Registration Act 2002, yet digital conveyancing has yet to arrive. The sun of digital conveyancing has risen across the horizon here first.[1] The basis for ARTL lies in a patchwork of provisions. They are:

- Automated Registration of Title to Land (Electronic Communications) (Scotland) Order 2006, SSI 2006/491
- Land Registration (Scotland) Rules 2006, SSI 2006/485[2]
- Bankruptcy and Diligence etc (Scotland) Act 2007 s 222
- Fees in the Registers of Scotland (Amendment) Order 2006, SSI 2006/600[3]
- Stamp Duty Land Tax (Electronic Communications) (Amendment) Regulations 2006, SI 2006/3427
- Solicitors (Scotland) (ARTL Mandates) Rules 2006[4]

And last but not least there are the Keeper's Terms and Conditions for access to the ARTL system.

Automated Registration of Title to Land (Electronic Communications) (Scotland) Order 2006

This Order is made under the Electronic Communications Act 2000, an Act which allows orders to be made amending primary legislation. It amends the Requirements of Writing (Scotland) Act 1995 so as to allow conveyancing documents within ARTL to be in digital form as an alternative to physical form. The new s 1(2A) of the 1995 Act says: 'An electronic document ... shall be valid for ... the creation, transfer, variation or extinction of a real right in land.' Then comes a new s 2A, which defines an 'electronic document' which is executed by a 'digital signature', and confers on the Keeper the power to issue 'directions' as to such documents. A new s 3A provides that such deeds are probative, ie raise a presumption of their own authenticity. Witnessing is unnecessary. The Order also

---

1 Within the UK. New Zealand and Ontario were there first, but Scotland may yet get the bronze medal in the English-speaking world.
2 Replacing the original Land Registration (Scotland) Rules 1980, SI 1980/1413.
3 For this, see p 67 above.
4 There was some chopping and changing between this title and 'the Solicitors (Scotland) (Automated Registration of Title to Land Mandates) Practice Rules 2006'. The shorter version seems to have prevailed.

amends the Land Registration (Scotland) Act 1979. Among other things, a new s 4(2A) of that Act makes it clear that ARTL can be used only for 'an authorised dealing'. That provides the basis for limiting ARTL applications to certain types of transaction.

Land Registration (Scotland) Rules 2006

The original Rules were the Land Registration (Scotland) Rules 1980, and they have remained in force until now, with only minor tinkering. The new Rules have been introduced because of the need to accommodate ARTL. They came into force on 22 January 2007.

On the whole, provisions unaffected by ARTL have been left alone. But one change worth noting which was not strictly necessitated by the introduction of ARTL is the abrogation of the rule that in an application for registration of a dealing it is necessary to submit the land certificate. That rule disappears, not only for ARTL cases but for all cases. Moreover, the Keeper has announced that, except for the first fortnight, he will not return any land certificates that are submitted to him with applications for dealings. At the same time the rule about substitute land certificates has been omitted from the new Rules. This is all part of a downgrading of the significance of land certificates. What matters, after all, is what the Land Register says. A land certificate is merely a certified snapshot of the Register on a particular day. Land certificates themselves will continue to exist, though applicants will have the choice between a physical certificate and a digital one in both ARTL and non-ARTL transactions.[1]

The forms have also changed, in respect of all Land Register applications. Matrimonial Homes Act documentation ('family homes' documentation for same-sex relationships) no longer has to be submitted. Instead, there is a 'TMDSM' question (TMDSM = 'tell me don't show me'). The applicant simply certifies the position to the Keeper. There is also a TMDSM question for the Register of Inhibitions. In form 1, the rather confusing questions about legal extent and occupational extent have been revised to make them clearer. In all forms there is now a box for the ingiver's email address. In some of the questions in some of the forms, the 'yes' and 'no' boxes have helpfully been joined by a third box, 'N/A'. There are numerous other changes, chiefly minor.

Letters of obligation normally refer to the numbered questions on the Keeper's forms. The Land Registration Rules 2006 mean that letters of obligation should be revised to take the new forms into account.

Digital signatures and Keeper's directions

The ARTL Order[2] provides for the Keeper to issue 'directions' specifying the requirements for digital signatures systems that will be acceptable for compliance

---

1 Form 8 (application to make a land certificate comply with the Register) is not included in the new Rules.
2 Ie the Automated Registration of Title to Land (Electronic Communications) (Scotland) Order 2006.

with the Requirements of Writing Act. At the time of writing the directions had not yet been issued. The Keeper is proposing to supply ARTL users with digital signatures in a PKI (Public Key Infrastructure) system specially commissioned for ARTL from Trustis Ltd.

Licensees, users, practice administrators and local registration authorities

To use ARTL it is necessary to be authorised by the Keeper.[1] Application forms can be found on the Keeper's website (www.ros.gov.uk), along with the terms and conditions. Those authorised to use ARTL will be 'licensees'. Licensees will be firms, rather than individuals, though of course a sole practitioner can be a licensee. Lending institutions can also be licensees. A licensee must have a 'practice administrator', who has the ability to set up other individuals in that firm/company as ARTL users. There must also be a 'local registration authority', who, despite the name, will be an individual within the firm/company who will be authorised by the Keeper to issue digital signatures to other individuals within that firm/company. The same individual can perform both practice administrator and local registration authority roles. 'Users' will be individuals who are authorised to operate the ARTL system. There will be different classes of user: a user without a digital signature will be able to carry out certain tasks but will not be able to execute deeds.

Solicitors (Scotland) (ARTL Mandates) Rules 2006

In practice few clients will have their own digital signatures, and deeds will have to be executed on clients' behalf. The authorisation from the client is known as the mandate. The Keeper does not need to see a copy of this. But he is prepared to accept mandates for preservation (by electronic scanning), and the new Law Society Rules (which came into force on 1 January 2007) require solicitors to send them to the Keeper: 'A solicitor shall, within 14 days of applying for registration in the Land Register within the ARTL System, send the principal of each mandate … to the Keeper for archiving and return to that solicitor.'[2] It is understood that the Law Society intends to publish suggested styles of mandate, but at the time of writing this had not yet happened.

A problem will arise when the granter of a deed is not legally represented. One possibility, of course, is for the transaction to proceed as a non-ARTL transaction. But the mass re-mortgage market is likely to shift to ARTL quickly. In such a case it is expected that the solicitors acting for the lender will have the borrower sign a mandate in their favour. Thus the standard security will be signed by the grantee's solicitor. It is understood that the Law Society considers this to be acceptable. It seems likely that the mandate style in such a case will be different from the style of mandate where the mandate is granted to the client's own solicitors.

---

1 Land Registration (Scotland) Rules 2006 r 10(1): 'An application for registration using the ARTL System may be made only by an authorised user.'
2 Rule 4.

Other provisions

Creditors sometimes wish to have standard securities registered for execution, but the Books of Council and Session can accept only physical deeds. Section 222 of the Bankruptcy and Diligence etc (Scotland) Act 2007 inserts a new s 6A into the Requirements of Writing (Scotland) Act 1995 which provides for the registration of an office copy of the electronic document. The provision came into force on 16 January 2007.[1] It brings about only a partial 'e-enablement' of the Books of Council and Session. Complete 'e-enablement' must await future legislation

The Stamp Duty Land Tax (Electronic Communications) (Amendment) Regulations 2006 enable the Keeper to collect SDLT on behalf of HMRC. They are made under the framework provisions of s 47 of the Finance (No 2) Act 2005.

Which transactions?

ARTL is not available for first registrations, or for any transaction in which Sections A or D of a title sheet would be altered. Thus it is not available for transfers of part, or for deeds in which new burdens or servitudes are created. It is available for such cases as (i) transfer from X to Y of the ownership of registered property, and (ii) the same, plus a discharge of the existing standard security and the creation of a new standard security by Y. Since most transactions do not affect Sections A or D, it follows that ARTL will be available for most transactions (other than first registrations and transfers of part). However, the Keeper has the power to limit ARTL further on a transitional basis. For example, he could, transitionally, decide that ARTL will be available only for properties in certain counties, or will be available only for Section C transactions, and so on. He has published on his website (www.ros.gov.uk/artl) a helpful list of the transaction types which are, and are not, ARTL-compatible, although this list will no doubt change over time.

Missives

It takes two to tango. ARTL requires both sides to co-operate. The Law Society's 'ARTL Practice Notes'[2] suggest this provision for offers:

> Provided the transaction is ARTL compatible, it will proceed under ARTL. Neither the purchaser's solicitor nor the seller's solicitor will withdraw from using ARTL during the progress of the transaction without reasonable cause and without reasonable prior notice to the other solicitor.

The Notes also say that 'in the absence of a provision in the missives there will be no obligation on either party to use ARTL', but nevertheless the recommendation is that, for the avoidance of confusion, if ARTL is not to be used then the missives

---

1 Bankruptcy and Diligence (Scotland) Act 2007 s 227(2).
2 In the 'ARTL' section of the Society's website (www.lawscot.org.uk/). The website also contains 'Guidelines on Operation of ARTL' and a useful opinion by Professor Robert Rennie which touches on a number of issues surrounding ARTL mandates.

should state this expressly, either in the offer (if the buyer's solicitors do not wish to use ARTL) or in the qualified acceptance (if the offer proposes ARTL but the seller's solicitors do not wish to use it).

COMPLETION OF TITLE AND NEGATIVE PRESCRIPTION

The story so far

We cannot do better, by way of introduction to the astonishing litigation of *Bain v Bain*,[1] than quote Lord Glennie:[2]

> The action concerns title to a property at 57 Main Street, Dreghorn … which was valued by the pursuer, when this action began in 1996, at something over £50,000. The pursuer is the father of the first defender and they have been fighting over the title to the subjects in a series of six actions since the mid 1970s. The present action, the latest of those six, has already been to the Inner House on three occasions. In an Opinion delivered in January 1994, in the third of the actions between the parties, Lord Maclean observed that this family battle between father and son bore some resemblance to a version of 'Bleak House'.[3] Events since then have done nothing to invalidate that comparison. However, there is one difference, which Dickens could not have anticipated: both the pursuer and the first defender are legally aided, and this family dispute is, therefore, in the first instance at least, being conducted at the public expense.

The story is a long one, even when stripped down to the essentials. John McMurtrie owned a house at 57 Main Street, Dreghorn. In 1910 he borrowed money, and granted to the creditor a bond and disposition in security over the house (ie the equivalent of a modern standard security). In 1947 the security was assigned to Robert Bain. Robert Bain took possession. He did so literally: he lived in the property as if it were his own, and still does so today. In 1941 John McMurtrie died, bequeathing his whole estate to his widow, Sarah McMurtrie. In 1951 she died, intestate. Her sole heir was her son Robert McMurtrie. Neither Sarah nor Robert took any steps to complete title to the property. Robert McMurtrie died intestate in 1971: his heirs were his two children, John and Mary McMurtrie. They too took no steps to make up title.

In 1970, the year before his death, Robert McMurtrie concluded missives to sell the property to Andrew Bain. This Andrew Bain was the son of Robert Bain. In 1976 the son obtained a decree for declarator and implement of the missives. But still having no completed title, in 1995 he raised another action to enforce

---

1 There have been various litigations between the Bains. 2006 produced two judgments in one of those litigations, both by Lord Glennie: see [2006] CSOH 142 and [2006] CSOH 189, 2007 GWD 6-84.

2 [2006] CSOH 142 at para 2.

3 For another endless battle, see *Sexton and Allan v Keeper of the Registers* 17 August 2006, Lands Tribunal, digested above as Case (48).

the missives. He obtained decree. This time he obtained a disposition in his favour, signed by the Deputy Clerk of Session; the disposition was recorded in the Register of Sasines.[1] But he still did not have possession: his father remained in possession.

Now back to the father. In 1986 he obtained a disposition of the house from John and Mary McMurtrie.[2] It appears, however, that this was not recorded and remains unrecorded to this day. In 1994 the son raised an action to reduce this disposition, and was successful. In 1996 the son raised an action to evict his father from the house. That action is, it seems, still continuing.

The position at the beginning of 2006 thus seems to have been as follows. The father was in possession. There was a disposition in his favour but it had never been recorded and had been reduced. The son had title completed in the Register of Sasines but was not in possession.

The current action

The current action, in which the father was the pursuer, had five conclusions, and they deserve to be reproduced in full, not least the fifth, which is for the reduction of a reduction:

1. For production and reduction of the pretended Missives between the late Robert McMurtrie and the first Defender dated 19 October 1970 to convey the subjects known as and forming 57 Main Street, Dreghorn to the first Defender.
2. For production and reduction of the pretended Decree of Implement of the said Missives pronounced and signed by the Honourable Lord Brand of 20 October 1976 and obtained at the instance of the first Defender against the second and third Defenders.
3. For production and reduction of the pretended Disposition granted by in favour [sic] of the first Defender recorded in the General Register of Sasines for the County of Ayr on 22 May 1996.
4. For production and reduction of the pretended decree of implement which decree was pronounced and signed on 26 April 1995.
5. For production and reduction of the pretended decree of reduction and interdict which decree was pronounced and signed by the Honourable Lord MacLean on 7 January 1994.

Does a personal right to land prescribe negatively?

The case raises many issues, but its core was the argument that any right Robert McMurtrie had to the property had prescribed 20 years after his father's death in 1941, so that by 1971, when he entered into missives of sale, his right had already disappeared. Everything following on from those missives, including the disposition, and three decrees, were also invalid. *Pettigrew v Harton*[3] was cited

---

1 We have some difficulty in imagining the terms of the clause of deduction of title contained in this disposition.
2 Here too it would be interesting to see the clause of deduction of title.
3 1956 SC 67.

as authority on the question of prescription. This argument was upheld and all five reductive conclusions were successful.[1]

With respect, we do not think that the argument should have succeeded. *Pettigrew* held that the right of a legatee to complete title was subject to the long negative prescription. If that is correct, then Sarah McMurtrie's right as legatee would indeed have prescribed negatively in 1961. But though Robert was his mother's heir, he did not need to trace his right to the property through his mother. For he was also, as we understand it, his father's heir. As such, his right was imprescriptible. To quote Millar: 'A *jus sanguinis* never prescribes. The person who is entitled to take up the heritable succession of a person deceased may do so at any time.'[2]

It is curious that there has been confusion on this matter. One of the cases relied upon by the Lord Ordinary was an unreported decision, *Redford v Smith*,[3] in which Lord Mackay of Drumadoon said:[4]

> In *Bain v Bain*,[5] the pursuer sought reduction of a disposition in favour of his father, the first defender. Amongst the issues that the Lord Ordinary, Lord MacLean, required to address were whether, prior to the coming into force of the 1973 Act, the right to be served as general heir to an ancestor and the right of an uninfeft proprietor to complete title were rights that could prescribe. In deciding the case in favour of the pursuer, Lord MacLean proceeded on the basis that such rights were imprescriptible. It is important to note, however, that his Opinion makes no reference to *Pettigrew v Harton*. That might suggest he was not referred to that authority. Moreover, later in 1994, when Lord MacLean came to decide *Porteous's Executors v Ferguson*,[6] his Opinion in that subsequent case made no mention of his earlier decision in *Bain v Bain*. In the latter case, applying the decision of the Second Division in *Pettigrew v Harton*, Lord MacLean proceeded on the basis that, prior to the coming into force of the provisions of the 1973 Act, the right of an uninfeft proprietor to complete title to heritable subjects had been extinguishable by operation of twenty years negative prescription. In these circumstances, counsel and I found those two decisions of Lord MacLean difficult to reconcile.

But the decisions of Lord MacLean are on different matters, and are both well founded on the authorities.

Finally, in arguing that the position taken by the pursuer in this litigation was unsound in law, we do not wish to imply that the defender's title was better than the pursuer's. The defender had, it is true, a disposition in his favour duly recorded in the Sasine Register. But whether it was a valid disposition is another question.

The nature of missives

Although the matter really ends there, the litigation raises a number of other issues of interest. Suppose that the pursuer had been right in saying that by 1970

---

1 The Lord Ordinary's decision to reduce three decrees raises procedural issues which cannot be entered into here.
2 J H Millar, *A Handbook of Prescription according to the Law of Scotland* (1893) p 87.
3 16 July 2002, Outer House.
4 Paragraph 17.
5 1994 GWD 7-410. This was an earlier stage in the *Bain* dispute.
6 1995 SLT 649.

Robert McMurtrie's right had prescribed. Would that have made any difference? We would suggest not, and that the action should still have failed. The pursuer's action was based on the theory that the 1970 missives were invalid on the ground that the seller's right had prescribed. But this is to misunderstand the nature of missives. Missives are a contract. They convey nothing. A seller with a bad title will have a problem implementing the missives, and the consequence may be liability in damages. But that does not mean that the contract is invalid.[1] Indeed, if the contract were invalid, the seller could never be in breach. The pursuer argued that 'the missives were invalid to pass any property to the first defender'.[2] But missives *never* pass any property. Missives are a contract whereby the seller undertakes that he *will* transfer ownership. The Lord Ordinary, however, seems to have taken the same view as the pursuer: 'Robert McMurtrie had no right of property with which to make a contract for sale to the first defender in 1970.'[3] But no right of property is needed to make a contract of sale. Nor is that all. Suppose that the missives had, after all, been invalid. It would still not follow that the disposition in favour of the defender fell to be reduced. A disposition does not stand on missives as a man stands on a ladder.[4] If missives are invalid, the disposition may be void, or it may be voidable, or it may be unimpeachable. All these are possible. To say that missives are invalid says nothing about the ensuing disposition.

Title to sue

Suppose that the missives were invalid. The pursuer had no right to reduce them: *res inter alios acta*. The same issue arises for the disposition. Even if the disposition was invalid, it is difficult to see what title Robert Bain would have had to reduce it. He was not the owner of the property.

Other arguments

Certain other arguments made by counsel call for comment. The Lord Ordinary, while recording them in his opinion, does not discuss them. It was argued for the pursuer that 'all personal rights ... were moveable property'.[5] With respect, this is not correct. The personal/real distinction is separate from the moveable/heritable distinction. Some personal rights are heritable property. The right of a purchaser under missives is an example. Equally, some real rights are moveable property, such as ownership of a moveable object.

---

1 This is trite law. For discussion see Mungo Brown, *A Treatise on the Law of Sale* (1821) p 111. Scotland follows Roman law on this matter: for the latter see D 18.1.28 (Ulpian). It is because this is the law that the Lands Tribunal does not hesitate to order local authorities to enter into missives to convey what they cannot convey, except with a third party's co-operation. For an example from 2006, see *Fletcher v South Lanarkshire Council* 2006 SLT (Lands Tr) 51, digested above as Case (52).
2 [2006] CSOH 142 at para 12.
3 [2006] CSOH 142 at para 14.
4 Stair II.3.14: 'we follow not that subtility of annulling deeds, because they are *sine causa* ... and therefore narratives expressing the cause of the disposition, are never inquired into, because, though there were no cause, the disposition is good....'
5 [2006] CSOH 142 at para 12.

Next, it was argued for the pursuer that 'any interest in heritage that is not recorded is a personal right'.[1] In fact there are many real rights in land that are outside the Land Register or Sasine Register. These are the rights that the Land Registration (Scotland) Act 1979 characterises as 'overriding interests'.[2]

Then it was argued for the defender that as a result of *Sharp v Thomson*[3] 'the law now recognised something in between a personal right on the one hand and a right of infeftment on the other'. We cannot agree: as Lord Hodge expressed the position in another 2006 case, *3052775 Nova Scotia Ltd v Henderson*,[4] 'Scots law does not recognise a right that lies between a real right and a personal right'.

Old law, new law

Pettigrew v Harton[5] held that the right of a legatee prescribes negatively. Is that still good law?[6] Might it mean, for example, that a person who holds on a docket transfer but does not complete title for 20 years has lost her right? What about a disposition that has not been recorded or registered for 20 years? There are some difficult issues here. But it seems that the effect of the Prescription and Limitation (Scotland) Act 1973 was to depart from the rule as laid down in *Pettigrew*. That Act provides that 'any right to be served as heir to an ancestor or to take any steps necessary for making up or completing title to any real right in land' is imprescriptible.[7] The first part of this provision is merely declaratory of the previous law, but the second part was new. There could be room for debate about the exact scope of the second part, but at all events it is clear that it would cover the case of someone who holds a disposition or a docket transfer but who has not completed title.[8]

The heritable creditor in possession

The concept of a heritable creditor taking possession is a familiar one. It is done as a preliminary to sale, because although it is possible to sell while the debtor is still in occupation, it makes sense to remove him first. Thus the creditor's possession is merely temporary, and with the purpose of facilitating sale. The creditor does not possess for himself. It would be strange if the Halifax, on enforcing a security, did not sell the property but just occupied it for its own uses.

There is, however, one situation in which a creditor can take and keep possession. That is where the enforcement is done by collecting the rent. Thus suppose the property is subject to a 25-year lease. The heritable creditor could

---

1 [2006] CSOH 142 at para 12.
2 Land Registration (Scotland) Act 1979 s 28(1).
3 1997 SC (HL) 66.
4 [2006] CSOH 147, 2006 GWD 32-675, digested above as Case (47).
5 1956 SC 67.
6 For a discussion, see D Johnston, *Prescription and Limitation* (1999) paras 3.52 ff.
7 Prescription and Limitation (Scotland) Act 1973 sch 3 para (h).
8 We will not enter into the question of the negative prescriptibility of succession rights in general (whether testate or intestate), other than to note that while the 1973 Act has specific provisions about legal rights and prior rights (sch 1 para 2(f)), it does not have specific provisions about legacies or about rights to the free intestate estate.

enforce either by selling the property, subject to the lease, or by requiring the tenant to pay the rent direct to itself instead of to the owner. This seldom happens, but it is competent.[1] Another possibility is where the debtor is in actual occupation. The creditor could remove him and let the property out, taking the rents. In both these cases the creditor would have 'possession' of an indirect nature (ie civil possession): the direct possession would in each case be in the hands of the tenant.

So a heritable creditor takes possession only for the purpose of selling, or for the purpose of collecting rents. Yet Robert Bain seems to have taken possession for his own personal use. Whether this was lawful or not is an interesting and somewhat difficult question, on which there is little authority.[2] At all events, a creditor who does this must be liable for a fair market rent.

Two dubious titles and the defensive advantage of the possessor

If the defender's title was dubious, so was the pursuer's. Indeed, the pursuer's argument on prescription, had it been sound, would have cut down the (unrecorded) disposition in his favour just as effectually as it would have cut down the (recorded) disposition in favour of the defender. The Lord Ordinary observes:[3]

> It will, of course, be open to the first defender in the present action, if the parties choose to continue this war of attrition, to seek to reduce the 1986 missives in a fresh action on a different ground, namely that, by the time of those missives, John and Mary McMurtrie's title, if any, to the subjects had prescribed. But it may be that there would be no point in him so doing.

The last words presumably mean that since Robert Bain is in possession, it does not matter that his title is bad, because his son, having no title, could not oust him. The observation is in substance correct.[4] As the Lord Ordinary says:[5]

> The pursuer is entitled to come to court to show that the title of the person seeking to evict him is no better than his own. His right to bring the action impugning the evictor's title does not depend upon any title of his own. It is enough that he is de facto in possession.

STAMP DUTY LAND TAX[6]

One gets the feeling that stamp duty land tax is like a new car which has not been designed very well. Its fans in the Treasury pore over its engine like any

---

1 Conveyancing and Feudal Reform (Scotland) Act 1970 sch 3 standard condition 10(3).
2 W M Gloag and J W Irvine, *Law of Rights in Security* (1897) in a brief passage at pp 99-100 seem to say that it is lawful.
3 [2006] CSOH 189 at para 11.
4 But not in detail, partly because Andrew would have no more title to reduce the 1985 missives than Robert had to reduce the 1970 ones, and partly because missives are merely contractual.
5 [2006] CSOH 189 at para 7.
6 This part is contributed by Alan Barr of the University of Edinburgh.

enthusiast, tweaking the gears here and the oil there, in an attempt to make it run better. And nasty tax planners are always trying to put sand in the petrol, in the form of convoluted avoidance schemes. There were significant further changes in 2006 to a tax only introduced in 2003, following substantial changes in each of the last two years. These occurred both in the normal Budget and Finance Act process, and also in the December pre-Budget report, with new Regulations coming into force on the day of the Statement.[1]

There was also a very significant administrative development. From 1 November 2006, the submission receipt which online customers receive when they successfully submit a return over the Internet has been accepted as a substitute SDLT 5 certificate. It can be printed off and sent to the Land or Sasine Register, along with the document being registered.[2] Early indications are that this system is working well, where electronic submission is being successfully achieved.

However, the particular need for early registration in Scotland still leads to heavy use of the services provided from Edinburgh alone – personal presentation in a limited category of cases, and the 16-day 'emergency' service where a postal certificate has not been received. And by all accounts the telephone Help Line remains a contradiction in terms.

Threshold for residential property

After last year's doubling of the residential threshold,[3] there was a much more modest increase, from £120,000 to £125,000, last year.[4] This took effect for transactions with an effective date on or after 23 March 2006.[5] Other rates and thresholds remain unchanged, including the £150,000 residential threshold in so-called disadvantaged areas.

Deregulation

A number of arrangements no longer constitute 'chargeable consideration'. Thus where, in a gift, the donee or beneficiary agrees to bear inheritance tax or capital gains tax, this will not constitute chargeable consideration.[6] Similarly, the payment of a landlord's reasonable costs on the grant or variation of a lease is excluded from being chargeable consideration;[7] but this does not extend to costs paid by an assignee to the assignor or the landlord. And although the exact treatment of single farm payment remains a little obscure, an agreement by the tenant to assign

---

1 The Stamp Duty Land Tax (Variation of the Finance Act 2003) Regulations 2006, SI 2006/3237. See further below.
2 See p 78 above, and the *Stamp Duty Land Tax (SDLT) Practitioners' News* (formerly *Newsletter*) issue 13 (Oct 2006).
3 *Conveyancing 2005* p 142.
4 Finance Act 2006 s 162(1), (2), amending Finance Act 2003 s 55(2) and sch 5 para 2(3).
5 Finance Act 2006 s 162(4).
6 Finance Act 2003 sch 4 paras 16A, 16B, inserted by the Stamp Duty Land Tax (Amendment to the Finance Act 2003) Regulations 2006, SI 2006/875, reg 3.
7 Finance Act 2003 sch 17A para 10(1)(g), inserted by the Stamp Duty Land Tax (Amendment to the Finance Act 2003) Regulations 2006 reg 4(1).

entitlement to the payment on termination of the lease will not be chargeable consideration.[1]

Partnerships

In 2006 there were significant changes to the partnership rules. These took the form of essentially deregulatory measures in the Budget in March, extended further over the course of the Finance Act, followed by heavy restrictions in the pre-Budget Report and the regulations which followed

Thus the formula for calculating SDLT on transfers to and from a partnership was restricted to the market value of the land in question, as opposed to a combination of market value and actual consideration.[2] And the charge on transfers of partnership interests was restricted to interests in property investment partnerships – a very welcome restriction for the large numbers of partnerships who hold land and whose partnership interests change from time to time.[3]

There were also new rules to prevent a double charge arising in relation to certain partnership transactions, for example where money is withdrawn from a partnership.[4]

Further changes following the pre-Budget report increased the number of situations where tax is chargeable on transfers into or out of a partnership, or of a partnership interest, where the partners are entities other than individuals. This was an anti-avoidance measure, to prevent the exploitation of the partnership rules, which had just been revised earlier in the same year.[5]

Anti-avoidance

The rules on new unit trusts, which were protected from stamp duty land tax by so-called 'seeding relief', had been exploited by significant property investors. Large quantities of commercial property are thus, somewhat surprisingly, now owned by Jersey unit trusts. In 2006 seeding relief was withdrawn, subject to transitional provisions.[6]

Much more significant and extensive anti-avoidance legislation was introduced after the pre-Budget report. This consisted of a new s 75A in the Finance Act 2003.[7] To quote from HMRC's explanation of this wide-ranging measure, it will apply:

- where one person disposes of a chargeable interest and another person acquires that interest, or one derived from it,

---

1 Finance Act 2003 sch 17A para 10(1)(h), inserted by the Stamp Duty Land Tax (Amendment to the Finance Act 2003) Regulations 2006 reg 4(1).
2 Finance Act 2003 sch 15 paras 10, 11, 18, 19, amended by the Finance Act 2006 sch 24 paras 2–7.
3 Finance Act 2003 sch 15 para 15, amended by the Finance Act 2006 sch 24 para 9.
4 Finance Act 2003 sch 15 para 17A, amended by the Finance Act 2006 sch 24 para 10.
5 See changes made to Finance Act 2003 sch 15 by the Stamp Duty Land Tax (Variation of the Finance Act 2003) Regulations 2006 sch para 2.
6 Finance Act 2006 s 166.
7 Inserted by the Stamp Duty Land Tax (Variation of the Finance Act 2003) Regulations 2006 sch para 1.

- a number of transactions (the 'scheme transactions') are involved in the disposal and acquisition, and
- the stamp duty land tax chargeable on all the scheme transactions is less than that which would have been chargeable on a single land transaction, the chargeable consideration for which is the total consideration given or received (the 'tax-saving' test).

The scheme transactions are then disregarded and there is a notional land transaction, the chargeable consideration for which is the total consideration given or received.

As with all anti-avoidance legislation, this is clearly capable of catching the innocent as well as the tax avoider. In an interesting explanatory method, HMRC has given a range of examples where it says the new rules will apply *if* the tax-saving test is satisfied – but it does not necessarily accept that the test is satisfied, indicating that it may yet challenge some of these schemes through the courts. The HMRC examples (which are obviously based on English law[1]) include:

(1) V grants a 999-year lease to N for no premium and a peppercorn rent. V assigns the freehold reversion to P for a nominal sum. P pays N £X in consideration of N's agreement to vary the lease by the insertion of a provision giving the landlord the right to terminate the lease for no payment. P exercises the right to terminate.

The notional land transaction is the acquisition of the freehold by P with chargeable consideration of £X.

(2) V grants a 999-year lease to N for no premium and a peppercorn rent. The lease includes a right for the landlord to terminate the lease on payment of £X to the tenant. V assigns the freehold reversion to P for a nominal sum. P exercises the right to terminate and pays N £X.

The notional land transaction is the acquisition of the freehold by P with chargeable consideration of £X.

(3) V grants a 999-year lease to P for no premium and a peppercorn rent. The lease gives the landlord a right to terminate it within 14 days of the date of grant. P offers to pay V £X if V allows the 14 days to elapse without exercising the right to terminate. V does so.

The notional land transaction is the grant of a 999-year lease by V to P with chargeable consideration of £X.

(4) V agrees to sell property to N for £10 million. N agrees to sub-sell the property to P for £5. Both transactions are completed at the same time.

The notional land transaction is the acquisition of the property by P and the chargeable consideration is £10 million (the largest amount received by any person in respect of the scheme transactions).

Leases

In 2006 a number of technical changes were made to the rules on leases. Some of these were deregulatory in nature. For example, the rule bringing a charge on

---

1 For instance a 999-year lease could not be granted in Scotland: Land Tenure Reform (Scotland) Act 1974 s 8; Abolition of Feudal Tenure etc (Scotland) Act 2000 s 67.

rent increases outwith the terms of the lease is now restricted to such increases within the first five years of the lease.[1] Increases beyond that period are now only dealt with by special rules on abnormal increases in rent; and the formula for calculating an abnormal increase has been simplified.[2]

The treatment of leases which are 'backdated' where they commence after the termination of a lease between the same parties of the same premises has been simplified and clarified. Any rent which has been taxable in the 'gap' will be allowed as a credit against the rent in the new formal lease; and the term of the new lease is now treated as beginning on the day it is expressed to begin (normally the day after the termination of the former lease).[3]

There is a small deregulatory measure, whereby it is made clear that assignations of leases originally granted for less than seven years only have to be notified if there is stamp duty land tax to pay.[4]

Alternative finance arrangements

The various reliefs available in connection with alternative finance arrangements (Islamic mortgages) were extended in 2006 to make them available to all persons, allowing parity of stamp duty land tax treatment to companies, clubs and other organisations.[5]

---

1 Finance Act 2003 sch 17A para 13, amended by the Finance Act 2006 sch 25 para 6.
2 Finance Act 2003 sch 17A para 15, amended by the Finance Act 2006 sch 25 para 8.
3 Finance Act 2003 sch 17A para 9A, inserted by the Finance Act 2006 sch 25 para 3.
4 Finance Act 2003 s 77(2A), substituted by the Finance Act 2006 s 164(1).
5 Finance Act 2006 s 168. It now seems that such entities can be deemed to have religious sensibilities. For the compatibility of 'Islamic mortgages' with the Conveyancing and Feudal Reform (Scotland) Act 1970 see *Conveyancing 2005* p 143.

❦ PART V ❧
TABLES

TABLES

CUMULATIVE TABLE OF APPEALS 2006

This lists all cases digested in *Conveyancing 1999* and subsequent annual volumes in respect of which an appeal was subsequently heard, and gives the result of the appeal.

Adams v Thorntons
2003 GWD 27-771, OH, 2003 Case (46) *affd* 2004 SCLR 1016, 2005 SLT 594, IH, 2004 Case (44)

Aerpac UK Ltd v NOI Scotland Ltd
31 March 2004, OH, 2004 Case (1) *affd* [2006] CSIH 20, 2006 GWD 18-365, 2006 Case (7)

Anderson v Express Investment Co Ltd
2002 GWD 28-977, OH, 2002 Case (5) *affd* 11 Dec 2003, IH, 2003 Case (13)

Armstrong v G Dunlop & Sons' JF
2004 SLT 155, OH, 2002 Case (48) *affd* 2004 SLT 295, IH, 2003 Case (39)

Bell v Fiddes
2004 GWD 3-50, OH, 2004 Case (8) *affd* [2006] CSIH 15, 2006 Case (13)

Bell v Inkersall Investments Ltd
[2005] CSOH 50, 2005 Case (28) *affd* [2006] CSIH 16, 2006 SC 507, 2006 SLT 626, 2006 Case (59)

Burnett v Menzies Dougal
2004 SCLR 133 (Notes), OH, 2004 Case (42) *rev* [2005] CSIH 67, 2005 SLT 929, 2005 Case (40)

Burnett's Tr v Grainger
2000 SLT (Sh Ct) 116, 2000 Case (21) *rev* 2002 SLT 699, IH, 2002 Case (19) *affd* 2004 SC (HL) 19, 2004 SLT 513, 2004 SCLR 433, HL, 2004 Case (24)

Cahill's Judicial Factor v Cahill
2 March 2005, Glasgow Sheriff Court, A2680/94, 2005 Case (49) *affd* [2006] CSIH
26, 2006 GWD 19-409, 2006 Case (88)

Caledonian Heritable Ltd v Canyon Investments Ltd
2001 GWD 1-62, OH, 2000 Case (69) *rev* 2002 GWD 5-149, IH, 2002 Case (61)

Candleberry Ltd v West End Homeowners Association
12 October 2005, Lanark Sheriff Court, A492/5 *affd* 2006 GWD 21-457, Sh Ct, 2005
Case (9) *rev* [2006] CSIH 28, 2007 SCLR 128, 2006 Hous LR 45, 2006 Case (15)

Caterleisure Ltd v Glasgow Prestwick International Airport Ltd
2005 SCLR 306, OH, 2004 Case (21) *rev* [2005] CSIH 53, 2005 SLT 1083, 2005 SCLR
943, 2005 Case (15)

Cheltenham & Gloucester plc v Sun Alliance and London Insurance plc
2001 SLT 347, OH, 2000 Case (63) *rev* 2001 SLT 1151, IH, 2001 Case (73)

Conway v Glasgow City Council
1999 SCLR 248, 1999 HousLR 20 (Sh Ct) *rev* 1999 SLT (Sh Ct) 102, 1999 SCLR 1058,
1999 HousLR 67, 1999 Case (44) *rev* 2001 SLT 1472, 2001 SCLR 546, IH, 2001 Case
(51).

Glasgow City Council v Caststop Ltd
2002 SLT 47, OH, 2001 Case (6) *affd* 2003 SLT 526, 2004 SCLR 283, IH, 2003 Case
(6)

Grampian Joint Police Board v Pearson
2000 SLT 90, OH, 2000 Case (18) *affd* 2001 SC 772, 2001 SLT 734, IH, 2001 Case
(17)

Hamilton v Mundell; Hamilton v J & J Currie Ltd
20 November 2002, Dumfries Sheriff Court, 2002 Case (13) *rev* 7 October 2004,
IH, 2004 Case (11)

Henderson v 3052775 Nova Scotia Ltd
2003 GWD 40-1080, OH, 2003 Case (58) *affd* [2005] CSIH 20, 2005 1 SC 325, 2005
Case (47) *rev* [2006] UKHL 21, 2006 SC (HL) 85, 2006 SLT 489, 2006 SCLR 626, 2006
Case (86)

Inverness Seafield Co Ltd v Mackintosh
1999 GWD 31-1497, OH, 1999 Case (19) *rev* 2001 SC 406, 2001 SLT 118, IH, 2000
Case (13)

Jones v Wood
27 October 2003, Dumfries Sheriff Court, 2003 Case (52) *affd* [2005] CSIH 31, 2005 SLT 655, 2005 Case (42)

Kaur v Singh (No 2)
1999 HousLR 76, 2000 SCLR 187, 2000 SLT 1324, OH, 1999 Case (34) *affd* 2000 SLT 1323, 2000 SCLR 944, IH, 2000 Case (26)

Kingston Communications (Hull) plc v Stargas Nominees Ltd
2003 GWD 33-946, OH, 2003 Case (35) *affd* 17 December 2004, IH, 2004 Case (31)

Labinski Ltd v BP Oil Development Co
2002 GWD 1-46, OH, 2001 Case (16) *affd* 2003 GWD 4-93, IH, 2003 Case (17)

McAllister v Queens Cross Housing Association Ltd
2001 HousLR 143, 2002 SLT (Lands Tr) 13, 2002 Case (26) *affd* 2003 SC 514, 2003 SLT 971, IH, 2003 Case (28)

Minevco Ltd v Barratt Southern Ltd
1999 GWD 5-266, OH, 1999 Case (41) *affd* 2000 SLT 790, IH, 2000 Case (36)

Moncrieff v Jamieson
2004 SCLR 135, Sh Ct, 2003 Case (20) *affd* [2005] CSIH 14, 2005 SC 281, 2005 SLT 225, 2005 SCLR 463, 2005 Case (6)

Robertson v Fife Council
2000 SLT 1226, OH, 2000 Case (84) *affd* 2001 SLT 708, IH, 2001 Case (82) *rev* 2002 SLT 951, HL, 2002 Case (69)

Royal Bank of Scotland plc v Wilson
2001 SLT (Sh Ct) 2, 2000 Case (53) *affd* 2003 SLT 910, 2003 SCLR 716, 2004 SC 153, IH, 2003 Case (40)

Scottish Youth Theatre (Property) Ltd v RSAMD Endowment Trust Trustees
2002 SCLR 945, OH, 2002 Case (3) *affd* 2003 GWD 27-758, IH, 2003 Case (8)

Souter v Kennedy
23 July 1999, Perth Sheriff Court, 1999 Case (69) *rev* 20 March 2001, IH, 2001 Case (81)

Spence v W & R Murray (Alford) Ltd
2001 GWD 7-265, Sh Ct, 2001 Case (9) *affd* 2002 SLT 918, IH, 2002 Case (1)

Stevenson v Roy
2002 SLT 445, OH, 2002 Case (67) *affd* 2003 SC 544, 2003 SCLR 616, IH, 2002 Case
(54)

Superdrug Stores plc v Network Rail Infrastructure
2005 SLT (Sh Ct) 105, 2005 Case (35) *rev* [2006] CSIH 4, 2006 SC 365, 2006 SLT 146,
2006 Case (62)

Tesco Stores Ltd v Keeper of the Registers of Scotland
2001 SLT (Lands Tr) 23, 2001 Case (30) *affd* sv *Safeway Stores plc v Tesco Stores Ltd*
2004 SC 29, 2004 SLT 701, IH, 2003 Case (25)

Thomas v Allan
2002 GWD 12-368, Sh Ct, 2002 Case (7) *affd* 2004 SC 393, IH, 2003 Case (22)

Wilson v Inverclyde Council
2001 GWD 3-129, OH, 2001 Case (29) *affd* 2003 SC 366, IH, 2003 Case (27)

TABLE OF CASES DIGESTED IN EARLIER VOLUMES
BUT REPORTED IN 2006

A number of cases which were digested in *Conveyancing 2005* or earlier volumes
but were at that time unreported have been reported in 2006. A number of other
cases have been reported in an additional series of reports. For the convenience
of those using earlier volumes all the cases in question are listed below, together
with a complete list of citations.

AIB Group (UK) plc v Guarino
2006 SLT (Sh Ct) 138

Burnett v Menzies Dougal WS
[2005] CSIH 67, 2006 SC 93, 2005 SLT 929

Henderson v 3052775 Nova Scotia Ltd
[2005] CSIH 20, 2005 1 SC 325

Marley Waterproofing Ltd v J H Lightbody & Son Ltd
2006 GWD 6-113

Superdrug Stores plc v Network Rail Infrastructure
2005 SLT (Sh Ct) 105

Warren James (Jewellers) Ltd v Overgate GP Ltd
[2005] CSOH 142, 2006 GWD 12-235